Black Eden

Black Eden

Black Eden

The Idlewild Community

Lewis Walker · Ben C. Wilson

Michigan State University Press
East Lansing

♾ The paper used in this publication meets the minimum requirements
of ANSI/NISO Z39.48-1992 (R 1997) (Permanence of Paper).

Michigan State University Press
East Lansing, Michigan 48823-5202
Printed and bound in the United States of America.

15 14 13 12 11 10 09 08 07   1 2 3 4 5 6 7 8 9 10

Paperback edition 978-0-87013-804-1
The Library of Congress has catalogued the hardbound edition as follows:

LIBRARY OF CONGRESS CATALOGING-IN-PUBLICATION DATA
Wilson, Ben C.
Black Eden : the Idlewild community / Ben C. Wilson, Lewis Walker.
p. cm.
Includes bibliographical references and index.
ISBN 0-87013-622-4
1. African Americans—Michigan—Idlewild—History. 2. African Americans—Michigan—
Idlewild—Social life and customs. 3. AfricanAmericans—Michigan—Idlewild—Social conditions.
4. Idlewild (Mich.)—History. 5. Idlewild (Mich.)—Social life and customs.
6.Idlewild (Mich.)—Social conditions. 7. City planning—Michigan—Idlewild—History.
I. Walker, Lewis. II. Title.
F574.I35 W55 2002
791'.09774'68—dc21
2001007860

Cover design by Ariana Grabec-Dingman
Book design by Sharp Designs, Inc., Lansing, Michigan

Cover photos are used courtesy of the Ben C. Wilson Collection,
Black Americana Studies Department, Western Michigan University.

Visit Michigan State University Press on the World Wide Web at *www.msupress.msu.edu*

Contents

Acknowledgments

IN PREPARING THIS VOLUME, THE AUTHORS ARE DEEPLY INDEBTED TO THE many past and present resorters. We interviewed numerous informants over the years and are truly grateful to them for their powerful voices and knowledge, which helped us immensely in cross-checking assertions by those who have written about the region. The oral tradition provided by these men and women gave the authors a glimpse of how the area's whites reacted to black resorters, the resorters' many adjustment problems, Idlewild as a stage for young black entertainers, the decline of the place, and much more. Their contributions assisted greatly in separating fact from fiction.

We owe a continuing debt to the Western Michigan University Lewis Walker Institute of Race and Ethnic Relations for its support of this project. Its director, Dr. William Santiago-Valles, gave the project his blessing and accepted it under the aegis of the institute. Support also came from the Black Americana Studies Program (also WMU).

Dr. Benjamin Wilson acknowledges his special indebtedness to his dad, Ben C. Wilson Sr.; his mother, Winifred J. Wilson; the Reverend Joseph E. Graves; the Reverend Van C. Graves; Dr. Arthur Truss; Mr. C.; and the countless other black men who were his mentors. Appreciation is also extended to Dr. Ruth Hamilton of the Sociology Department at Michigan State University, Dr. Joseph McMillan of the University of Louisville, graduate assistant Ronald B. Coleman, undergraduate assistant Stephen Johnson, and others.

We wish to acknowledge the special service of Ms. Carrie Jordan and Ms. Mae O'Neal of the Western Michigan University Library. They were most helpful in combing the collections to find information on Michigan's black heritage. Ms. Patty DeLoach, administrative assistant in Black Americana Studies, has our thanks for her typing skills and encouragement. Ms. Patricia Martin is owed an enormous thanks for her critical reading, editing, and substantive contributions to the manuscript.

Finally, Dr. Lewis Walker extends a special word of appreciation to his wife, Georgia, for her patience and encouragement throughout this work. His mother, Thelma Freeman, is owed a debt for providing numerous nutritional delights to the authors throughout the writing of the manuscript. Dr. Richard MacDonald, a longtime friend and colleague, is appreciated for his interest in the project and his insightful contributions regarding the revitalization of Idlewild.

Introduction

Before the oral history is lost, there is a need to chronicle the black towns and rural communities that emerged in various parts of the United States in the aftermath of the Civil War and during the early part of the twentieth century. The black towns in Kansas, Oklahoma, Mississippi, Michigan, and other places deserve to have their histories recorded for posterity. Of those black rural communities whose history has not yet been adequately chronicled, Idlewild, Michigan, is one, and thus this book is an effort to capture the enormous richness of a black experience from which valuable lessons may be learned.

Idlewild may be viewed as a microcosm of the larger society. It is emblematic of the collective history of a people who have faced insurmountable odds, yet survived; a people who have made enormous contributions to the growth and development of a nation, yet are despised by many because of the color of their skin. Sociohistorically, Idlewild was established as a black resort community in northwest Michigan as a worthwhile if inadequate response to the serious problems of segregation and discrimination in this state and the country as a whole. Not unlike the black church, Idlewild represented many things to many people. It became a Mecca for thousands who wanted to escape, among other things, the sweltering summer heat of Chicago, Detroit, Indianapolis, Cleveland, and other big cities. Idlewild was their salvation; it provided them safe haven, a place to escape the rigorous demands of daily life. It was a place many people came to love and cherish, and today many would love to see it reclaim some of its past glory.

This work is not an attempt to provide answers to race problems, unemployment, welfare dependency, and drug addiction; neither is it a recipe or guideline for political correctness and ethnic awareness. The primary intent of this volume is to present a sociohistorical perception of chosen eras in the history of Idlewild. The thread that ties this together is the black experience in out-state Michigan as expressed in the oral tradition and incredible photos of the common, everyday folk who were the Idlewilders. (Unfortunately, however, it was impossible to include all of the rich experiences and personal voices of those who contributed to the Idlewild experience, both past and present. Another volume of a different nature would be needed to do justice to such a task. At any rate, it falls outside the purview of this work.)

This volume addresses the history of the resort, its significance to black entertainers and their audiences, the economic impact of the Civil Rights Act of 1964 on the resort, and the hard times and downturns leading toward the formation of a ghost town. It also looks at revitalization efforts and the need for a comprehensive strategic plan for future growth.

Lake County, within which Idlewild resides, has been identified by a Lake County Demographic Study (2 August 1999) as one of the poorest counties in Michigan. Idlewild is a rural community characterized largely by petty crimes and some violence, joblessness and welfare dependency, drugs, vacant buildings, and abandoned land. The area conjures up negative images and conveys only a part of the truth about the actual conditions of the troubled community. It is also an area where the population is largely elderly, with an average age of sixty-five, and where the average income was roughly $9,500 in 1999. Consequently, many of the residents are viewed as "clients," or consumers of services, especially as the population ages, with no real prospect of them becoming producers.

Idlewild is thus in the unenviable position of becoming a client community, as more of its residents become powerless to affect their own or their community's future. As more residents, young and old alike, become dependent on the largesse of social institutions, such as social service agencies and government programs, they ironically tend to fall victim to the very institutions established to help them become self-sufficient and responsible citizens.

A significant challenge with welfare reform has been to overturn the tragic tendency for residents to come to accept themselves as "fundamentally deficient" or as victims who are simply incapable of reversing the deficiencies in their lives. A social environment that enables a significant proportion of its people to remain solely dependent on its welfare agencies and governmental programs for survival is an environment that robs its people of dignity and any sense of purpose. Moreover, the community suffers as a result of this dependency relationship. Consequently, Idlewild—as a community—must seek alternative routes if the problems of complacency, unemployment, welfare dependency, and other social ills are to be addressed anytime soon.

Sociologically, it seems imperative that policies, programs, and activities be developed to aggressively address the problems associated with old age, poor health, unemployment, single parents, crime and delinquency, and environmental issues. At the same time, it is also vital that the community's assets, capabilities, and abilities be identified and mobilized to attack those concerns. Not to do so would be to ignore the fact that there are resources, even in poor communities, that can be utilized, in conjunction with outside resources, to mount a more effective defense against poverty and its attendant problems.

Since it is Idlewild itself, rather than any particular person or group, that is the main character in this book, our primary goal is to provide some in-depth information about the geophysical, economic, social, and historical aspects of that community. Between 1912 and 1964, African Americans by the thousands sought out Idlewild as a place to rest and relax, sheltered from the battles associated with racism. The original resort was located in the section of the community called "the Island," but the resort eventually came to comprise all of the subdivisions within Yates Township, as well as parts of Pleasant Plains. For the sake of simplicity, we will refer to the entire area as Idlewild—the place that became the most popular black resort in the Midwest.

Establishing the Foundations
of a Black Resort in Michigan

A UNIQUE SET OF SOCIAL AND HISTORICAL CIRCUMSTANCES SET THE STAGE FOR the Idlewild drama. Among them were the drastic overcutting of prime timberland and the shifting of sizeable numbers of black people from the South to the North. The convergence of these two necessary conditions helped establish the foundation on which a special group of men and women built a black resort community in the woods of northwest Michigan at a time when segregation and racism were rampant in every state in the Union.

EARLY HISTORY: A LOGGING COMMUNITY IN MICHIGAN

The Manistee National forest is 40 miles from the shores of Lake Michigan; roughly 75 miles north of Grand Rapids, Michigan; 270 miles east of Chicago, Illinois; and 250 miles west of Detroit, Michigan. Nearly 1,340,000 forested acres encompass large portions of the counties in the northwest part of Michigan's Lower Peninsula. The heart of this forest covers parts of ten Michigan counties: Manson, Newaygo, Oceana, Wexford, Manistee, Muskegon, Isabella, Montcalm, MeCosta, and Lake. The red and white pine trees, which grew in abundance on the sandy loams, specifically in Lake County,

Loggers harvesting the pines and hardwoods for home construction west of the Mississippi, prior to the creation and development of Idlewild. Courtesy of the Ben C. Wilson Collection, Black Americana Studies Department, Western Michigan University.

provided a livelihood for many residents who lived there. Between 1870 and 1890, loggers exploited the land and added to the population in such settlements as Baldwin, Luther, and Chase. Rebecca E. Dinsmore, in "Archaeological Perspective of the Lumber Industry in Northern Lower Michigan, 1865–1920," mentions that

> The race to meet the lumber demands of burgeoning eastern and midwestern cities, coupled with the lenient land management practices of post Civil War government, spawned the exploitation and inevitable destruction of Michigan's virgin forests. As the last stand of prime timber in one area fell under the axe and saw, the industry moved up river into the next watershed. . . .[1]

According to census figures, in 1884 there were twenty-five sawmills in Lake County, employing some 1,200 people. R. G. Peters, Justus Stearns, Volney Lacy, L. A. Blodgett, Alvin Joiner, Thomas R. Lyon, Elhanan Copley, and Jack Hackley of Muskegon were among the businessmen who operated on a large-scale basis.[2] Most took advantage when

> The federal government, during the thirty years, 1841–1871 . . . opened up a gigantic era of what might be termed land-happy generosity on a national scale. The standard government price for land was cut to $1.25 per acre . . . timber speculators began a scramble for choice pine lands when more than ten million acres of unsold government lands were disposed of or tied up in various land grants. . . . Some grants were made to the state of Michigan under the label of "swamp" lands but they were actually good pine lands, and sold at $1.25 per acre to private individuals and companies.[3]

Most of the pine logs, later oak and maple, too, were moved to Manistee and Ludington via the Pine, the Little Manistee, and the Pere Marquette Rivers. Eventually, the railroads became involved in the movement of timber from the area. Years of excessive cutting in Lake County resulted in the gradual disappearance of jobs related to the logging and lumber industry. Jobs associated with the railroads, hotels, and saloons and taverns were among

Log haulers working in the Idlewild area before it became a resort for African Americans. Courtesy of the Ben C. Wilson Collection, Black Americana Studies Department, Western Michigan University.

those lost as the demand for workers in these categories declined. Other industries did not move into the county, as many had anticipated they would. In this connection, there was an attempt to introduce the Great Northern Cement Plant in the village of Marlborough, but it was a futile effort. In the meantime, due to back taxes, vast acreage of former timberlands in Lake County went into receivership.

Around the same time that the logging communities in Michigan were being formed, large numbers of blacks had begun to move out of the South. By the time the land had been drastically overcut, a sizeable black population had arrived in Michigan and many other northern states. The black population had actually decreased for several decades in some northern cities before the Civil War. However, the black presence in these cities increased steadily after the passage of the Thirteenth Amendment to the Constitution, which freed the slaves; the Fourteenth Amendment, which provided for citizenship; and the Fifteenth Amendment, which granted the vote to black males. Between 1870 and 1890, over 80,000 blacks left the South, and between 1890 and 1910, over 200,000 additional blacks moved to the North and the West. The black populations in large cities in Illinois, Indiana, and Michigan increased twofold during that time. In spite of its numbers, however, this migratory trend was only a prelude to the so-called Great Migration, which began during World War I and involved over a million blacks moving from the rural South to the industrial centers in the North.

By the turn of the century, in Detroit blacks numbered 5,741 out of a total population of 465,766. Chicago's black population numbered 44,103 out of 2,185,283; in Cleveland they totaled 8,448 out of 551,925; and they numbered 15,931 out of 233,650 in Indianapolis. During that same period, the midsize city of Kalamazoo, Michigan, had a population of roughly 39,437, with 685 blacks. The Population Abstract of the United States Census reveals that blacks numbered roughly 600 to 800 in Grand Rapids, Michigan, which had a total population of 112,571 at the time.

The northern auto industry, the steel plants, the meat processing shops, and other auxiliary businesses were thriving and dominated the economies of the aforementioned cities and other northern and midwestern localities from 1910 to 1920. In this context, a condition most favorable to both management and labor was created by virtue of the fact that factories needed huge workforces and the new laborers from the "Deltas" and "Black Bottoms" of the South needed good-paying jobs.

These cities became magnets and terminals of the 1914–1920 Great Migration. By the summer of 1916, an estimated one thousand blacks were arriving monthly in Detroit. By 1920, out of a total population of 993,678 in that city, African Americans numbered 40,838. Ten years later there were over 120,000 blacks in Detroit, out of a total population of 1,568,622.[4] During the outward migration, many blacks in rural areas paid little attention to their black leaders, especially those who were suspected of being the paid stooges of white patriarchs, when they were advised to remain in Dixie. Leon Litwack, in his seminal piece *Trouble in Mind: Black Southerners in the Age of Jim Crow*, cited a prominent black who conceded that "any leader who argued against migration invited serious doubts about his leadership."[5] In addition, Litwack's informant said that "a businessman he knew wrote an article opposing migration. Clergymen, who preached against the migration, saw their congregations dwindle. To retain their clientele and congregations, many businesspeople, professionals and clergy chose to follow the sheep Northward. For so many, 'freedom was free-er and better in the Norf.'"[6] Many black leaders of progressive organizations, such as the National Urban League and the National Association for the Advancement of Colored People, encouraged the move.

RACIAL SEGREGATION, NORTHERN STYLE

Although the grass appeared greener in the North, many blacks who made the journey were disappointed when the North proved to be neither the "Beulah" nor the "Promised" land. Here, too, blacks faced physical, psychological, and mental abuse along with social and economic barriers. For example, housing shortages pitted blacks against whites, fueling tensions, which sometimes boiled over into race riots. These conditions gave rise and persistence to the so-called black ghettoes that soon characterized many black neighborhoods in northern cities. The most available jobs were the underpaid or the least desired occupations in the service sector. Merely surviving from day to day was difficult, and, for many, barely eking out a living stifled aspirations. Stagnation was neither wholesome nor beneficial.

In the midst of these conditions, black professionals who had middle-class economic status and disposable incomes sought sanctuaries in the resorts located on or near inland spring-fed lakes. These places of unsullied Arcadian innocence became areas of "recreation and relaxation without humiliation." Idlewild soon emerged as one of the most popular resorts in the Midwest.

THE FORMATIVE YEARS AND THE IDLEWILD RESORT COMPANY, 1915–1927

Pehyun Wen, in "Idlewild—A Negro Village in Lake County, Michigan," suggests that

> By definition a resort is a "place providing recreation and entertainment especially to vacationers." Therefore the recreation and entertainment businesses catering to the lumberjacks were probably the first beginnings of resorts in the frontier life. . . . Aside from church attendance or the occasional demonstration, there were few regular centers of social life. Newaygo county (the Southern neighbor of Lake County) has old records in the platbook which show that the first area platted out as fishing and hunting resorts was done in 1887, a second one appeared in 1889, and a third one was platted in 1895. More platted areas appeared from 1900 onward. All were developed on small lakes. The E. G. Branch family, which developed the resort as Idlewild for the Negroes, developed a resort in 1912, . . . [7]

In her article on Erastus Branch, which appeared in the *Grand Rapids Press,* Audrey D. Strophpaul said that as the lumbering activities faded out, Branch was one of the first in the community to realize the possibilities of the tourist trade. He got busy in that direction, platting the Diamond Lake Resort and stocking the lake with fish. Then, with that project underway, he developed a similar resort on Robinson Lake in Newaygo County.[8]

A loan from an area bank of $35,000 allowed Erastus and his brother Adelbert to purchase what is called the Island. According to a letter from a family member, "A small hut was built for Erastus and his wife Flora, and they lived there for two years, satisfying the government that he had established

6

Among the founders of the IRC were (clockwise from top left) Alvin Wright, Adelbert Branch, Erastus Branch, and Wilbur Lemon. Courtesy of the Ben C. Wilson Collection, Black Americana Studies Department, Western Michigan University.

residence and had a legal right to the land. A clear title was given. In spite of the hard economic times, they plugged away at the principle and paid off the loan. While paying the notes, the Branches and their brother-in-law cut streets, pulled stumps, and erected street signs. They called it Idlewild Terrace."[9]

Fundamental to the establishment and the subsequent development of the resort community was the relationship between the key principal financial investors. In addition to Erastus Branch, his brother Adelbert Branch, and other family members, other names associated with the resort were: Dr. Wilbur Lemon, Mamye Lemon, Alvin E. Wright, Madolin Wright, Albert Flogaus (a trustee of the city of Chicago), and Charles Wilson (a Chicago attorney between 1912 and 1927). According to Nicole Christian's article in the *New York Times,* this group purchased nearly 2,700 acres of overcut timberland from lumber concerns and from a Michigan railroad company that were then in receivership for back taxes.[10] They envisioned a resort project involving blacks exclusively. They would be blacks who were hungry for land, and their ownership of a piece of resort property would be evidence that they had made the American Dream work for them. The site would be east of Baldwin and would include the following lakes: Crooked (renamed Idlewild), Paradise, Little Idlewild, Switzer, Connamra, Little Bullhead, Watermill, and Tank. There is little doubt that some whites were apprehensive about this development in light of the racial tensions as exhibited in the 1919 "Red Summer" riots, which occurred in some northern cities.

THE CONTRACTUAL AGREEMENT

While the Branch brothers are credited with starting the resort, its growth and development could very well have depended on the action of a single individual who found it necessary to enlist the assistance of many others. Dr. Wilbur Lemon of Chicago was that individual. It is clear that the awesome responsibility of ensuring the business success of the resort fell on his shoulders. What is not clear, however, are the particular circumstances leading up to his acceptance of that burden as reflected in an interesting copartnership agreement created when the group formed the Idlewild Resort Company (IRC).[11] The agreement is presented below in its entirety. It is interesting not only for its historic relevancy, but also because it identifies the principal parties involved, it explains who owned what, it specifies the arrangements made between the parties, it identifies the trustee of the land, and it specifies the terms of dissolution in the event of defaults. After a careful reading of the agreement, several intriguing questions are raised:

1. What was the nature of the copartnership?
2. Who stood to benefit the most from the copartnership?
3. Who was willing to give up what, and for what gain?
4. How was the total sum of company assets derived?
5. What party stood to lose the most under the agreement and why?
6. Were the terms of the agreement fair and equitable to all parties?

Before attempting to answer these questions, we would like to present the complete document.

WHEREAS, the parties hereto are now conducting a resort development and real estate and business in lands situated in Lake County, Michigan, as copartners under the firm name of Idlewild Resort Company, by virtue of Articles of Copartnership existing between them bearing date of June 1,1925, and

WHEREAS, said copartnership is the owner of lands situated in Idlewild Plats and Idlewild Terrace Plats duly recorded in said County of Lake, as well as unplatted lands, certain numerous contracts for the sale of lands, and certain lots, cottages, office equipment, books of account, and other properties relating to said copartnership business and constituting the assets thereof and hereinafter referred to as copartnership assets, and said first parties are the owners of a forty percent (40%) interest in the said partnership assets and said second party is the owner of the remaining sixty (60%) interest in said assets, and

WHEREAS, by virtue of the agreement existing between said copartners, the legal title to all of said lands and contracts for the sale of lands owned by said copartnership is held in the name of said second party as trustee for the use and benefit of said copartnership, and

WHEREAS, the parties hereto desire to dissolve said copartnership and to liquidate their several rights and interests in the assets thereof and said second party desires to purchase the interest of said first parties therein, and to furnish them adequate security for the performance of his agreement of purchase.

THEREFORE THIS AGREEMENT WITNESSETH AS FOLLOWS:

1. That said first parties hereby agree to sell, transfer, convey, and assign unto said second party, and said second party hereby agrees to purchase, the forty (40%) interest of said first parties in and to the assets of said IDLEWILD RESORT COMPANY, a copartnership, for the sum of $50,000.00, which sum said second party hereby covenants and agrees to pay to said first parties as follows: $5,000.00 within ninety days following the date of this contract; $5,000.00 within twelve months following the date of this contract; and installments of $5,000.00 each and every six months thereafter until the entire purchase price has been paid in full, together with interest at the rate of six percent per annum from the date hereof on the portions of said purchase price which remain from time to time unpaid, which said interest shall be payable in weekly installments commencing one week from the date of this contract; all payments of principal being represented by promissory notes of even date herewith and all principal and interest to be paid at the office of Branch Brothers, White Cloud, Michigan;

with the privilege of making additional payments at any time in multiples of $1,000.00. Time shall be deemed to be of the very essence of this contract.

2. That in further consideration of the foregoing, said second party hereby covenants and agrees that he will indemnify and save the said first parties harmless against any and all expenses, accounts, debts, obligations, and other liabilities of whatsoever name or that may be now existing or outstanding against said IDLEWILD RESORT COMPANY, a copartnership, or that may be incurred by said second party on its or his own behalf after the date hereof, as well as against any claims and demands whatsoever by reason of or arising out of their membership in or their connection with said copartnership.

3. It is expressly agreed that upon the performance of this contract by said second party, all existing obligations, liabilities, and debts from said second party are liquidated and discharged, the same having been taken into consideration in fixing the purchase price herein. All the debt hereof shall be paid by said second party.

4. That said second party shall also on the 10th day of each month render a full and complete statement to said first parties of all lands sold by him during the preceding month in relation to said copartnership assets, and until the fulfillment of this contract, said first parties shall at any time be entitled to examine all books, records, contracts, and other documents of said copartnership as well as of said second party in relation to any business that may hereafter be conducted by said second party in connection with said copartnership assets, the intent being that said first parties shall at all times be entitled to be fully advised and informed of all transactions affecting said copartnership assets to the end that their security for the performance of this contract may not be unduly diminished.

5. It is further expressly understood and agreed that said first parties shall be entitled to all the security for the performance of this contract upon the part of said second party that the nature of the case affords, and that they are and shall remain the owners of their forty percent interest in said copartnership assets until the full performance of this contract upon the part of said second party. As further security for the payments of principal and interest herein agreed to be made by said second party, said second party does hereby pledge his sixty percent interest in said copartnership assets to said first parties.

6. In that event it shall become impossible for said second party to perform this contract and carry out his agreement to purchase said interest of said first parties at the time the first payment of principal herein specified becomes due and payable, then

all payments of interest which shall have been made by him to the said first parties shall be considered as dividends paid out of said copartnership business to said first parties on their forty percent interest therein, the same effect as if said copartnership had continued to exist, and this contract shall thereupon terminate and become wholly null and void, and said copartnership shall thereupon be revived, and the interests of the several parties hereto inland to said copartnership, IDLEWILD RESORT COMPANY, shall become reinstated and said copartnership shall continue as before, as though it had not been dissolved and terminated.

7. In the event of any default upon the part of said second party in paying any installment of interest or principal that shall become due and payable under the terms hereof after the first installment of principal has become due, that is, after the expiration of the period of ninety days from the date hereof, and provided that any default as to making a payment of principal (after the first payment) shall continue for thirty (30) days, then it is expressly understood and agreed that the sole and absolute equitable and legal title and ownership in and to all of said copartnership assets, as well as all title and interest hereafter acquired by said second party, as trustee of otherwise, in and to lands situated in the County of Lake, State of Michigan, shall thereupon become immediately vested in said first parties as the sole and absolute owners thereof, and for the purpose of making said transfer of title effective, said second party in his own right and as trustee does hereby sell, transfer, convey, and assign unto said first party all the rights, title, and interest now owned or hereafter acquired by said second party as trustee, or otherwise, in and to any and all lands situated in said County of Lake, which said conveyance shall become operative only in the event said second party shall make any default in the payment of any installment of principal or interest becoming due and payable under the terms of this contract after the date of maturity of the first payment of principal of $5,000.00 hereunder, and in that event, said first parties may cause a duplicate of this instrument to be recorded in the office of the Register of Deeds for said County of Lake, and upon being so recorded, all the rights, title, and interest of said second party as trustee, or otherwise, in and to any and all land situated in said County of Lake, whether the same be represented by deeds of conveyance, or shall be the form of contracts for the purchase of the sale of such lands, shall thereby immediately become vested in said first parties, and this instrument shall constitute a deed of conveyance and assignment to said parties to the same effect to all intents and purposes as though said second party in his own right and as trustee had, by ordinary deed of conveyance and assignment, conveyed and assigned to said first parties, for valuable

considerations, his title and interest as trustee or otherwise, in and to all such lands, contracts for the sale or for the purchase of lands, and other assets. In that event also, said second party shall immediately surrender possession and deliver over to said first parties all books of account, contracts, records, and other documents belonging to the assets of said copartnership or relating to any business hereafter transacted by said second party in connection with the subject matter of this contract, and said first parties shall thereupon be entitled to sell and dispose of said lands and other assets, in the exercise of their discretion, for the best price or prices they may obtain therefore, and out of the proceeds of said sale, shall retain an amount sufficient to pay the obligation herein incurred by said second party to said first parties together with interest thereon until the date of satisfaction, as well as any damage that they may have sustained by reason of the default upon the part of said second party in the terms of this contract, as well as any and all reasonable expenses of conducting the business of winding up and disposing of said lands and other assets, and when the same shall have been paid to said first parties, the remainder of said lands and assets, if any, shall be surrendered and transferred and conveyed to said second party.

8. It is further expressly agreed that said second party shall not make any disposition of any property affected by this contract in any manner other than the usual and customary manner in which the assets of said copartnership have heretofore been disposed of, without the written consent of said first parties, and a violation of this condition shall constitute a default upon the part of said second party.

9. It is further expressly agreed that said copartnership, IDLEWILD RESORT COMPANY, is hereby mutually dissolved and terminated, subject only to be revived in the event of the failure of said second party to make payment of the first installment of principal herein provided for.

10. It is further expressly agreed that in the event of the insolvency of bankruptcy of said second party such insolvency of bankruptcy shall constitute a default upon the part of said second party, and all the terms and conditions herein contained for the use, benefit, and protection of said first parties shall become operative and all the rights, title, and interest of said second party in and to all lands situated in said County of Lake, and other property and assets affected by this contract, as aforesaid, shall immediately become vested in said first parties with the right to liquidate said assets as above mentioned.

11. Upon the fullment [*sic*] of this contract upon the party of said second party in the manner and within the time above specified, said first parties shall, by good and

sufficient instruments, transfer, convey, and assign unto said second parties all their rights, title, and interest in and to said copartnership assets.

In WITNESS WHEREOF, the parties have hereunto set their hands and seals the day and year first above written.

In the Presence of

Harry D. Reber, Adelbert Branch, L.S.

Johanna Smalligan, Erastus Branch, L.S.

Wilbur M. Lemon L.S.

STATE OF MICHIGAN,

: ss.

County of Newaygo,

On this 29th day of November, A.D. 1926, before me, the subscribed, a Notary Public in and for said County, personally appeared ADELBERT BRANCH and ERASTUS G. BRANCH, to me known to be two of the same persons described in and who executed the within instruments, and acknowledged execution of the same as their free act and deed.

Notary Public, Newaygo Co., Mich.,

My Com. Expires

(STATE OF ILLINOIS,) : ss.

(County of Cook,)

On this day of November (usual acknowledgement clause for Wilbur M. Lemon). Signed by Notary in Cook Co., Illinois[12]

———————

Since Adelbert and Erastus Branch (the first parties) owned 40 percent (valued at $50,000) of the copartnership, it stands to reason that Wilbur Lemon's 60 percent would be worth $75,000, for a combined total of $125,000. How was this price arrived at? This is just one of the many unanswered questions which exist concerning the relationships between the key investors in the black resort community.

Though many such particulars are not known, Dr. Wilbur M. Lemon did become the "trustee" of a copartnership in whose operation the Branch brothers did not appear to be interested in having a hands-on role. Neither did they appear to be interested in owning or purchasing total control of all assets in

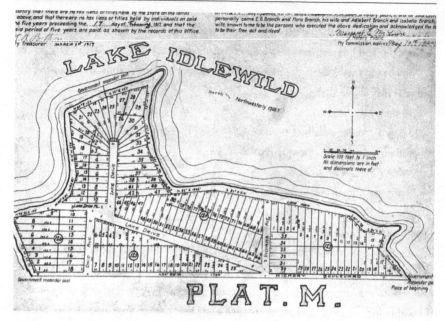

This map shows the layout of the platted lots south of Lake Idlewild. Courtesy of the Ben C. Wilson Collection, Black Americana Studies Department, Western Michigan University.

the company via any formal agreement. This observation is consistent with the fact that the copartnership was formed in such a manner that Mr. Lemon was allowed to serve as trustee while at the same time being allowed to purchase the interests of the brothers under terms of a formal contractual arrangement. The fact that he was given only a five-year period within which to purchase their interest further seems to suggest that they did not want a long-term relationship with the resort.

Restricting comments to the terms of the formal contract, it seems that Adelbert Branch and Erastus Branch, who owned 40 percent of the copartnership, stood to make a substantial gain in the case of a default on the formal agreement. That the brothers were astute businessmen is reflected in the language of the formal contract. For example, if Lemon was unable to make the "first payment" on the principal, but had made interest payments (which were to be made in weekly installments, commencing with the signing of the contract) then those interest payments would be treated as dividends for the brothers and, according to the contract, the situation would revert to a copartnership. However, in the event of any default in making subsequent payment on the principal (after the first payment) or interest, the Branch brothers would become the "sole and absolute" owners of all assets, and Lemon would have to sell and transfer "all the rights, title, and interest now owned or hereafter acquired" by him. (The contract language is silent on what Lemon would receive in the event of a default. This is an aspect of the contract that is ambiguous and appears to be inequitable to Lemon. On the other hand, the contract language is explicit insofar as what the Branch brothers would receive in the event of a satisfactory fulfillment of the contract.)

Wilbur Lemon appeared to be a man willing to take substantial risks. It is not known whether his 60 percent interest in the copartnership was owned solely by him, or whether he had silent partners to share that risk. The Branch brothers, it is clear, however, put none of their 40 percent interest at risk throughout the duration of the agreement with Lemon, who had to pledge his 60 percent interest to the brothers as further security regarding the performance of the contract. Moreover, the brothers were indemnified, in that the

Four-legged bathers make use of the lake before the summer resorters arrive at Idlewild (1920s). Courtesy of the Ben C. Wilson Collection, Black Americana Studies Department, Western Michigan University.

agreement held them "harmless" with respect to any debts, obligations, or liabilities that existed or would be incurred by the company or copartnership. Further, to help safeguard their interests under the terms of the agreement, Lemon was obliged to make a "full and complete" accounting of all business transactions to the brothers, and he had to receive their written consent to conduct business under certain circumstances. Finally, their interests were protected in the event of insolvency and bankruptcy, at which point all assets would be vested in the Branch brothers for disposal.

Although the satisfactory fulfillment of the contract would result in the transfer of all the rights, title, and interest in the copartnership to Lemon, he had no way of knowing what the value of their 40 percent interest would be worth at that time. Again, it was a risk that Lemon assumed for doing business under the terms of the contract. On the other hand, upon satisfactory completion of the contract, the Branch brothers would have received $50,000 (plus 6 percent annual interest) without any substantial risk to their assets in the copartnership.

Without adequate historical documentation, it can only be surmised that, since the terms of the contract placed Lemon's interests at a substantial risk, he was spurred to both form new business arrangements and vigorously engage in those activities that maximized his chances of satisfactorily fulfilling the terms of the contract. To do less would only have maximized his chances of failure. Thus, it seems that Wilbur Lemon—more so than Adelbert and Erastus—was the prime mover, the dynamo, behind the establishment of the resort and its subsequent growth and development.

Accordingly, besides the Idlewild Resort Company, there was also a Michigan business association created under the name of the Idlewild Corporation, with William E. Sanders as its president and an Illinoian, Albert Flogaus, serving as its first secretary. Dr. Wilbur and Mayme E. A. Lemon and Alvin and Madolin Wright were the other members of this fledgling organization. Arthur Riffe, William Green, and Marion and Carl Arthur were among the men in Cleveland who were anxious to sell lots to blacks for these companies. Another group, known as the Chicago Illinois Idea Premium Department Advertisers, organized and incorporated by Albert Flogaus, was awaiting the opportunity to canvas the black communities in downstate Illinois. The driving force behind all these initiatives was Chicagoan Dr.

Excursion bus from Chicago with a group of potential buyers. Courtesy of the Ben C. Wilson Collection, Black Americana Studies Department, Western Michigan University.

Wilbur Lemon and his wife, Mayme. A perusal of the Libers in the Records of Deeds Office in Baldwin (the Lake County seat of government) reveals that, on many quit claim deeds, the aforementioned individuals were heavily involved in acquiring additional property.[13] Outside of the auspices of the Branch family and the agreed upon notarized document, Dr. Lemon's networking abilities with colleagues, other business persons, and friends—both black and white—helped to fulfill the vision of a "Black Eden."

Once the contract had been fulfilled, the Lemons, the Wrights, the Flogauses, and others turned developers and, while studying the practicability and possibilities of the Idlewild venture, drew up a strategic plan in 1915. Pursuant to the implementation of this plan, the company opened a sales campaign in a booth at the Chicago Coliseum during the Lincoln Jubilee.[14] The response of middle-class blacks to this campaign was very gratifying, and shortly after the close of the Jubilee, the first excursion from Chicago visited Idlewild, followed by an excursion from Grand Rapids, then bus excursions from Detroit, Cleveland, and Indianapolis. All who visited were impressed with the lakes and the general environment as well as the plans for future development.

THE IRC PLAN

In 1912, African Americans Lela Wilson and her husband, Herman, joined an excursion from Chicago to look over the area at Idlewild. While impressed with the area, this husband-wife team did not return to Idlewild until 1921 at which time the Wilsons bought 80 acres surrounding Paradise Lake. To help recover some of their investment dollars the Wilsons found that "Rental cottages was one answer. . . . Selling real estate was another. They . . . acquired, as fast as they could, [an additional] 320 acres." Eventually Lela Wilson built a hotel, a store, and the Paradise Night Club on Paradise Lake.[15]

The Paradise Club and some of the patrons. One of the two women sitting on the steps is Mrs. Lela Wilson who, with her husband, purchased large tracts of land and established several businesses in the community. Courtesy of the Ben C. Wilson Collection, Black Americana Studies Department, Western Michigan University.

Resorters at the Idlewild Club House around 1926. Courtesy of the Ben C. Wilson Collection, Black Americana Studies Department, Western Michigan University.

Lela's travels also attracted many southerners to Idlewild. Eventually, the Wilsons brought the area its first paved roads and electric lights.[16] In addition, Mrs. Wilson bought from Darthula H. Jones of Havana, Cuba, "for one dollar and other valuable considerations . . . lots twenty (20), twenty-one (21), twenty-two (22), twenty three (23), twenty-four (24), twenty-five (25), twenty-six (26) and twenty-seven (27) of block four (4) and lots eleven (11) and forty five (45) of block seventy-six (76)" of Idlewild, according to the recorded plat.[17]

In the spring of 1916, the Idlewild Club House was started and the construction of cottages began by lot owners. The pace of cottage building accelerated very rapidly during this period, with many of them costing several thousand dollars. In fact, on the deeds recorded for lot owners George A. Thompson, Harriet Brooks, and Phebbe Ford, as well as countless others, it was stipulated that:

> No store, pool or billiard room, factory shop or other public place shall be created or maintained on the above described land. No buildings to be erected on said

One of the first sets of cabins built in Idlewild. Courtesy of the Ben C. Wilson Collection, Black Americana Studies Department, Western Michigan University.

above described land shall be used otherwise than as a private dwelling. No dwelling house or cottage shall be erected on the said described land at a less cost than two hundred (200.00) dollars. No spirituous, . . . or intoxicating liquors shall be manufactured or sold on said above described land. . . .[18]

These covenants helped establish the desired tone and quality of the environment, which meant that not everyone was happy when liquor licenses and sales came to the community in later years.

In addition to the more substantial cottages, many tiny bungalows were built. First-generation Idlewilders called the one-door, eight-by-ten bungalows "dog houses." The door of each of these bungalows opened onto a narrow boardwalk, while a window at the opposite end faced Lake Idlewild. Each cottage contained two cots, a crude nightstand, a pitcher and bowl, a kerosene heater, a bucket for drinking water, and a vintage hot plate. A "thunder mug" or chamber pot was placed under the bed because the privies were located far behind the living quarters.

After the completion of the Club House, a hotel with modern laundry facilities, some twenty-five guest cottages, ice houses, an electric plant, a dancing pavilion, a barbershop, a billiard hall, a superintendent's cottage, improved roads, an athletic field, tennis courts, baseball fields, an athletic track, a railroad station, a post office, telephone service, a school, and a tabernacle were added. All contributed enormously to the rapid growth of Idlewild between 1917 and 1920. As a matter of fact, Idlewilders of that era "boasted of property valuation upwards of $900,000."[19]

Many middle-class professional blacks were lured to the "rustic retreat" by the hyperbolic language contained in the company's pamphlets and in the *Chicago Defender* newspaper. Both sources described the Eden-like playground for blacks as having sandy beaches, new hotel accommodations, unpolluted water, boating, swimming, golf and tennis, horseback riding and nightclubbing. A publicity brochure in one Chicago branch office claimed that "the 2,700 acres of land, both cleared and uncleared, was parceled out into some 19,000 small plats 25 × 100 feet in size with a price tag of $35 each, $6 down and $1 a week."[20] In addition, the brochure read:

If you buy a lot in Idlewild you will be investing your money in a growing, rapidly developing locality where it will work for you while you sleep and where it should pay you handsome profits through increased values;

If you buy a lot in Idlewild you will help, encourage and make yourself a part of one of the biggest, best, most beneficial, most progressive movements of the day;

If you buy a lot in Idlewild you will place yourself, your family and your friends in position to reap the innumerable benefits that spring from personal contact and social intercourse with the deepest thinkers, the most active, most progressive people of the times;

If you buy a lot in Idlewild you will always have a place to go where you can enjoy your vacations to the fullest extent, build up your health, increase your business efficiency, and increase your producing powers;

If you buy a lot in Idlewild as long as you keep it you will not be dependent or homeless;

If you do not buy a lot in Idlewild you will have neglected an opportunity— a real opportunity comes but seldom, and you will always regret it. Your children will always regret it. Is it better to say I'm glad I did or I wish I had?

Act now! Fill out one of the coupons below and mail with a money order covering the first payment and we will select a choice location for you. Every lot is guaranteed high and dry and suitable for building purposes.[21]

Also included in the pamphlets were eloquently written letters by black notables of the era who described and promoted the resort. One such letter was written by Madame C. J. Walker, the first black female millionnairess, who on 23 December 1918 wrote:

Idlewild Resort Company,
Chicago, ILL.

Gentlemen:

I consider Idlewild a great national progressive movement . . . it supplies a great pressing necessity to our people, namely, a national meeting place where the leading spirits from the various sections of the country may gather each year and discuss problems of national and race importance. Great good cannot help but result from such a movement[,] and Idlewild[,] being located as it is in the heart of the Great Resort Sections of Michigan[,] makes it ideal for the combination of business and pleasure.

I have purchased a beautiful lake front location and intend to build my summer home at Idlewild . . . [and] also a school for teaching Hair Culture and expect to have the school completed and in operation during the season of 1920. Wishing you every success and assuring you of my hearty co-operation, I am

Yours very truly,
C. J. Walker[22]

Though Madame Walker died before realizing her dream of a school at Idlewild, she indeed did entice countless blacks, especially from Indianapolis, to purchase property in the community. A'Lelia Bundles, great-great-granddaughter of Madame Walker, mentioned that her famous relative invested in the resort because

. . . it represented a place that was beautiful, relaxing and showed African Americans all the things they could do and have their own enclave of special-ness. . . . It also provided youngsters with positive role models because of all the professionals who were there. . . . Networking was quite common. It showed what we could accomplish in spite of the bombardment of racial stereotypes. It represented the best example of successful blacks. [23]

Initially suspicious of the white developers' intentions, "land-hungry urban blacks" quickly began buying Idlewild lots by returning the coupons in the pamphlets or brochures with a cash deposit (see appendix 1 for samples of coupons).[24] Dr. Lemon hired black salespeople to canvas large- and inter-mediate-sized midwestern cities. For example, Charlie Gass, while employed as the shoeshine man at the Pantlind Hotel, formerly in downtown Grand Rapids, used his worksite to hawk Idlewild property. Eventually, he became a successful property holder there. As a matter of fact, he was responsible for selling to those who settled in a section known as the Grand Rapids Beach area. Gass's successes prompted the IRC office to submit a letter to him with several incentives. It reads:

Undoubtedly you have friends who would be interested in securing lots. . . . If you get them interested enough to buy, either from you directly or our nearest agent or through this office, we will give you a lot for every customer you get, that is to say, one of the lots that we have been selling for $10 each. All you have to do is to get your friends interested; then call or write our nearest agent or com-municate with the Chicago office. If you can handle the sale yourself, a location will be sent to you. If it is handled through our agent, he or she has locations on hand to offer. If you would prefer to take out an agency yourself and work on a commission basis in place of receiving a lot for each sale you help make, you will receive a cash commission of $2 for every lot you sell, together with regular agents outfit and assignment of lots to sell.[25]

Most of the black salespersons were familiar with the resort project; some had visited the community with earlier excursion parties. Between 1915 and 1930, chartered buses from Chicago quite frequently transported

"Ma" Buckles from Medicine Hat, Canada, claimed that the resort was a place where the men were "idle" and the women were "wild." Courtesy of the Ben C. Wilson Collection, Black Americana Studies Department, Western Michigan University.

prospective buyers to the area. In addition, black social clubs from the Milwaukee area contracted with the Lake Michigan ferry lines to transport potential buyers to the resort. Mary Frazier was among those who came across Lake Michigan in 1919 to inspect the resort community and decided to purchase some lots. She was prompted to buy because she felt that "A lot of these white resorts, you know, wouldn't accept colored folks." So, in 1925, she built herself a cottage on the lake and started spending summers in Idlewild, taking in boarders to make ends meet. About the resort, she recalls, laughing, "Oh, it was jumping. . . . Yeah, we had big crowds here. All kinds of amusement."[26]

Some salespeople were tremendously successful in getting blacks to purchase land in Idlewild, even selling lots sight unseen. The dream of Idlewild as a "Black Eden" in Michigan reverberated throughout the black communities, especially in the Midwest. The constant ringing of Randolph 2315, the telephone number at the company's office on the eighth floor of the Hartford Building in Chicago, proved that the developers had reached an untapped desire by many middle-class professionals for a black resort. Solicitation campaigns were so successful that trains departing from urban areas such as Detroit were often crowded with passengers bound for Idlewild, in search of lots for purchase. For example, in the Wayne County area, the Chesapeake and Ohio Railroad trains were boarded by many purchasers at the Second and Fort Street station in Detroit. Crowded trains left the station at 11:30 P.M., and by the next morning they would unload their passengers at Idlewild, ready to scrutinize the area for promising lots. For those who drove, the resort was five hours from Detroit via Woodward Avenue north to U.S. 10.

The Idlewild Chamber of Commerce in the 1920s took great pleasure in inviting progressive blacks

> . . . to the cool, pleasant environs of this great national playground. Here nature has lavished beauty, grandeur, loveliness, in blue inland lakes surrounded by sandy stretches of beach, lush green valleys and cathedral forests. This great vacation empire is near your home by fast train or splendid paved highways. Delightful are our summer days and pleasant are our nights with cool lake breezes sweeping through carrying the fragment scent of pine trees and wild

In Baldwin, Michigan, drivers await the arrival of the train to take vacationers to Idlewild Resort. Courtesy of the Ben C. Wilson Collection, Black Americana Studies Department, Western Michigan University.

floral life making sultry, sleepless nights something relegated into the unknown. In this exhilarating summerland all outdoors is your playground. Here is the finest fishing on the continent, swimming, hiking and horseback riding on unusual trails, picnicking in virgin forests, and a hundred other recreations. You will find friendliness and hospitality everywhere in this vacationland, so why not treat yourself to a delightful, ideal vacation among the lakes and fragrant pines of WESTERN MICHIGAN at "America's most distinctive national resort?" Make new friends and become one of the thousands who call Idlewild their "vacation home."[27]

Sociological Illuminations

The Quakers, a white religious group, conscientiously risked their lives and property in an organized effort to help dismantle slavery in this country. Their actions during antebellum years, deliberately designed to help black people as a group, played a big role in the growth of the black population in Michigan. Such behavior was not common among whites in Michigan, or in any other northern state, for that matter. The small group of whites that purchased the acreage in Lake County, Michigan, that would become Idlewild was thus an exception. Though they bought it to make an economic profit— a profit that could have been made by selling the lots to other whites—there appears to have been a conscious effort by this group to provide a place for blacks that they could call their very own.

Contextually, it is significant that this occurred at a time when segregation was a way of life in virtually every state in the Union. This was also a time when it appeared that America would forever be a "white man's country." Consequently, the pattern was for black people to carve out a niche for themselves as best they could, knowing that segregation was the "order" of the day.

The fact that segregation was so widespread was largely responsible for the development of the numerous so-called all-black towns and communities around the country. In addition to Michigan, they were formed in such places as Kansas, Oklahoma, and Mississippi, to name a few. Of interest here is the fact that most of these places were formed as a result of the initiatives of blacks themselves who were courageous and bold enough to strike out on their own. Idlewild is an exception to that pattern. Though Idlewild, too, was formed as a direct result of racial segregation, its existence is the result of the work of a small group of white entrepreneurs that, while hoping to make a profit, intentionally sought to help blacks help themselves.

Despite the IRC's dependence on black salespeople, some blacks were suspicious of the endeavor because the developers were white. W. E. B. Du Bois, an outstanding intellectual, writer, and reformer, articulated their doubts even as he gave the white entrepreneurs credit. He states:

> No one will accuse me of over partiality toward my paler neighbors. I deeply regret that as I grow older a white face is to me a sign of inherent distrust and suspicion, which I have to fight in order to be just. Now white men developed Idlewild. They recognized its beauty, bought it and attracted colored people there. They have made money by the operation. That was their object. But they have not been hogs. They have not squeezed the lemon dry, and they have apparently been absolutely open, square and just. Idlewild is worth every penny. . . . It is worth a good deal more than most people paid for it. . . . White men developed it because they knew how. We pay for their experience, but we pay a very low sum. Our hats are off to the Idlewild Resort Company.[28]

Though most of the earlier resorters were recruited from the black bourgeoisie category—la crème de la crème—not every white citizen in Lake County was overjoyed or welcomed their presence in the black resort. "Negrophobia" over the vote and other issues was widespread in Michigan, especially in those communities where there was already a sizeable black population. The area experienced some growth between 1915 and 1929 because blacks were able to purchase inexpensive virgin land in Idlewild.

The black presence in Michigan and the development of the resort community in Idlewild occurred at a time when more blacks were celebrating their racial progress. In Michigan and elsewhere, a new class of African Americans was emerging, and they were eager to prove that they could "achieve wonders on their own." Idlewild was simply another exemplar where black people could come together and prove to themselves and the world that they could accomplish greatness. Again, recalling the words of A'Lelia Bundles, the great-great granddaughter of Madame Walker, "it

[Idlewild] represented a place that was beautiful, relaxing and showed African Americans all the things they could do and have their own enclave of specialness. . . . It represented the best example of successful blacks."[29]

Though overcut and virtually unsuitable for farming, the land—with its beautiful scenery, lakes, and wildlife—became irresistible for many black citizens who could afford the price of a plot of land and who, at the same time, wanted to be part of a progressive movement to enhance the status of the black race. A movement that promised to bring together the country's finest black minds to tackle race and other important issues was heady stuff. To be able to relax and have a holiday and also be a part of discussions and developments on race was an exciting and exhilarating experience for many.

Continuation of
a Good Deal

IDLEWILD FROM ITS INCEPTION WAS BOTH NATIONAL AND INTERNATIONAL IN
scope, and between 1915 and 1927, annual African American visitors to
Idlewild increased from a few hundred to five or six thousand. Pioneers came
from Illinois, Michigan, Ohio, Massachusetts, New York, Kentucky, Georgia,
Indiana, Missouri, Texas, and Canada. Furthermore, it is said that there also
were visitors from Hawaii and Liberia during the early twenties. According to
a 1927 booklet entitled *A History of Idlewild,*

... 16,895 lots have already been deeded to approximately 5,630 lot owners.
Approximately 3,000 lots are now being bought under contract by ... 1,000 owners, making a total of 6,630 people throughout the country who are financially and
substantially interested in this wonderful project, and one of the outstanding features is the fact that these lot owners represent the cream of the colored population, men and women of the highest type of education and intelligence, members
of all of the professions and various enterprises, people ambitious to do something
meritorious, people whom it is a pleasure and an inspiration to meet. These facts
and figures prove that Idlewild is now an established institution resting on the

most substantial foundation conceivable and it follows that its future can only be one of constructive progress.[1]

The Formation of Idlewild Summer Resort Company

In the summer of 1926, Dr. Wilbur Lemon initiated the first carnival and chautauqua as a way of spreading the fame of Idlewild throughout the country. He also decided to capitalize on the resort venture by selling shares, after six weeks of haggling with Mr. William B. Gilmore, deputy chair of the Michigan Securities Commission.[2] In the late summer of 1927, the Idlewild Summer Resort Development Company (ISRDC) was incorporated for the purpose of uniting the six thousand active and energetic resorters into one large, disciplined body, bringing Lemon's vision into reality.

Since he was driven by the notion of bringing the "best class of colored" to Idlewild, Lemon thought that it would be wise to have two blacks on the ISRDC board. Reverend R. L. Bradby, pastor of Second Baptist in Detroit—the oldest black church in Michigan—was viewed as an ideal candidate. In a letter dated 6 July 1927 to Dr. Wilbur Lemon from W. C. Osby, president of Dunbar Hospital in Detroit, Reverend Bradby is described as "a man of exemplary character, tempered with an indomitable will to do . . . right; a man of vision, diplomacy and business efficiency which is the foundation of his present responsibility as pastor of a 5,000 membership church, president of the local branch of the National Association for the Advancement of Colored People (NAACP), and president of the State Baptist Convention; a man whose personal property and other investments approximate $50,000."[3]

Once the ISRDC was incorporated and chartered to do business, Bradby became first vice president. The other black board member was Chicago attorney Charles A. Wilson. Edgar F. Olson, cashier of Franklin Trust and Savings Bank of Chicago, in a letter dated 7 July 1927 to the Michigan Securities Commission, stated that ". . . we have known Mr. Charles A. Wilson . . . for a number of years, during which time he has carried a satisfactory account in this bank, and on a number of occasions we have referred clients to him, who have been well pleased with the service rendered. We feel confident that any statements that Mr. Wilson makes can be relied upon."[4] Wilson became the legal counsel for the ISRDC. The other key players were

David Manson and Herbert F. Kandler, both white, who were chosen as second vice president and secretary and treasurer, respectively.

An advisory board, composed of black men and women from throughout America but limited to three per city or community, was created, and acted in a special advisory capacity to the officers. Those chosen for the board had to be accomplished role models in their particular line of endeavor and be reputable individuals in their respective communities. Each member of the board was furnished with special emblems of distinction and granted special privileges, and their names and addresses appeared on the stationary and literature of the ISRDC. Between the late 1920s and the 1960s, the management of the resort depended heavily on the opinions and advice of this board, which became the Idlewild Lot Owners Association in the late 1920s.

Buying stock in the ISRDC was thought by many to be one of the best and most beneficial investments for black professionals. Stock sold for $25.00 per share, in blocks of four shares for $100.00, payable in installments of $10.00 for each block and $5.00 per month.[5] At the outset, Dr. Wilbur Lemon owned 2,040 shares, Reverend Robert Bradby owned 120, David Manson, 20, Charles Wilson, 18, and Herbert Kandler, 2. With the passing of years both Bradby and Wilson sold a few of their shares to colleagues of comparable status in Detroit and Chicago. Once an individual purchased stock in the company, he or she received a copy of the important Articles of Association. Again, because of the historical importance of this document, it is presented in its entirety. It reads:

ARTICLES OF ASSOCIATION
THE IDLEWILD RESORT DEVELOPMENT COMPANY

We, the undersigned, desiring to become incoporated under the provisions of Act 230 of the public Acts of 1897, entitled "An act to provide for the formation of corporations for the purpose of owning, maintaining and improving lands and other property kept for the purposes of summer resorts for ornament, recreation, or amusement, and to repeal all laws or parts of laws in conflict herewith" etc., do hereby make, execute and adopt the following articles of association, to wit:

ARTICLE I

The name assumed by this association, and by which it shall be known in law, is The Idlewild Summer Resort Development Company.

ARTICLE II

This corporation intends to proceed under section 10034, chapter 192, summer resort, sports and amusement associations.

ARTICLE III

The purpose or purposes of this corporation are as follows;

To form a corporation owning, maintaining and improving lands and other property for the purposes of a summer resort or a park for ornament, recreation or amusement in that section of Lake County known as Idlewild, situated about five miles from the town of Baldwin, Michigan.

ARTICLE IV

Principal place where company will operate is 8 South Dearborn Street, Chicago, Illinois, County of Cook.

[The] Address of [the] main office in Michigan is on the Idlewild grounds at Idlewild, Michigan.

[The] Address of main office outside of Michigan is Room 808, 8 South Dearborn Street, Chicago, Illinois.

ARTICLE V

The total capital stock authorized is One Hundred Thousand, ($100,000.00) dollars.

The amount subscribed is Fifty-Five Thousand ($55,000.00) dollars.

The amount paid is Fifty-Five Thousand ($55,000.00) dollars.

The number of shares of common stock is Four Thousand (4,000) of the per value of Twenty-Five ($25) dollars each.

Such shareholders shall be entitled to participate in dividends or assets of the corporation as follows; equally.

Amount of common stock paid for in cash is . . . Fifty-Five Thousand ($55,000.00) dollars . . . the description and valuation at which each item is taken is as follows, viz:

That part of the West fractional half of the Northwest fractional quarter of Section Eighteen (18), Township Seventeen (17) North, Range Twelve (12) West Lying North of the plat of Idlewild Terrace two (2) containing 26,500 acres more or less in Lake County, Michigan Fifty-Two Thousand Five Hundred ($52,500.00) dollars.

Lots Twenty-Two (22) and Twenty-Three (23) in Block Ten (10), Plat "HE" of Idlewild Terrace, Lake County, Michigan, Twenty-Five Hundred ($2,500.00) dollars, containing fifty (50) by one hundred (100) feet, making a total of 26.72 acres more or less.

The amount of actual capital, in cash or property of both, which this corporation owned and possessed at the time of executing these articles is Fifty-Five Thousand ($55,000.00) dollars.

ARTICLE VI

The term of this corporation is fixed at Thirty (30) years.

ARTICLE VII

Names of incorporates, their residences and shares subscribed by each, are:

NAME	RESIDENCE	NO. OF SHARES
Wilbur M. Lemon	808, 8 South Dearborn St., Chicago, Ill.	2,040
Robt. L. Bradby	441 Monroe St., Detroit, Michigan	120
David Manson	5401 South Michigan Blvd., Chicago, Ill.	20
Chas. A. Wilson	3451 Michigan Blvd., Chicago, Ill.	18
Herbert F. Kandler	808, 8 South Dearborn St., Chicago, Ill.	2

ARTICLE VIII

The names and addresses of officers and directors (or an attorney in fact) for the first year of the corporation's existence are as follows:

NAME	RESIDENCE	OFFICE
Wilbur M. Lemon	808, 8 South Dearborn St., Chicago, Ill.	President
Robt. L. Bradby	441 Monroe St., Detroit, Michigan	1st Vice President
David Manson	5401 South Michigan Blvd., Chicago, Ill.	2nd Vice President
Chas. A. Wilson	3451 Michigan Blvd., Chicago, Ill.	Corporation Council
Herbert F. Kandler	808, 8 South Dearborn St., Chicago, Ill.	Secretary and Treasurer

ARTICLE IX

In Witness Whereof, we, the parties designated as provided by law, by the parties associating as shown under articles of these articles, for the purpose of giving legal effect of these articles, hereunto sign our names this 27th day of May A.D. 1927.

Wilbur M. Lemon	808–8 South Dearborn St, Chicago, Ill.
Robt. L. Bradby	2116 Pennsylvania Ave, Detroit, Mich.
David Manson	5401 Michigan Ave, Chicago, Ill.
Chas. A. Wilson	3451 Michigan Ave, Chicago, Ill.
Herbert F. Kandler	808–8 Dearborn St, Chicago, Ill.

STATE OF MICHIGAN (COUNTY OF NEWAYGO) On this 27th day of May A.D. 1927, before me, a Notary Public in and for said County, personally appeared Wilbur M. Lemon, Rob't L. Bradby, David Manson, Chas. A. Wilson, Herbert F. Kandler, known to me to be the persons named in, and who executed the foregoing instrument, and severally acknowledged that they executed the same freely and for the intents and purposes therein mentioned.

Erastus G. Branch

Notary Public

My commission expires Jan. 18,1928.[6]

———

THE IDLEWILD SUMMER RESORT COMPANY
PLAN OF DEVELOPMENT

The company and its advisory board felt properly built and furnished cottages were necessary for the success of the operation. It was suggested that they should range in size from one to five rooms, with porches and verandas, furnished and equipped to accommodate families that preferred cottage life. Further, consideration should be given to establishing completely furnished tents in desirable locations for those who preferred to "rough it."

By 1927, nearly eight hundred summer homes had already been constructed by lot owners on their own initiative. However, for those who did not have sufficient personal resources, there was a plan to offer them some financial assistance. The ISRDC and its advisory board planned to establish, own,

Vacationers outside the original "dog houses" that had canvas tops. Courtesy of the Ben C. Wilson Collection, Black Americana Studies Department, Western Michigan University.

and operate a lumberyard, along with a hardware store, so that building materials could be purchased on a wholesale basis and, in turn, sold on terms to those not as blessed financially as others. They hired their own contractor/builder, Archie Brott, who inaugurated a building campaign. Over the years, among the workers employed were: Rollo Branch, John Simmons, Charles Scott, Andy White, Herman Wilson, and George Webb.[7]

The plan was a progressive one and, according to *A History of Idlewild*, the idea was to

... enable the lot owner to select the style of cottage desired and start paying ... in monthly installments. When a certain percentage of the cost, to be determined later, has been paid in the cottage shall be erected and the lot owner will give a mortgage on the property to the company for the balance and continue the monthly payments until the cottage is paid for in full. The company will be able to build on a much less cost basis than under the present system of the individual contractor, who must seek here and there for his material and pay, in many cases, exorbitant prices. We believe that where one cottage is now built, ten cottages can easily be built within the same period of time. The company will receive a reasonable profit on the material, labor, financing, etc., which should make it exceedingly beneficial to the stockholders and at the same time reduce the cost and increase the convenience and possibilities for the cottage builder. The cottage builder will not only derive the pleasure and benefits from the possession of a home of his [or her] own, but will have no difficulty in renting . . . during the season when he [or she] does not occupy it himself [or herself]. . . .[8]

The next item in the line of development was the establishment of high-grade entertainment and amusement devices. Prior to 1927, virtually all visitors enjoyed the pleasures of beautiful scenery, swimming, boating, sun-bathing, picnicking, fishing, and hiking. They also enjoyed social gatherings to a limited degree, but those forms of entertainment, while beneficial and satisfying to some, left other resorters unfulfilled. Thus the advisory board thought that what was needed was a line of high-grade amusement

A group of resorters outside of their rented cottages known as the "dog houses." Courtesy of the Ben C. Wilson Collection, Black Americana Studies Department, Western Michigan University.

rides, activities, and facilities such as those found in first-class white resorts. What they had in mind were activities involving water sports, skating, formal dancing, and drama. They also wanted a dance pavilion, theaters, riding stables, tennis courts, horseshoe courts, croquet grounds, bowling alleys, and chautauqua and carnival sites.

The company and advisory board also planned a clubhouse that they envisioned would be the heart of the resort. It would be constructed on the island, and the contractor and builders were instructed to include a huge shaded veranda and an artistically designed lobby that would lend charm, ease, comfort, and convenience to its guests. The clubhouse would also include rooms for afternoon teas, card parties, and committee meetings, and space for small convention meetings. The clubhouse was eventually built, and it was located on a hillock on the island. It quickly became the central gathering place for visitors. Upon arrival at the resort, Florence Powell Washington, a resorter from Columbus, Ohio, mentioned that "[once] we unpacked our luggage, we all went to the clubhouse to see what was going on and who was already on the Island." She further stated that inside "there was a piano, reading rooms and a big picture of Dr. Booker T. Washington hanging in the foyer."[9]

Besides the clubhouse, the group also proposed to erect an elegant executive mansion that they thought would be the "pride of the race." It would be the home of the president (Dr. Wilbur Lemon) of the ISRDC. It was to be of colonial architecture, with a large audience room that had a huge fireplace, leading to a balcony. Off of the balcony would be sleeping rooms, sleeping porches, and committee rooms. On the first floor would be the executive office, dining room, and kitchen. According to *A History of Idlewild*,

The audience room shall be used for the Annual Stock Holder meetings, Board of Directors Meetings and all other purposes pertaining to the . . . management of the Affairs of the company. The sleeping rooms and dining rooms shall be used and occupied by the President and his family, attaches, and invited guest. In connection with the Executive Mansion there will be a Museum and Library. . . . [T] he Museum, Library and Executive Mansion . . . shall be furnished and decorated with relics and antiques; such as, rare skins, skulls, horns and taxidermy specimens, war, hunting and fishing implements, musical instruments, works of music and art from all countries having a colored population. It is proposed that this building and its furnishings shall be magnificent enough to attract the attention of the entire country and will be a source of unlimited pride. . . . [It] has been proposed that this Executive Mansion, Library and Museum shall be erected by popular subscription . . . and have a personal interest and pride in this great race monument. The names of all those who contribute $1.00 or more will be enrolled in a register which will be kept in the Executive Mansion. . . .[10]

A fire station was constructed and volunteer firefighters were trained to operate the fully equipped fire truck, which cost $10,000. That achievement was brought about through the keen foresight and efforts of the advisory board, the township board, and donations from resorters.[11]

Unfortunately, the mansion never materialized. Business meetings pertaining to the development of the resort took place in the clubhouse, which itself was perceived as a symbol of "race pride" by many of the pioneer resorters. To realize their dream of building new facilities and the amusement park theme, the company thought it would be necessary to attract more resorters. To attract prominent and nationally known blacks to the resort, the ISRDC commissioned a group of filmmakers from the *Chicago Daily News* to produce a promotional film on the resort. Shown primarily in black theater houses in the North and Midwest, "A Pictorial View of Idlewild" was successful in disseminating information about the resort. It was at least in part responsible for getting a number of black notables to notice Idlewild. More bait was added to the hook when the advisory Board hosted its second annual carnival and chautauqua between July 25 and August 6, 1927. A promotional letter, written on the company stationery and signed by President Lemon, reads:

> . . . you are not only invited to be present, but you are also cordially invited and urged to take an active part in these exercises. We want you to get a glimpse of the tremendous program of development that we are now inaugurating. We want you to have the best time you ever had in your life and we want you to join with the other lot owners and put your shoulder to the wheel and help us to bring our tremendous program to a successful conclusion. We are enclosing the program

for the carnival and chatauqua [*sic*] to be held this year. Will you kindly read it over carefully and if possible, take part in some of the . . . events. The basket picnic will be an exceedingly enjoyable event. We want the largest automobile parade of the most beautifully decorated cars ever seen in Idlewild. We want the best swimmers for the swimming contest, that it is possible to secure. We want the largest number of most beautifully decorated boats in the boat regatta that has ever graced the waters of Lake Idlewild. All of these events will carry suitable prizes. We want the most gorgeous display of beautiful girls and costumes in the bathing beauty contest ever put before the public, and the winner will be crowned Miss Idlewild and receive an appropriate prize. The winners of all the athletic events will receive appropriate prizes. Decide now on what part you can take and register your name and address with your choice of the event[s] you wish to enter, with Mr. Chas. [Charles] A. Wilson, general director of athletics, 808 Hartford Bldg., Chicago, ILL: Any information you may desire or suggestions you may have to offer regarding the Chataqua [*sic*] should be addressed to Rev. R. L. Bradby, director of Chatauqua [*sic*], 2116 Pennsylvania Ave., Detroit, Michigan. The Idlewild Summer Development Company is now incorporated and the time ripe for all Idlewild lot owners to do their bit towards making this great development and progressive program a tremendous success. Will you kindly fill out and mail to this office at your early convenience the stock subscription certificate mailed to you recently in a previous letter. Free camping space for those bringing camping equipment. Yours for a Greater Idlewild! Let's Go![12]

Without a doubt, the biggest drawing card to Idlewild was Dr. Daniel Hale Williams, the most influential black in the field of medicine, and an acquaintance of an executive board member of the ISRDC, Chicago attorney Charles Wilson. Dr. Williams was the founder of Chicago's Provident Hospital and the first to operate successfully on the human heart. He traveled in influential circles from coast to coast and talked highly and often about the resort. Dr. Williams bought a large portion of land both on and near the island in Idlewild in the 1920s, naming it the Daniel Hale Williams Subdivision.[13]

Dr. Williams sold most of his property to his friends, associates, and fellow professionals. Among them were attorney Charles Chestnutt (a Cleveland resident, who authored the novels *Conjure Woman*, *The Wife of His Youth*, and *The House behind the Cedars*), Lemuel Foster (of Nashville, a distinguished

Dr. Daniel Hale Williams, a pioneer heart surgeon from Chicago, was one of the major landholders in Idlewild. He built a summer cottage that he named Oakmere. He also died at Idlewild. Courtesy of the Ben C. Wilson Collection, Black Americana Studies Department, Western Michigan University.

Fisk University alumnus who became manager in the late 1920s of the black-owned Victory Life Insurance Company), Ed Wright and Louis B. Anderson (both of Chicago, the latter an alderman), Oscar De Priest (of Chicago, the first northern black representative elected to Congress), Mary McCleod Bethune (of Daytona Beach, Florida, and founder of Bethune-Cookman College[14]), and other reputable blacks. The presence of these luminaries attracted other people from all walks of life to the resort. Helen Buckler, in her study entitled *Daniel Hale Williams: Negro Surgeon*, states that he built a little health center for emergencies at Idlewild.[15]

Dr. Williams's presence was highly visible, and he had a tremendous impact on the development of Idlewild. He created a little park across the street from his summer home that was enclosed by a white picket fence and white arches with the words "Oakmere Park" carved over the gates. He later constructed a small hexagonal summer pavilion in the park where he and guests could sit and watch the sunset. He was a friend of the environment, leaving everything as natural as possible. Gravel walks wound under the trees, their edges kept neat by his own efforts. Early risers saw him out at dawn, down on his knees, clippers in hand, working his flower garden. His prize tulips, many varieties of roses, and blood-red peonies were given to the postmistress (Ms. Elsner) and others in the vicinity.[16]

Dr. Williams located his house, a simple bungalow made luxurious with electricity and Oriental rugs, on a high knoll facing eastward over the lake. He cut down only those trees necessary to make room for the house. His chicken house, tool workshop, and garage were all nestled under the inviting shelter of green tree branches. Later in life, he began to lose dexterity in his hands and adjusted to his handicap by ceasing to perform major surgery. Although he recovered from his first stroke, it signaled the end of his career as a surgeon.

His rally from the first stroke was short-lived, as his life was threatened by other strokes during the last five years of his life, and he gradually lost his mental power. The end came on Tuesday, 4 August 1931, at his beloved Oakmere at Idlewild. The editor of the *Lake County Star* wrote a very fine tribute to him, and not once in two columns of type felt it necessary to mention that he was of Negro ancestry. In part, the obituary reads:

The Idlewild Post Office with a gas pump in front of the building. Courtesy of the State Archives of Michigan, Stanley Kufta Collection.

. . . an invalid for nearly five years . . . his departure from Idlewild was attended with honors and reverence of exceptional character. With the summer season at its height and several thousand residents and visitors at the resort, all activities were suspended for the day and in the evening a memorial service was held in which all joined in paying tribute to the splendid character of a beloved associate. . . . It is remarkable that so famous a man should carry his honors so lightly. In 1920, he built his beautiful cottage in Idlewild and went there during summers to rest. He did not practice, but he never turned a deaf ear to a call for help. One of our bankers owes his life to the skillful ministration of 'Dr. Dan,' and many others found him willing and ready to serve without pay in the cause of humanity. . . . Modest, retiring, unassuming, he found his little world here full of reverent, loving friends. To the children he was 'Dr. Dan' and a friend, even though regarded awesomely as a miracle man. Like many other truly great men he found peace, solace and instruction in nature. He loved his flowers and his garden was filled with lovely native and exotic plants. He loved the woods and waters and the living things in them. . . . To have known him was a pleasure— to know him intimately was a priceless privilege. He was at once an inspiration and an aid. To emulate his simplicity, his kindly spirit and his great modesty is to pay tribute to the truly great. The world has lost greatly. . . . Perhaps the publicity brochure was not all hyperbole when it suggested that "if you buy a lot in Idlewild you will place yourself, your family and your friends in position to reap the innumerable benefits that spring from personal contact with the deepest thinkers, the most active, most progressive people of the times."[17]

Eventually, the ISRDC gave rise to other organizations such as the Idlewild Lot Owners Association, the Original Idlewilders, and later five regional Idlewilders clubs. Their existence was helpful in attracting other African Americans to Idlewild, as visitors, vacationers, purchasers of lots, and builders of cottages.

Harry Solomon, from Cleveland, said his parents eventually bought property after becoming aware of the resort. The former township supervisor recalled:

In August of 1928, at the age of 12, my father, mother, sisters, and brother made the trip to Idlewild. I remember it took 24 hours to get there from Detroit in a

Model-T Ford after many flat tires. I remember my sister becoming car sick from the trip. I remember that Idlewild was rugged, natural and beautiful with dirt roads, trails and very few modern conveniences. . . . I saw for the first time in my life snakes, porcupine[s], deer, bear[s], rabbit[s] and a variety of birds. I saw my father shave by the light of the sun. We spent two very beautiful weeks in a cottage owned by a Mrs. Hattie Martin. We had many camp type meals. This was my first real experience of what a vacation was like.[18]

For those vacationers who were from Michigan, quite often women and children stayed the whole summer while the husbands and fathers worked in the cities and came to Idlewild on weekends and holidays.[19]

The Business District in Idlewild

As a result of the growing black population between 1917 and 1930, especially between Memorial Day and Labor Day, the business district at Idlewild began to grow. Strolling through the area, one would find a dress shop, a gift shop, grocery stores, a car wash, a bike rental shop, a Swedish massage parlor, a cement company, a propane gas distributor, six cafes, two hotels, twelve motels, boarding houses, at least four nightclubs, a post office, a telephone operator office that served seven to fifteen customers on the island, a brick-making facility, a dry cleaning/laundry shop, and a small food cannery.

During the summer months especially, the money introduced into the area's economy by the black resorters allowed Idlewild to boost its business district in record time. Those same resorters, however, also helped sustain the economic development in Lake County, a county that had depended primarily on the logging industry before it turned to tourism. Without a doubt, it is fair to say that Lake County was not an island of racial tolerance. Blacks, regardless of social status, simply were not welcomed at white resorts during this time. It is interesting and noteworthy that the white developers of Idlewild—Lemon, the Branch brothers, the Wrights, and others—also developed another resort in the area, the Big Star Lake. Located near Baldwin, Michigan, this recreation site was for whites only. It was widely known that the black butlers, maids, and chauffeurs of the white vacationers were forbidden to spend the night at any time. Such segregation notwithstanding,

Log cabin grocery store where resorters could buy food and gas. Courtesy of the State Archives of Michigan, Stanley Kufta Collection.

many blacks were so content with their piece of "Eden" at Idlewild that few, if any, even entertained the thought of purchasing and resorting at Big Star Lake.

Sociological Illuminations

The Idlewild Resort Company's marketing strategy had several key features that made it possible for that company to achieve some great strides in the development of Idlewild as a resort community. Those strides meant that they had to be successful in getting black people to purchase one or more lots in a place that was a considerable distance from any large city in the Midwest. Fundamentally, they were successful because they hired black salespersons to sell lots to black people and they took advantage of a purchasing habit commonly found in the black community that involved spending a small amount of money on important things. For example, black ministers and other leaders in the community were often relentless in pressuring black people to join burial societies where they were expected to pay a few cents each week.

Participating in the various self-help societies was an idea strongly emphasized as the right thing to do, racially. Adults were assured that purchasing a burial policy was good insurance against the unforeseen future. It was the right thing to do, and one was obliged, as a member of the black community, to join and actively support the various societies because that support was needed for the survival of the black community.

Though reluctant at first, white insurance companies took advantage of the black community by sending in salesmen to push so-called penny policies that eventually supplanted the burial societies. They made it appear as if they had better benefits for less money, and that they were doing black people a favor by allowing them to hold policies in a major white company. A few black-owned companies eventually emerged and were able to compete with the white companies. The North Carolina Life Insurance Company is one such black-owned-and-operated company that gave some of the white companies a run for the black dollar. In a big family, each member could be insured for a few cents a week.

Sellers and a potential buyer at the resort. Courtesy of the Ben C. Wilson Collection, Black Americana Studies Department, Western Michigan University.

So, for many African Americans, purchasing a lot in Idlewild—which called for $6.00 down and the balance in sums of $1.00—conformed very well with a buying tradition that they had embraced for decades. A small amount down and a negligible amount due on an ongoing basis was a well-entrenched purchasing habit that made life bearable, if not affordable. This habit of purchasing made it possible for some blacks to buy lots sight unseen. It seems that with the sale of each lot the black resort movement gained both momentum and size. Also, the appeal to racial pride was another major reason for their success. On the national scene, racial pride had acquired high currency, as evident in the Harlem Renaissance Movement, in Garvey's Universal Negro Improvement Association, in the "era of the New Negro," in the writings of scholars, and in the expressions of various artists who accepted the challenges found in a protracted struggle against Jim Crowism.

The Popular Place
to Be

WITH THE ADDITION OF MORE HOTELS, MOTELS, AND BOARDING HOUSES, MORE places to eat, more entertainers to enjoy, and a plethora of other activities, Idlewild's popularity skyrocketed as it became "the place" to be. African Americans arrived in waves at "the place" in the woods in Lake County, Michigan. Over time the character of the resort community changed, and it experienced some intragroup tensions as a result of its transformation from a homogeneous community to one that was more heterogeneous in nature. This chapter considers the impact of promotional activities, the various waves of visitors to the resort and their interactions, facilities built at the resort, and several pieces of music and poetry written about the area.

PROMOTION OF THE RESORT

To supplement the sales brochures, various black daily, weekly, and biweekly newspapers carried advertisements about the resort. Among those used were the *Chicago Defender*, the *Idlewild Herald Magazine*, the *Chatter Box*, the *Chicago Daily News*, and the *Idlewild Challenger*. The *Negro Digest*, a nationally circulated magazine, also carried information about the resort. These differ-

Well-dressed resorters at the summer cottage in Idlewild. Courtesy of the Ben C. Wilson Collection, Black Americana Studies Department, Western Michigan University.

ent print sources were used in tandem with a twenty-three-minute silent promotional film that the ISRDC commissioned.[1] The results suggested that they did a splendid job of disseminating information and interesting blacks in the resort.

Because of the marketing activities undertaken by the Idlewild Resort, more people became interested in finding an attractive weekend getaway. A larger number of visitors came to Idlewild and, since the down payment on lots was still so affordable, many purchased one, because it was "the thing to do." Charles English, a Battle Creek native and Idlewild property owner, remarked that "Five dollars down was nothing, and lots of people bought just to own land—a piece of the earth itself." Many of these people had no intention of becoming permanent residents at the time, but returned to Idlewild in the post–Second World War years and built cottages there.[2]

The success of the promotional activities, however, meant that as more and more people came to the resort, they wanted more than the beautiful scenery. A burgeoning population provided more opportunities for entrepreneurs to profit by catering to the needs of the resorters and lot owners. To fill those needs, Lemon and his ISRDC had to find businesspeople who were willing to build new facilities. There was no problem with respect to physical space; land was plentiful and could be purchased at a reasonable price. All that was required were entrepreneurs willing to take advantage of the opportunity that was being offered them. An example of what was needed had already been established in the 1930s by a black architect and builder from Detroit. Mr. Robert Jones came to the resort and built the first modern hotel in the area. He entered the contracting business and proceeded to construct permanent, year-round homes for retired pioneer resorters who had no desire to leave the community.

In addition to Mr. Jones, other entrepreneurs from such cities as Detroit and Chicago played either a direct or indirect role in the construction of buildings in the community. He modernized a decrepit hotel and built a plush hotel nightclub. Over time, then, people began to enjoy the activities at such places as the Paradise Club (built in 1922), the Club El-Morocco, the Eagle's Nest, the Polk Skating Rink, Pearl's Tavern, the White Way Inn, Trillie Stewart's Place, Maceo Thomas's Place, and the Hotel Casa Blanca

Bra-Haven, a bed and breakfast, was built in response to a demand for more facilities to accommodate the vacationers in Idlewild. Courtesy of the State Archives of Michigan, Stanley Kufta Collection.

The White House Tearoom was at full occupancy during the summer months. Courtesy of the State Archives of Michigan, Stanley Kufta Collection.

The Oakmere Hotel was owned by Phil Giles, a former Detroit hotel man and former president of the Idlewild Chamber of Commerce, who realized the need for more room accommodations. Courtesy of the State Archives of Michigan, Stanley Kufta Collection.

(these latter places were constructed in the 1940s and 1950s). The Fiesta Room, a new section of the Paradise Club, was also completed in the 1950s.

Other places that attracted resorters were the Purple Palace, the Idlewild Club House, Morton's Motel, the Sweetheart Motel, the Oakmere Hotel, the Lydia Inn on the Lake, the White House Tearoom, the Bra-Haven Boarding House, Douglas Manor, and Sonny Roxborough's new Rosanna Tavern (later known as the Red Rooster Tavern). The family picnics, boating, swimming, excellent entertainment, and just plain "rest and relaxation" found at the resort made Idlewild the destination of choice for many African Americans for nearly fifty years, with its heyday between 1940 and 1965.

Special Music and Poems Written for Idlewild

The resort became so popular that Robert Belton, writing in Negro dialect, wrote a poem entitled "If You Ebber Want to Get to Hebben Quick, Come to Idlewild." This poem also was used to advertise the resort in many black communities. In addition to the poem, several songs were written about the place by those who wanted to express their affection for the "Black Eden." One such song was written by Dr. Wilbur Lemon, the manager of the IRC and a major stockholder in ISRDC Incorporated. It reads:

> Dear I—dle—wild, ____my I—dle—wild I hear the birds a calling, I see the rain drops falling to I—dle—wild, Dear I—dle—wild, ____ the can—dle lights are burn—ing, my thots of you are turning, to I—dle—wild, (oh boy) Dear wild.[3]

Major N. Clark Smith, the *Chicago Defender* bandmaster, later expanded that version to read:

> In a big Lake Count-y, not man-y miles a—way, the count-less pil-grims gath-er, for rest and play; It's trees of oak and love-ly folk, it's Ta-ber-na-cle or a church, where ma-ples grow with state-ly birch, 'Tis na-ture's won-der-child, Dear I—dle—wild Fern Gar—den, A dream of life come true, and old Pere Mar—quette riv-er, so clear and blue, God made its wa-ters sing a strain, to bub—bling brook an' spring re-main, they chant and sing a sweet re-frain, with na-ture's mu-sic dream, Dear

CHORUS

I—dle—wild ____ my I—dle—wild ____ I hear the birds a—calling, I feel the dew—drops fall-ing; To I—dle—wild,—Dear I—dle—wild, ____The can-dle lights a—burning, My thoughts of love are turn-ing, To I-dle-wild (oh boy) Dear wild, ____[4]

Ray Kamalay, a Lansing, Michigan resident, tried to capture the impact of music and the livelier times of the resort, during the 1950s and 1960s, when he wrote:

> Idlewild, wild and free
> our jumpin' rhythms always calling me,
> country air, sweet and strong,
> packing up my suitcase
> so it won't be long,
> sing and dance 'til sundown,
> It's such a rat race in Chicago town,
> still I feel like a child,
> cuz I'm heading up to Idlewild[5]

The passing of the years has not dimmed the desire of those familiar or still connected with Idlewild to express their thoughts in songs and poems about the rustic retreat. A contemporary poem entitled "Idlewild Is the Face of God" was written by Audrey Bullett, a former township supervisor. In July 1998, she wrote:

IDLEWILD IS THE FACE OF GOD

> looking at me daily.
> I see the face of God in the change of the seasons
> in the storms of life
> in the coldness of winter.
> I see the face of God in the greenness of spring
> in the barrenness of fall
> and the warmth of summer.
> I see the face of God in the birds, bees, and trees

in the frogs in the swamp
in the soft white clouds that drift by
that hang over the downpour of rain.
I see the face of God throughout this community
in every place, person, creature
and phase of life.
Idlewild is the face of God
looking at me daily.

THE EMERGENT CLEAVAGES AT IDLEWILD

As mentioned at the outset of this chapter, African Americans flocked to the resort in different waves and at different times, some waves overlapping others. Over time, the initial homogeneous character of the resort changed, with each new wave of visitors resulting in a more diverse population at the resort. Numerous publications have referred to the pioneers on what is called the "Island" as "Gold Coasters," or as "the thinking, progressive, active class of

Views of a summer cottage in Idlewild. Courtesy of the Ben C. Wilson Collection, Black Americana Studies Department, Western Michigan University.

people who are the leading spirits of their communities."[6] However, African Americans of all social, educational, and philosophical levels came to be visitors at the "Ideal Sylvan Retreat," and thus it should not be a surprise that some tensions and intragroup cleavages did occur. The following section discusses some of the new elements added to the mix and their impact on the changing nature of the resort community.

A new black element was introduced into Lake County by a little-known Chicago real estate firm that decided to capitalize on the resort's notoriety. The realtors purchased large blocks of land near, but not actually within, the resort. In an area north of the county seat of Baldwin, they sold land with the implication that it was part of the Idlewild resort community. Some of the sales techniques used in this nearby project were thought to be scandalous, a perception also reserved for many of their customers.

Much of the land was platted in five-acre lots and sold as retirement places. Lots were advertised on streetcars, given as door prizes, and merchandised using the full gamut of high-pressure techniques. These "new people" who lived on the periphery of the actual resort were quite different from the aristocratic pioneer Idlewilders. Many came from steel-mill towns and the poorer industrial districts located in the Midwest metropolitan areas. Their educational, social, and economic levels were lower than those of the original Idlewild community. Black pioneers condescendingly referred to them as "less progressive," or simply "them." Whether from the rural or urban areas of the South, the majority of the new arrivals found coping with northern city life to be very difficult due largely to poor education, nonsalable or nontransferable skills, overcrowded living conditions, lack of transportation, and more. Viewed through the eyes of the black bourgeoisie, these new residents were considered economic failures.

Another group that became acquainted with the resort in the late 1930s and early 1940s was attributed to the automobile. Car ownership and an improved state highway infrastructure made the resort community increasingly accessible. By the late 1950s the love affair with the automobile was deeply entrenched in the fabric of the American way of life. The proud owners of automobiles most often had good jobs and aspired to a better way of life for themselves and their families. Though their values may have differed from those of the more elite blacks, they nonetheless were pleased with their

A view of the sleeping cottages called the "dog houses." Courtesy of the Ben C. Wilson Collection, Black Americana Studies Department, Western Michigan University.

station in life. Furthermore, not unlike their elite counterparts, upon arrival at the resort these visitors went straight to the motel, hotel, or boarding house lobby to reacquaint themselves with old friends. Invariably, the automobile and their travel to the resort became topics of conversation: the long drive, getting lost, the overheating of the radiator, the number of flat tires, the horsepower of the cars, their top speeds, and other topics associated with the love affair with the automobile were avidly discussed. In the late 1950s and 1960s, the bumper-to-bumper traffic at the resort was a primary irritant. The Yates Township Police Department was established in 1955 primarily for crowd and traffic control. Its chief, Bill Morton, an interesting and unique individual, also served as a public relations officer during the resort's most prosperous era.[7]

Between the late 1920s and 1950s, a third group appeared on the scene— the weekenders. Some were independent business owners and came from the same social and economic levels as the resort's pioneers. Also found among this group were a few policy bosses, numbers bankers, and runners.

These men's "slightly" shady backgrounds, most often well known in the community, were readily overlooked, however, by the aristocrats, who tolerated them because of their cash flow and "manners." They were not looked upon with contempt because many of the numbers men and policy bosses were indeed longstanding friends of some of the pioneers. Often friendships developed between these two elements as a result of banks denying loans to the pioneers, who then received favorable responses from policy bosses.

A case that illustrates the closeness of the two elements at Idlewild involved the flashy Sunnie Wilson from Detroit and the Jones boys (Mac, George, and Ed) from Chicago. They were well-established and popular Idlewilders. Sunnie Wilson and John Cohassey, in their book, *Toast of the Town: The Life and Times of Sunnie Wilson*, let it be known that:

> These brothers [Mac, Ed, and George] made millions in the numbers. All of them were good-looking and very intelligent. As a young man I loved to spend money. The Jones Boys enjoyed watching me spend money and liked to give me cash. I didn't care where they got it as long as I could spend it. . . . In Chicago the Joneses ran policy out of milk depots. They owned hotels and Ben Franklin stores. They were very enterprising individuals. . . . The family owned a Chateau in France. Their daughters spoke French and Spanish. . . . The numbers made them multimillionaires. After their father died, their mother was the backbone of the outfit and Ed was the boss.[8]

Sunnie revealed that The Jones Boys led tough lives. As Wilson recalls in his memoir, Ed went to prison because he took the income tax evasion "rap" for the family, but while there found himself at the mercy of Chicago mobsters. Their extortion continued after Ed was released from prison, and, on one occasion, his brothers were kidnapped, forcing him to pay a ransom. While driving to a cabaret, Mac Jones hit an embankment and was killed. Later, George received an empty casket at his home; it was a warning from the mob, and he quickly left Chicago and moved to Mexico for his own safety.

Though the Jones Boys were multimillionaires and familiar to many in Idlewild, they did not have a monopoly on the policy game, nor did they control access to the resort. Owing to its popularity, in the 1950s other sporting men from such cities as Saginaw, Detroit, Flint, Cleveland, and Indianapolis began to seek out Idlewild as their summer haven. Some of them even made financial contributions to the cultural events of the resort. That policy bosses participated in this manner was not an unusual, because many of them had "bought" respectability in their own communities. The buying of respectability took many forms, and the case of the Jones Boys is illustrative of this fact, in that:

> Most "respectable" people . . . , when they defend policy, do so on the basis of the achievements of men such as the "Jones Boys." For instance, one legitimate businessman said, "I'm glad to see our group go into business enterprises no matter where the money comes from." Businessmen frequently cited the "racketeers" as "the ones who have taken the lead in the business world," as persons who "give employment to a large number of people and give the race a rating among the people of the white business world that we have not enjoyed before." One successful entrepreneur, after listing a half-dozen prominent racketeers, said, "All of these men are known as racket men, but at least they have opened places that give employment to our own people." One female tavern owner doesn't "know how to explain it, but the people who have opened the best businesses are those who have made money from policy." Occasionally, these encomiums are associated with a criticism of the "respectable" businessmen, who "always had large sum of money at their disposal, but none of them have opened anything worth mentioning."[9]

Speaking of respectability, it would be difficult to find a policy boss anywhere who commanded more respect than that which was bestowed upon the Jones Boys, according to Drake and Cayton, when they opened their store on one of the main streets in Chicago. On the program, along with other dignitaries and celebrities, was heavyweight champion Joe Louis, who also was a popular figure in Idlewild.[10]

African Americans in the military made up a fourth wave of blacks to the resort. These black G.I.s were inducted in their respective home states but were stationed in the Great Lakes area with specific assignments to either Ft. Custer (Battle Creek, Michigan), Selfridge Field (an air force base near Mt. Clemens, Michigan), Great Lakes (a naval station near Waukegan, Illinois), Scotts (an air force base near Lebanon, Illinois) or Wursmith (an air force base near Oscoda, Michigan). Unfortunately, their military uniforms did not safeguard them against the prejudice in the various local communities in Michigan and Illinois. Though the men were encouraged by their commanding officers to leave their military bases and interact with the local people during social events and church services, stereotypes were widespread about single military men in general, and doubly so for men of color, and therefore families were excessively careful in monitoring the behavior of their children, especially their daughters. Thus, people in the local communities were not eager for these men to participate in their social life. The lack of civility and cordiality in the local communities added enormously to these men's loneliness and caused many to question their role as inductees in the military of the United States.

The black military personnel at Ft. Custer, just outside Battle Creek, Michigan, found the Douglass Community Center in Kalamazoo and the Hamblin Center in Battle Creek to be favorite facilities on the weekends. These centers sought to serve the needs of the black community in these towns, often holding dances and other social events, and they welcomed the lonely and homesick young black military men. Time permitting, the military men also traveled to Idlewild, where they spent not only their furlough time but also their money. Between World War II and the Korean Conflict, many shots of liquor were poured and paid for by these men in the local bars. They were good spenders, and a few occasionally overindulged, to the consternation of the black elite. On several occasions, the soldiers exhibited their military prowess by becoming involved in brawls.

Finally, a fifth wave of visitors came to the resort during the late 1950s and the 1960s. These people, who were unable to adjust to northern urban life, were "squatters," who did not own a cottage or any lots at Idlewild but simply unhitched their mobile homes and set up camp on someone else's property. Some broke into summer homes and cottages and made themselves at home until the vacation season began. Of course, homeowners were disappointed and disgusted upon arriving at Idlewild to discover their property stolen, vandalized, or both.[11] This prompted a few property owners in the area to invest in security systems.

The Skin Color Factor: Intraracial Strife and Problems of Social Distance

During the early days of the resort, whether consciously or unconsciously, it seems that many African Americans who were targeted to purchase lots or become involved with the development of Idlewild as a resort were those of a lighter skin color. Though there was no preference for a certain skin color printed on the leaflets and marketing materials or broadcast on the radio, this was indeed a factor that affected interactions among black people. The proportion of light-skinned African Americans was higher among the more affluent people in Idlewild

> . . . than among the rank and file. This, of course, has nothing to do with the superiority of their "white blood." It is the result of a social process which has, in the past, made it easier for the lighter Negroes to get ahead, and of the tendency for the more successful men to marry women lighter than themselves.[12]

According to an observation made by St. Clair Drake and Horace R. Cayton,

> When "fair" (i.e., light-skinned) Negroes seem inordinately proud of their skin-color, or when darker Negroes have a predilection for association with very light ones or encouraging their children to do so, Bronzeville calls them "color-struck." One color-struck woman told an interviewer that she liked dark-skinned people "in their places . . . I mean I like them, but not around me. Their place is with the rest of the dark-skinned folks." Another woman says much the same: "I have no ill-feeling for the 'less fortunate,' but I don't care to entertain them outside of closed doors. I really feel embarrassed when people see me with black persons. I do have a friend who is quite dark. I love her and really forget that she is black until we start outdoors. I never go very far with her, though." Of such people, a dark-brown-skinned professional man observed: "Somewhere in their early childhood these light-skinned people who think they are better than the dark Negroes are taught that the nearer they are to white the better they are. They have a superiority complex. This attitude, just like the attitude of white people toward Negroes, is the result of propaganda."[13]

Though some African Americans from the more fortunate families were horrified at the sight of their beautiful Idlewild being "invaded" by their uncouth, unscrupulous, and uneducated darker-skinned brothers and sisters, color was by no means always the dominant factor in intraracial relations at the resort. There were other factors—such as ability, competence, and loyalty—in the mix, which lessened or mitigated the importance of color at Idlewild, as well as in the larger society.

In addition to the skin color factor, the coming together of waves of people from differing walks of life and social positions also led to some intraracial strife. The pioneers wanted to isolate themselves from the "new people," but found it impossible to do so. Still, there was a proclivity among many to maintain a clannish existence in all phases of life at the resort. They had the good manners to be cordial but rarely the tolerance to be social. A good example of this behavior was seen on those occasions where people from the various socioeconomic levels would attend a function; often, the pioneers would socialize only with those of "their own ilk."[14] Even having the same socioeconomic background did not guarantee acceptance; some newcomers, with their "tainted values," simply did not fit. Yet, for some, color was a factor.

Lawrence Otis Graham described this notion in *Inside America's Black Upper Class: Our Kind of People*. He mentioned that there were those families who made what some called

> ... "a handsome picture" of people with "good hair" (wavy or straight), with "nice complexions" (light brown to nearly white), with "sharp features" (thin nose, thin lips, sharp jaw) and curiously non-Negroid hazel, green or blue eyes. . . . In fact . . . some . . . not only had complexions ten shades lighter than that brown paper bag, and hair as straight as any ruler, but also had multiple generations of "good looks, wealth and accomplishments. . . ."[15]

However, a few of the newcomers who were dark in complexion were the sporting men who had money to invest in Idlewild ventures. Arthur "Daddy" Braggs was a striking example of those who risked their dollars in ventures throughout the 1950s and 1960s. Braggs was seen by many as a premier promoter. He brought numerous well-known performers to the resort. Many of his entertainers were from either the Chicago or the Detroit area.

Exterior view of the Club El-Morocco. Courtesy of the State Archives of Michigan, Stanley Kufta Collection.

If they could afford it, the darker-skinned characters patronized the Fiesta Room in the Paradise Club, the El-Morocco, the Eagle's Nest, the Polk Skating Rink, Pearl's Tavern, Trillie Stewart's Place, or Maceo Thomas's Place. On the other hand, the older aristocrats held more closely to their traditional functions at the Purple Palace and the Idlewild Club House. Nevertheless, it was not uncommon to see the aristocrats' children dismiss their class distinctions in order to "frolic" with whatever group appeared to have the liveliest activities. Crossing the social class lines was not too difficult for some adults in the aristocratic circle. They simply would party with everyone. It did not matter to them, for example, if the games (Georgia skins, coon-can, poker, bid whist, pinochle, bridge, canasta) were played in the homes of the elite on Idlewild's Gold Coast or in Idlewild's Flamingo Club. Their interest was in playing with people who were enthusiastic about these games and who could present them with a competitive challenge.

In the 1950s, regardless of social and economic distinctions, many adults could be found at Sonny Roxborough's new Rosanna Tavern downing a cold brew (served by either Chickie Wilson, day barmaid, or Hazel Burrell, night barmaid). At the roller skating rink it was hard to distinguish the children of the upper crust—who spent weeks at a time at Idlewild—from those belonging to blue-collar workers—who were there just for a weekend.

Exterior view of the Paradise Club, constructed by the husband and wife team of Herman and Lela Wilson, which overlooked Paradise Lake at Idlewild. Courtesy of the State Archives of Michigan, Stanley Kufta Collection.

OTHER RELATED DEVELOPMENTS

In the late 1920s and early 1930s, chautauquas, or open-air forums, were commonplace at Idlewild. They reflected a deep concern about the plight of black people in this country. The chautauquas were in keeping with the early notion that Idlewild would be a place where, among other things, the best thinkers in the race would come together and share their views with those of a like mind. A sampling of the topics handled in 1926 and 1927 provides some insight into the issues and concerns of the leadership of the day. The topics discussed included: "The Future of Idlewild," "The People of Idlewild," "The Negro Women's Contribution to History," "The Church's Role in Race Relations," "Education of the Handicapped," "The Unpublished History of the Negro versus the Published," "Negro Poets and Musicians," "The Inner City Insurance Cancellations," "Poems of Negro Life," "The Negro in Transition," and "The Crisis of Negro and White Leadership in a Free Society."[16]

In 1927, Dean William Pickens, national field secretary for the National Association for the Advancement of Colored People (N.A.A.C.P.), lectured on the value of having an organization that would speak for and represent black needs and desires throughout America.[17] In 1926, Chandler Owens (editor-organizer-champion of *Race Rights* in Chicago) and Robert A. Bagnall (director of branches of the N.A.A.C.P. and lecturer and organizer in New York City) were major presenters at the resort.[18] In 1927, the Chautuaqua Committee invited Governor Fred Green of Michigan to address the meetings at the resort, but he declined the invitation.

Though there were some social problems at the resort, they were, for the most part, petty, and they were not allowed to assume any major moment. The leaders of the community remained ever steadfast in their vision of developing a significantly better resort. Toward that end, according to an article in the *Idlewild Challenger* in 1952,

> Phil Giles, former Detroit hotel man and president of the Idlewild Chamber of Commerce, injected new life in the resort business here, with his many and varied enterprises all in keeping with the idea of providing the vacationer to Idlewild with modern and up to date accommodations and attractions. . . . [H]e has foresight in recognizing latent opportunity. . . . This has given the local people work and jobs. A new eatery, Giles Grill, which overlooks picturesque Lake Idlewild is nearing completion. Buildings for concession are completed, which will house new business being brought to the island. An amusement park, providing clear and wholesome recreation for the children will feature a merry-go-round and Ferris wheel and many other attractions. For the water lovers: water cycles will be the thing. . . . The Giles Dude Ranch is now open. Giles['s] riding stables will provide good mounts for the riding crowd. Lake Cruises in the motor boats will be planned daily. In keeping with the thoughtfulness of this one man dynamo, who seems to think of everything for the comfort and care of his guest, an ambulance is another addition which will be on hand to dispatch quickly and safely the sick or accident victims, to the local and nearby hospitals. . . .[19]

The proposed amusement rides, like the proposed executive mansion, never materialized. Yet, on a more positive note, the resort did emerge as an important stop on the "Chitlin Circuit" for many fledgling young black entertainers, much to the chagrin of some pioneers, which had a major influence on the growth and development of music and entertainment at the resort. This will be discussed in more detail in the next chapter.

The Flamingo Bar. Courtesy of John English.

In late 1928, after making a sizeable profit over and above their initial investment of $75,000 (and the purchasing of the Branches' interest for $50,000), Dr. Wilbur Lemon and his Chicago associates sold their shares in the ISRDC to the Idlewild Lot Owners Association (ILOA) for at least $20,000. Former Idlewilder and real estate agent Mr. John Reynolds in 1982 estimated that "Lemon and his group made at least one million dollars before parting ways with Idlewild."[20]

> The ILOA was an exclusive non-profit private club dedicated to promote [sic] a spirit of fraternity, co-operation [sic] and brotherly love among the Idlewild lot owners. No one except those who own lots in Beautiful Idlewild could become members of this Association, but all lot owners were invited and urged to do so. The money received from the membership fees was used, after the expenses of [the] organization were paid, to purchase all public utilities at Idlewild—including the clubhouse, ice house, rental cottages, electric plant, pier, boats, the eighty acres set aside for the golf link and other parcels of land throughout which had not been sold as lots and which were wonderfully adapted to being little picnic parks and scenic views.[21]

The board of managers for the association also made and enforced all the rules, regulations, and laws governing the resort. They pledged to use their best efforts to preserve the name, honor, and integrity of Idlewild. A branch or subsidiary club of the ILOA was organized in each city where there were at least ten lot owners. Each club elected its own officers and was mandated to meet once a month to discuss issues concerning the resort or the physical, intellectual, and spiritual welfare of its members.[22]

Sociological Illuminations
Social Adjustments in a Segregated System

Minority populations—whether in urban ghettoes or rural, agricultural environments, in this country or foreign places—have always had to bear the burden of adapting to the various patterns of segregation. Aside from living apart from others, they have often been forced to adjust their behavioral patterns to conform to the dictates of a segregated society. Additionally, often against tremendous odds, they have had to build social and economic infrastructures to meet their own special internal needs. For African Americans, Idlewild was a setting where it was necessary for them to build the requisite infrastructures to make it the "mecca" that it ultimately became. In the process, many African Americans benefitted economically because of the numerous opportunities and challenges available to those with the skills and money needed to help develop the resort community.

Acceptance, out of necessity, of the infrastructural challenges brought success to Idlewild in a context where there was widespread segregation and a relative lack of intraracial competition. This condition probably sent the wrong message to the planners, leaders, and entrepreneurs in Idlewild, leading them to believe that "Segregation will last and we will continue to make money." Thus, in time, it appears that they became satisfied with their own level of success, feeling that because black people were coming in throngs to and spending their money at the resort community, this trend would continue indefinitely.

The view that segregation would last and that the leaders of the resort would continue to prosper proved to be a myopic one, because it led to an unpreparedness or unwillingness to build the infrastructures needed to position the community to compete successfully with any challenges that might come from the outside world, race notwithstanding. Because the resort's leaders became satisfied with their successes, they gradually stopped planning and building to make Idlewild a truly world-class resort, and such plans as an amusement park and other attractions fell by the wayside. Rather than being satisfied with the very modest accommodations then available at the resort, Idlewild's leaders would have found the building of substantial restaurants and hotels to accommodate large numbers of people a risk worth taking, especially since land was plentiful and reasonably priced and thousands of people were visiting the community every year, prior to the time of the civil rights movements.

Living in a segregated society can be a powerful motivator. It can also be an awesome impediment, in the sense that life in such a society frequently can cause one to limit one's own actions because of a sense of reality as defined by segregation. If the perception in a segregated society is that black performing artists will never be allowed to play in major white clubs or the large white resorts, for example, then those artists are likely to limit their aspirations to playing in small black clubs or the black "Chitlin Circuit."

Arguably, segregation places a minority people in a subordinate status and forces them to adjust their social world to comply with the dictates of the segregated system. That very status, however, can be a forceful motivator, in the sense that people adopt lifestyles that tend to maximize the quality of life and the likelihood of their very survival. Idlewild is an excellent example of a subordinated people who were motivated to use their innovative skills to create and support a resort community that added immeasurably to the quality of the black experience in a segregated America.

Intraracial Social Cleavages

The small group of white entrepreneurs who were determined to sell lots in Idlewild to those African Americans who shared the same social values and aspirations and who came from the same social class—the black bourgeoisie or the upper crust—found their success in this venture to be short-lived. Thus, the potential for intraracial strife was an inherent part of the process from the very beginning. Since there was no monolithic black social structure in America, it was very difficult for the entrepreneurs to create and maintain a homogeneous resort community, based on social class.

As Idlewild's popularity grew, so did its diversity, as reflected in the various waves of visitors who came from different stations in life and yet who all wanted to experience the "black mecca" in Michigan. Though these different groups of black people shared a sense of peoplehood, based on historical identification, continuous harmonious relationships were not guaranteed. Simply put, a common history falls short of guaranteeing that internal divisions will not emerge as people come into contact with one another.

Though some elements at Idlewild sought to distance themselves from others, it was virtually impossible to deny the reality that all, regardless of skin color and economic status, were in the same boat with respect to being "a Negro" in America, where one drop of "Negro blood" made one "a Negro." Phenotypically, a person could pass for white, but if his or her black ancestry was known, no matter how remote, then that individual was considered to be black. Therefore, possessing thin lips, straight hair, light-colored eyes, and keen facial features did not automatically bestow upon a person a blanket of immunity from racism. Hence, though they may have come with different skin gradations and from different social classes, a sense of historical identification was the social glue that held the Idlewild community together in a virtual "rainbow of colors" and a common community of peoplehood. This was a peoplehood that manifested a diversity held together because of the shared experience of being "a Negro" in America. This race factor was not unique to Idlewild; it was a phenomenon duplicated in virtually every African American community in the United States.

An Emergent Black Entertainment Showcase

HARRY A. REED, IN HIS ARTICLE ENTITLED "THE BLACK TAVERN IN THE MAKING of a Jazz Musician: Bird, Mingus and Stan Hope," stated that young black musicians have always served a considerable period of an apprenticeship in juke joints and back bars. There they have learned acceptable professional standards and worked to improve their techniques, expand their repertoire, extend the range of their instruments, and internalize positive attitudes toward improvisation. Additionally, the entertainment site has been the place to experiment with new ideas. If the novices' competence has not matched their confidence, the negative response usually has spurred them to greater effort and sometimes final achievement or failure. The bar, among other things, has provided a location where companionships could be made and maintained. "In this setting a new language was learned, a new type of dress was adopted, and, new social modes were accepted. . . ."[1]

Besides making the rounds of the bars in the large urban areas, talents of all stripes found their way to Idlewild, where they contributed enormously to the growth and development of that area as a resort community. The contributions of these entertainers were complementary to such other summer activities as family picnicking, boating, and horseback riding. At one time or

another, many of the most notable intellectual, musical, and artistic talents
were nurtured at Idlewild, bringing that community in close harmony with
the Renaissance movement in black communities such as that found in New
York City. Desiree Cooper, a writer for the *Detroit News and Free Press*, makes
the observation that:

> That movement was later dubbed the Harlem Renaissance, an era in the 1920s
> when blacks used music, art, literature and intellectual discourse to exhibit their
> humanity to the rest of the world. The hope was that, through their contributions
> to American culture, racism and bigotry would eventually evaporate.
>
> During the Harlem Renaissance, New York became the cultural capital of
> black America, spawning famous writers such as Langston Hughes and Zora
> Neale Hurston; musicians such as Duke Ellington and Louis Armstrong; painters
> such as Palmer Hayden and William H. Johnson; and social activists such as
> W. E. B. DuBois, founder of the National Association for the Advancement of
> Colored People. That Renaissance also touched little Midwestern towns such as
> Idlewild.[2]

Some of the people mentioned in her article spent some time at Idlewild en
route to becoming national and international figures. This chapter highlights
many of the entertainers and a few of the other activities that made Idlewild
"the popular place to be" during its heyday.

The Chitlin Circuit

In much the same way that Jewish entertainers, between the 1930s and
1960s, got their start in the "Borscht Belt" resorts of the Catskill Mountains
in New York and elsewhere, many up-and-coming black performers began
their long road to fame and fortune via the Idlewild resort.[3] In the 1950s,
Chicagoan Wendell "Paw" Lawhorn and the original Chicago Idlewilders
began to hold benefit amateur shows consisting of dancers, bathing beauties,
comedians, male and female singing groups, and impersonators.[4] The admission fee for adults and children ranged from $0.65 to $1.25.[5] These shows
became the forum for many soon-to-be famous entertainers. Furthermore,
many already-established black performers exhibited their talents in either

Vacationers canoeing on Lake Idlewild. Courtesy of the Ben C. Wilson Collection, Black Americana Studies Department, Western Michigan University.

the Fiesta Room in the Paradise Club, the Flamingo Club, the Club El-Morocco, or the Idlewild Club House. Word-of-mouth about the splendid performances put on by Sammy Davis Jr., the leggy dancers, and the booming voice of Billy Eckstine made a trip to the resort a must for those who had never before visited the area. Idlewild in short order became a showcase for the talents of both well-known and lesser-known black entertainers. Because many of these entertainers went on to become nationally and internationally known, and because some, if not many, of them may be unfamiliar to the reader, we have provided a brief sketch of many of the notables who performed at Idlewild, followed by a description of some of the professional black athletes who frequented the resort. Among the performers who exhibited their talents at Idlewild were:

Louis Armstrong (4 July 1900–9 July 1971). Born in New Orleans , he was raised in very humble surroundings in an economically depressed neighborhood in New Orleans. Besides selling newspapers and delivering milk, Armstrong's early interest in music led him to earn pennies by singing on the streets. Growing up poor, not a rarity among African American families at the time, did not deter Armstrong from becoming one of the world's greatest jazz musicians. However, it was while he was at the Negro Waif's Home, for firing a gun, that he received some formal study in music, learning to read music and play the bugle and cornet. He subsequently built on this foundation and became proficient enough to perform in various jazz bands in New Orleans. By this time Joe "King" Oliver, his former music teacher, was enjoying some success with his own band, and he invited Armstrong to join his organization in Chicago. Armstrong accepted, and in short notice displayed his musical talents with King Oliver's band by cutting his first recordings. The "Hot Fives" and "Hot Sevens" were two of the bands that he formed and led after leaving King Oliver in the early 1920s. Earl "Fatha" Hines, a musician who later became famous in his own right, joined Louis Armstrong's quintet in Chicago in 1927. Armstrong later left Chicago and joined Fletcher Henderson in New York City. Though Armstrong was known by various nicknames, he was perhaps best known as "Satchmo" (which is a distortion of satchelmouth, first coined when he was in England), "Pops," or "Sweet Papa Dip." Besides entertaining audiences in Idlewild and at other stops in the United States, he became an international phenomenon with a style of jazz that continues to influence contemporary musicians around the world. He popularized the scat style of singing, and popular songs enjoyed by his many fans include: "Mack the Knife," "Hello Dolly," "West End Blues," "I Will Wait For You," "Mame," and many more. Armstrong appeared in many films, including "Pennies from Heaven," "Every Day's a Holiday," "Going Places," "Dr. Rhythm," "Cabin in the Sky," "The Strip," "Glory Alley," "The Glenn Miller Story," and "A Man Called Adam." Two of the Broadway shows he appeared in were "Hot Chocolates" and "Swingin' the Dream." His creative mind combined jazz and pop music in a fashion that was easily embraced by his many fans. He was on top of his profession, touring and singing, until serious heart problems beginning in 1968 slowed this musical gaint. For many years, he was known as one of this country's greatest musical ambassadors—the ambassador of jazz.

ALBERTA ADAMS (born circa 1925). Detroit resident Roberta Louise Osborne, or Alberta Adams, as she is more popularly known, has been singing the blues since the late 1930s. She was born in Indianapolis but was raised by her aunt in Detroit. Adams gained a foothold in the Detroit entertainment industry as a dancer through her former husband, Billy Adams. During one show she asked the club manager if she could sing. He responded, "OK, but keep the dancing in." Afterward, the manager told her to learn more tunes. Word of her vocal prowess spread, and she has been singing jazz and blues ever since. She has performed with Duke Ellington, Eddie "Cleanhead" Vinson, and T-Bone Walker, as well as with other notable jazz, rhythm and blues, and blues groups in Detroit and other Midwestern cities. Adams was influenced by the styles of Big Joe Turner, Dinah Washington, Sarah Vaughan, and LaVern Baker. She eventually became known as Detroit's Queen of the Blues. Her two most recent recordings, "Born with the Blues" and "Say Baby Say," were produced by Cannonball Records.

JULIAN "CANNONBALL" ADDERLEY (1928–1975). Born in Tampa, Florida, Adderley studied brass and reed instruments while in high school in Tallahassee. He continued his music studies at Florida Agricultural and Mechanical University (FAMU). Because he had such an insatiable appetite, high school friends nicknamed him "Cannibal," from whence the name Cannonball derived. Upon leaving FAMU, he became the band director for the formerly segregated Dillard High School in Ft. Lauderdale, Florida. While serving in the army during the early 1950s, he was the leader of the 36th Army Dance Band. He viewed his music as a chronological evolution from be-bop. He recorded a number of hits for the Riverside, Savoy, Blue Note, Mercury, and Veejay record companies.

WILLIAM "COUNT" BASIE (21 August 1904–26 April 1984). Born in Red Bank, New Jersey. In addition to audiences at Idlewild, music lovers in New York, Kansas City, and many other cities enjoyed Basie's piano music during the 1920s and 1930s. In his early years as a musician, he travelled the black theatre/vaudeville circuit, which took him from one black community to another. He later became one of the major contributors to the "Big Band" era. Basie gained an enormous amount of experience playing with bands such as Walter Page's Blue Devils. When musician Bennie Morton was killed in an automobile accident in 1935, Basie took over the leadership of his band and transformed it into a new organization. Subsequently, Basie went on to play at many of the major clubs, and to record many successful tunes on the MCA and Decca labels. Besides being known for his strong right-hand piano-playing style, Basie also was widely recognized as a great composer. He was the recipient of a Grammy Award. A few of his most popular tunes are "One O'Clock Jump," "Harvard Blues," "Dickie's Dream," "Lester Leaps In," "I Left My Baby," "Miss Thing," and "Don't Worry 'Bout Me."

"PEG LEG" BATES (died 6 December 1998). At a very young age, Bates narrowly escaped death in a cotton gin accident, which cost him a leg. Hence, the name "Peg Leg." Undaunted by this unfortunate accident, he found the courage and determination to pursue a career in show business. With a wooden leg he became proficient as a dancer who dazzled and electrified audiences at Idlewild with his performances. Not only was he a welcomed performer on the vaudeville circuit, he was virtually a regular performer on the very popular "Ed Sullivan Show," appearing more than twenty times. In the 1960s and early 1970s "Peg Leg" Bates was a household name in this country, and people flocked to see his performances as he toured the United States.

BROOK BENTON (19 September 1931–9 April 1988). Born Benjamin Franklin Peay in Camden, South Carolina. Like many African American singers, Benton got his start in the black church. In fact, he spent some time on the gospel circuit before turning his enormous talents to secular music. He was a popular vocalist who attracted large crowds to Idlewild. The sale of his recordings reflected his popularity, as seven of his songs made it to the number-one spot on the Rhythm and Blues (R&B) charts and eight more made the list of Top Ten hits. Benton's silky-rich baritone voice distinguished him from other singers and his relationship with writer/producer Clyde Otis proved to be very rewarding. Some of his most memorable tunes are "It's Just a Matter of Time," "The Boll Weevil Song," "Rainy Night in Georgia," "Thank You Pretty Baby," "So Many Ways," and "Kiddio." Another smash hit, "Baby (You've Got What it Takes)," was recorded with Dinah Washington.

JAMES BROWN (3 May 1933–). Born in Macon, Georgia. James Brown grew up in poverty, and like most black secular recording artists, he began singing in the church choir. After a bout with the law he organized the Famous Fame and his career took off. He eventually became the most important figure in the development of all forms of American popular music. He was responsible for turning rhythm and blues into soul and funk. His exuberance, theatric presentations, and passionate delivery, coupled with funky instrumentals and vocals, helped him to become known as "Soul Brother Number One," "The Godfather of Soul," and "Mr. Dynamite." He has recorded 116 charted number-one R&B hits. A few of his top numbers are: "Try Me!," "Please, Please, Please," "Papa's Got a Brand New Bag," "It's a Man's World," "Ain't It Funky," "Sex Machine," and others. His "Say It Loud, I'm Black and I'm Proud" became the anthem for black activists during the 1960s and 1970s. This innovative musician's rags-to-riches-to-rags story has heroic and tragic dimensions of mythic resonance.

THE MILLS BROTHERS (Herbert, 1912–1989; Harry, 1913–1982; Donald 1915–). Born in Piqua, Ohio, the group (including a fourth brother, John Jr., who played guitar and sang

The Mills Brothers. Courtesy of the Ben C. Wilson Collection, Black Americana Studies Department, Western Michigan University.

bass until his death in 1936) got its start performing in small-town vaudeville and rural tent shows. Initially they performed for all-black audiences, but in the late 1920s they began to attract white audiences due to the group's appearance as balladeers for ten months on a white radio station in Cincinnati. Eventually, the group was engaged by theaters and clubs outside the Midwest, and in the early 1930s began performing in New York City. With this exposure came record contracts and eventually small parts in movie musicals. One of their most popular hits was "Paper Doll" (1942). Six million copies were sold, which helped to distinguish the Mills Brothers as being among the first black vocal groups to achieve a national following. Their style of singing was very similar to that of a barbershop quartet.

THE BENNY CAREW BAND (c. 1913–5 June 1982). Grand Rapids, Michigan resident Benny Carew was a drummer for his own group, called "Pieces of Dreams." They entertained for more than forty years in southwestern Michigan's bars, cabarets, and clubs, with regular appearances at Idlewild. Carew died of cancer in 1982. He was an important player on the Kalamazoo Jazz scene.

Benny Carew, band members, and fans. Courtesy of the Ben C. Wilson Collection, Black Americana Studies Department, Western Michigan University.

THE SIGNIFICANCE OF IDLEWILD CLUBS TO ENTERTAINERS

Liquor licenses were difficult to obtain, but at least four were granted to night-clubs, bars, and hotels in the Idlewild community in the 1950s. Liquors and fine wines at the Fiesta Room in the Paradise Club sold for between $0.90 and $3.00, with most being in the $1.00 range.[6] Professional entertainment, coupled with the legalization of liquor, drew even more vacationers to Idlewild.[7] According to Sunnie Wilson, "following the legalization . . . , along with the winning of vacation time by the United Auto Workers Union, more working class customers came streaming in from Saginaw, Grand Rapids, Lansing, Flint, and other car manufacturing towns."[8]

It might be mentioned that a few from the bourgeois element "on the island" drew an imaginary line separating the quieter and more subdued fam-ily-oriented environment from the more rowdy and boisterous nightclub atmosphere. For example, Florence Powell Washington, former resident of Columbus, Ohio, wondered, "When are we going to get beyond all this loud stomping, primitive spiritual sounding rock and roll music?" In the late

MENU OF LIQUORS & FINE WINES

WHISKEY BLENDS

Sunny Brook	.85
Hill and Hill	.85
Seven Crown	.85
Schenley	.85
Calvert Reserve	.75
Carstairs	.85

IMPORTED CANADIAN WHISKEYS

Four Roses	.85
Barclay's Royal Canadian	
Canadian Club	
Seagram's V.O.	.80
MacNaughton's	.80
Lord Calvert	.80

BOTTLED IN BOND

Bourbon or Rye	.90
Irish Whiskey	.90
Scotch Whiskey	.90
Scotch Whiskey, 25 years old	1.25

MIXED DRINKS

Rum Cola	.85
Whiskey High Ball	.85
Manhattan	.85
Martini	.85
Tom Collins	.80
Whiskey Collins	.80
Stinger	.80
Whiskey Sour	.90
Gin Fizz	.90
Side Car	.90
Sherry Flip	.90
Pink Lady	.90
Alexander	.90
Fruit Lemonade	.90
Planter's Punch	1.25
Singapore Sling	1.25
Frozen Daiquiri	1.25
French 75	1.25
Fiesta Special	1.25
Zombie	3.00

BEER and SOFT DRINKS

Local Bottle Beer	.50
Premium Bottle Beer	.65
Soft Drinks, per Bottle	.50
Champ ale	.75
Lemon Seltzer	.85

CORDIALS and WINES IMPORTED

Domestic Cordials	.75
Liqueurs, Cordials and Imported Cordials	.85
Domestic Wines — 16%	.90
Domestic Wines — 20%	.75
Imported Wines	.85
Domestic Wines — 16%, per btl.	6.00
Domestic Wines — 20%, per btl.	7.50
Champagne Cocktail	1.25
Domestic Champagne, per glass	1.25
Sparkling Burgundy, per glass	1.50
Imported Champagne, per glass	1.50
Domestic Champagne, per btl.	10.00
Imported Champagne, per btl.	12.00

BRANDY

Domestic	.75
Imported	.85
Rums	.75

TO AVOID MISTAKES, KINDLY CHECK PRICES WITH MENU

ABOVE PRICES ARE SUBJECT TO FEDERAL TAX

The Fiesta Room's drink menu. Courtesy of George and Idella Anderson.

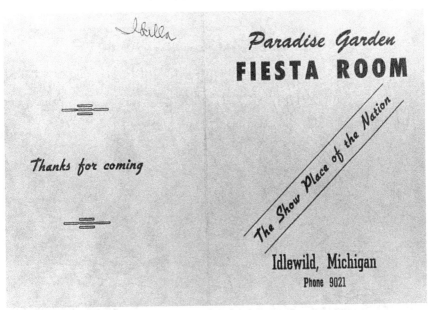

Paradise Garden
FIESTA ROOM

The Show Place of the Nation

Thanks for coming

Idlewild, Michigan
Phone 9021

The flip side of the Fiesta Room's drink menu. Courtesy of George and Idella Anderson.

Ziggy Johnson. Courtesy of John English.

Professional dancers in the Fiesta Room. Courtesy of John English.

fifties, "the aunt of Ms. Chipchase, resident of Kansas City, Missouri, telephoned the Paradise Club so that the staff would inform B. B. King that he played his music too loud. She came to the resort to rest."[9]

To handle the large crowds, George Anderson mentioned that especially on the Fourth of July weekends, "the Michigan National Guard was employed to keep the traffic flowing. The crowds were estimated at between twenty thousand and twenty-four thousand between Memorial and Labor Day. The bulk of the traffic involved resorters who went from club to club, which was part of the fun, checking out the different entertainers. It would not be unusual to start at the Fiesta Room and party, then to the Flamingo and party, then to the Club El-Morocco and party, and finally to the Morton's Motel to crash."[10] Anderson, the former president of the Kalamazoo Horseshoe Club, further said that the same routine would be repeated day after day.

An interesting story about the Club El-Morocco, an after-hours place at Idlewild, was shared by members of the Eddie Burns Band, which played at Idlewild. Allegedly, the El-Morroco was raided by the police and one of the

Law enforcement officers in Yates township. Courtesy of John English.

officers set up a table and started writing down the names of the patrons. Suddenly a Ms. Lela Wilson, one of the pioneering black developers, came in and told the policeman in no uncertain terms to get "his honkey ass out" of the place, which he did without any protestations. It seems that Ms. Wilson was a well-known figure in that community at the time and had acquired sufficient political power to control the behavior of certain police officers, not an easy task for any African American, especially at that time in the history of the State of Michigan.

There were several moderately sized hotels to accommodate the large crowds. In addition to Phil Gile's Hotel, the Casa Blanca was built in 1949 by W. C. M. Coombs, a Detroit architect and builder. Margaret Walker owned the Rainbow Manor.[11] Later, the Holiday House was constructed, primarily for boarding the entertainers who performed at the Fiesta Room.[12] Among those who might have stayed and performed at this newly constructed establishment were:

THOMAS "BEANS" BOWLES (1926–1999). Born in South Bend, Indiana, he was nicknamed "String Bean," then later "Beans" because of his six-foot-five-inch frame. He began playing clarinet at the age of nine and began working professionally as a saxophonist at age sixteen. In 1944, he attended Wayne State University in Detroit. He toured with musicians such as Bill Doggett and Lloyd Price. Bill Doggett performed at Idlewild and so did Bowles. In the early 1960s, he formed and led a Detroit band called the Swinging Dashikis, which often backed up Motown acts. He mentored young, up-and-coming stars such as Stevie Wonder, the Supremes, Martha Reeves, the Temptations, the Marvelettes, and Gladys Knight, to name a few. He also served as chairman of the Grayston Jazz Museum in Detroit and as a member of the board of the Rhythm and Blues Museum in Cleveland, Ohio. Stevie Wonder sang at his funeral, held at the Central United Methodist Church in Detroit.

JERRY BUTLER (18 December 1939–). Born in Sunflower, Mississippi. At the age of twelve, he sang for the Northern Jubilee Gospel Singers as a baritone, later teaming up with Curtis Mayfield to form the Impressions in 1958. When he was eighteen he drew national attention to the group with a song that he wrote: "For Your Precious Love." That song helped launch a thirty-seven-year career, which included producing and composing as well as performing. As a solo artist after he broke away from the Impressions,

Butler's big break came with the recording of "He Will Break Your Heart" and "Moon River." He went on to further greatness with the top hits "Western Union Man" and "Only the Strong Survive." The "King of Love Ballads" is still seen on public television stations that feature rhythm and blues artists.

CHOKER CAMPBELL (21 March 1916–20 July 1993). Born in Shelby, Mississippi, Campbell moved to Cleveland, Ohio, and eventually settled in Detroit. While in Detroit he formed a sixteen-piece ensemble, known as the Choker Campbell Orchestra, that was considered one of Motown's leading background bands. As a tenor saxophonist, he also worked with Big Joe Turner, King Curtis, Lowell Fulson, and various other rhythm and blues performers. Vacationers at Idlewild danced to the music of this band that played in the background for other artists. Though the Choker Campbell Orchestra did not become a household name, it did have a single: an instrumental version of "Mickey's Monkey," that was released in the United Kingdom.

BETTY "BE-BOP" CARTER (16 May 1930–26 September 1998). Born Lillie May Jones in Flint, Michigan, she followed her family to Detroit, where she received piano training at the Detroit Conservatory of Music. Inspired by the careers of Sarah Vaughan and Billie Holiday, she became intrigued with jazz while still in high school. By the age of eighteen, her fascination with jazz had earned her a praiseworthy reputation as a singer who had toured and performed in clubs in Michigan as well as Ohio. On her road to stardom she performed in a variety of venues, including Idlewild, and in the process crossed paths with such well-known artists as Dizzy Gillespie and Charlie Parker. She toured with several different bands, including Lionel Hampton, who hired her for several years as a regular with his organization. This outstanding and versatile singer of both jazz and blues also toured with Ray Charles and performed with blues sensation Muddy Waters and jazz artists Miles Davis and Thelonious Monk. The nickname "Be-Bop" is attributed to Hampton, who became upset with Betty because he felt that she had more of a predilection for the modern music ("bebop") of Charlie Parker, Dizzy Gillespie, and Miles Davis than for his musical genre. She eventually left Hampton's group due to this and other disagreements. With Ray Charles, she recorded a successful album entitled *Ray Charles and Betty Carter* (1961), followed by such widely acclaimed tunes as "The Audience with Betty Carter" and "Whatever Happened to Love," recorded in 1981 and 1982, respectively. She won a Grammy Award for each tune, receiving a total of three nominations for her work. Carter continued to work and inspire other musicians until the end of her life. In fact, in 1997, a year before her death of pancreatic cancer at the age of sixty-six, she released her critically acclaimed album *I'm Yours, You're Mine.*

CAB CALLOWAY (25 December 1907–18 November 1994). Born Cabell Calloway III in Rochester, New York, but raised in Baltimore. His interest in music was inspired by his mother and siblings. Though multitalented, he was one of the few African American musicians who became famous as a result of radio broadcasts. Starting in the early 1930s, he and his band were periodically broadcast live from the Cotton Club in New York. Prior to forming a band that carried his own name, Calloway was the leader of the Alabamians, later named the Missourians. Patrons of the Savoy Ballroom in Harlem also enjoyed the music of the man who wrote and made "Minnie the Moocher" one of the most famous songs of that era. "Minnie the Moocher" also became a success in several European countries, and "The Hi-De-Ho-Man" from Rochester, New York, became even more famous after he began playing at the Cotton Club. His music was broadcast live into the homes of music lovers throughout the 1930s. Through the years, white zoot suits became one of his trademarks, along with his "hi-de-ho" chorus. Calloway was known for his flamboyancy and diversity. This gifted "scat" musician composed "St. James Infirmary," "Lady with a Fan," "That Man's Here Again," "The Scat Song," "Jumpin' Jive," "Zaz Zuh Zaz," "Are You Hep to the Jive?" and others. As an actor, he appeared in numerous films, among them *International House, The Big Broadcast, The Cincinnati Kid, The Singing Kid,* and *Stormy Weather.* He also appeared on stage in *Hello Dolly* (with Pearl Bailey) and in *Porgy and Bess.* After more than sixty years in the business, he was awarded the National Medal of Arts by President Bill Clinton in 1992. Health concerns and age caused the singer, bandleader, and actor to become less active prior to his death in 1994 at the age of eighty-six.

CAROL CHILTON (13 December 1907–1995). Born in Chicago, Illinois. Carol was inspired by her foster mother, Lucille Bacon Chilton, and her cousin, Roberta Bacon, as well as by Ethel Waters (a blues vocalist and later a Hollywood actress) and Butterbeans and Susie (blues vocalists and dancers), who kindled a strong desire in her to become a professional singer and dancer. Before she turned six, Carol was dancing and performing on stage such tunes as "Mother," "Pretty Baby," and "China Doll." Her formal instruction included studies with Hazel Thompson Davis, a top tap instructor in the Windy City, and Nicholas Tsouklas, who taught Russian ballet. Chilton proved to be a quick study and absorbed her instructors' knowledge and techniques so completely that she started her own dance studio, instructing hundreds of children from her settlement neighborhood, by the time she was thirteen. Chilton, who was given away by her birth parents two weeks after her birth to Lucille Chilton, a probation officer, got her first major break in 1925, when she and her dancing partner, Earl Partello (one of her former students) became the first African Americans to perform on the Chicago Theater stage without black makeup on their faces, customarily worn by many men and women of both races. Though they were very popular on the Theatre Owners Booking Association (TOBA) circuit in this country, Chilton and her entertainer husband, Maceo Thomas, enjoyed enormous popularity in such European countries as France, Germany, Italy, Switzerland, and England. It was in England, in 1930, that she and her husband became the first African Americans to play a command performance before British royalty. Chilton and Thomas retired from show business in the 1940s, but not before they made an appearance in Idlewild. Their circle of friends included virtually thousands of entertainers, both black and white, including George Burns and Gracie Allen, the Berry Brothers (a dance team), John Bubbles, Bill "Bojangles" Robinson, Milton Berle, Mae West, Butterbeans and Susie, Eddie Cantor, and Al Jolson.

BILL COSBY (12 July 1937–). Born in Philadelphia, Pennsylvania, Bill Cosby represents the voice of the common person. Everyone seems to identify with his characters and the situations he presents in his various comedy routines. His humor often centers on the basic cornerstones of our existence as men, women, family members, children, and parents. He is a hilariously funny comedian whose appeal is not limited by race or ethnicity. He created such memorable characters as Fat Albert, Old Weird Harold, Dumb Donald, Weasel, and Heathcliff Huxtable. As an actor and producer, Cosby, who holds a doctoral degree in education from the University of Massachusetts, Amherst, was involved in the following feature movies: *Man and Boy, Hickey and Boggs, Uptown Saturday Night, Let's Do It Again, Mother, Jugs and Speed, A Piece of the Action,* and *Jack.* He further polished his acting skills in the television programs *I Spy, The Bill Cosby Show, Cos, The Cosby Mysteries, Fat Albert and the Cosby Kids,* and *Cosby.* He has also appeared on children's daytime specials such as *Sesame Street* and *The Electric Company.* He has written a bestselling book, produced twenty-one albums and a number of documentaries, and has earned eight gold records and five Grammy Awards. A crusader throughout his career for a better world, he and his wife, Camille, have made substantial financial contributions to charitable organizations, various social services, historical black colleges and universities, and civil rights organizations. The world was shaken by the death of his son Ennis, whom the public knew vicariously through Bill's characterization of boys and sons. Without a doubt, Bill Cosby is one of the most influential performers of the twentieth century.

SAMMY DAVIS JR. (8 December 1925–16 May 1990). Born in New York City, Sammy Davis Jr. has been called "The Greatest Entertainer in the World." At the tender age of two, Sammy toured with his uncle's family troupe—the Will Mastin Trio—which traveled the Orpheum circuit. Though he appeared in the 1930 film *Rufus Jones for President,* Sammy was first known as a dancer, along with his father and uncle, who had been performing long before he was born. Indebted to these two people, Sammy also owes a deep debt of gratitude to Bill "Bojangles" Robinson—tap-dance king—who helped him develop his own style of dance. Sammy became a member of the Mastin Trio in the mid-1930s and began to steal the show as a talented "hoofer." Life on the road was not easy for Sammy and his entertaining relatives. The act was later billed as the "Will Mastin Trio, starring Sammy Davis Jr." After his uncle and father retired in 1948 from show business, Sammy continued as a single and in time became known as the dazzling "Mr. Entertainer" for his versatility and enormous talents. He added singing to his repertoire, followed by acting in films and on stage. His relationship with the infamous "Rat Pack," which included such greats as Frank Sinatra, Dean Martin, and Peter Lawford, helped him land a co-starring role in the motion picture "Oceans 11" in 1960. A 1954 car accident cost him his left eye and nearly his life. His work in the film *Porgy and Bess* (1959) and the Broadway play *Golden Boy* (mid-1960s) is some of his most memorable. He starred in numerous movies, including *Johnny Cool* (1963) and *Robin and the Seven Hoods* (1964). On stage he was widely known for his role in *Mr. Wonderful* (1956). He fought a courageous battle against throat cancer, dying in 1990.

White Music Lovers at Idlewild

Once the cabarets and clubs began to feature professional performers and to serve alcoholic drinks, whites who summered in northern Michigan began to visit Idlewild. They came from such places as Petoskey, Northport, Glen Arbor, Harbor Springs, Charlevoix, and as far away as Mackinac Island. On weekend nights they would come to see quality black entertainment, but would immediately return to their "whites only" hideaway at the conclusion of the shows. Sometimes Idlewild nightclub staffers would reserve seating space for them, especially for celebrities like Mel Torme. As Sunnie Wilson so poignantly mentioned, "That's been the white man's pattern: Keep blacks in their own section and as soon as we start making music and entertainment [they] come flocking to our neighborhood."[13]

There were occasionally incidents such as that which occurred during a Brook Benton performance when a white patron at the club yelled out what was considered to be a racial insult: "Boy, play 'Boll Weevil.'" Authur Braggs, Ernest Saunders, and Edward Bracy, Saginaw numbers men, walked over to the young man and bodily escorted him out of the club. Such incidents were not common, however, and white patrons usually tried to imitate the behavior of blacks in the audience. At times, the responses from the audience became so loud that they momentarily drowned out the entertainers. The verbal responses were often accompanied by hand-clapping; foot-stomping; head, shoulder, hand, and arm gesticulations; and a spontaneous high-energy dance. Audience participation was important, because it let the performers know how much they were appreciated. It also, in turn, encouraged them to explore the full range of their artistic abilities and demonstrated the single most important criterion by which black artists determine whether they are living up to audience expectations. To hear individuals in the crowd say "they cooked," "they jammed," "the cat's a hip dude," the "boys were a mutha," or "they're bad" was a good indication that the performers would be invited back at some future date. With that in mind, many performed as if their next meal depended upon audience satisfaction.

Undoubtedly, audience and entertainer interaction was considered a bit bizarre by whites, who were unfamiliar with the black cultural experience of participatory crowd behavior. With the passage of time, however, some whites began to sing along on familiar refrains and choruses, snap their fingers, clap their hands, and move with the beat. Invariably, however, some among those participating would sheepishly check out the blacks in attendance to see if their responses were appropriate. Some of the entertainers popular among white audiences were:

BILL DOGGETT (16 February 1916–13 November 1996). Born William Ballard Doggett in Philadelphia, Pennsylvania, he was a very precocious child musically and was inspired

Bill Doggett. Courtesy of the Ben C. Wilson Collection, Black Americana Studies Department, Western Michigan University.

by his mother, Wynona, who was a pianist at her church. While in high school, Doggett formed his first combo and became known as a fine swing-base pianist. That reputation enabled him to make a living playing with Jimmy Gorman's fifteen-piece band, a band he later acquired and led for a very brief period before selling it to Lucky Millender. Besides playing with the Millender band, Doggett bounced around over the next decade or so, teaming up with many different musicians and musical groups. He was with the Millender band when "Little Old Lady From Baltimore" and "All Aboard" were released in 1939, the first two of his numerous recordings. Doggett developed musical arrangements for the Ink Spots from 1942 to 1944 and, as their pianist, cut five singles with that group. Additionally, he was a key performer with Louis Jordan's Tymphany Five from 1948 to 1951; he was Wild Bill Davis's replacement with that organization. Though he toured and recorded with some of the top singers and bands in the country, Lionel Hampton, Ella Fitzgerald, and Eddie "Lockjaw" Davis among them, it took the tune "Honkey Tonk" (1956) to push Doggett over the top to stardom in the music world. It was recorded on the King label, which had already released more than a dozen of his more moderately successful singles. He accompanied Ella Fitzgerald on three recordings: "Rough Riding," "Smooth Sailing," and "Airmail Special." Though his career had its ups and downs, this multifaceted pianist, organist, and arranger continued to perform and record until shortly before his death in 1996.

BILLY ECKSTINE (8 July 1914–8 March 1993). Born in Pittsburgh, Pennsylvania, as William Clarence Eckstine. Following an education at Armstrong High School and Howard University, Eckstine worked in local nightclubs and cabarets as an emcee and singer. His genre was modern jazz vocals accompanied by an orchestra. He worked with Earl "Fatha" Hines between 1939 and 1945, and he also led a modern jazz orchestra until 1948. He became a distinguished songwriter during the be-bop era, and his career flourished until he abandoned the big band for smaller combos. During his career he worked with such musical greats as Dizzy Gillespie, Fats Navarro, Budd Johnson, and Todd Dameron. He is also known to have been influential in the careers of many performers during the transition from jazz to "be-bop."

DUKE ELLINGTON (29 April 1899–24 May 1974). Born in Washington, D.C., Edward Kennedy Ellington grew up in an elegant and decorous lifestyle, as his parents were of solid middle-class means. Consequently, Ellington's background and regal air earned him the "Duke" sobriquet. Both parents played the piano, and Ellington was therefore introduced to that musical instrument at an early age. His interest, however, was in the area of commercial art, and he did not take seriously the opportunity to advance his formal piano training until he was in high school. In spite of his early lackadaisical attitude toward piano lessons, he eventually became learned enough to be known as one of the most prolific composers in the history of jazz. During his long career, he composed more than two thousand songs, as well as a number of movie scores. He received an Academy Award nomination for *Paris Blues* in 1961. He cut his first recording when he was twenty-five years old, and "In A Sentimental Mood," "Mood Indigo," "Jump for Joy," "Take the 'A' Train," "Hot and Bothered," "Sophisticated Lady," "Caravan," and "It Don't Mean a Thing (If It Ain't Got That Swing)" are among the compositions his audiences came to know and love. A Mr. Strayhorn, who joined his orchestra in 1939, is credited with writing the band's theme, "Take the 'A' Train." In addition to Idlewild, Duke and his band played Carnegie Hall, had several overseas tours, and recorded with some of America's greatest singers and musical talents. Ellington also became a fixture at the Newport Jazz Festival. In addition to several Grammy Awards, Ellington received many other awards, including the prestigious Springarn Medal from the National Association for the Advancement of Colored People in 1959. In 1974, five years after receiving the coveted Presidential Medal of Freedom from President Richard M. Nixon, he died of lung cancer.

ARETHA FRANKLIN (25 March 1942–). Born in Memphis, Tennessee, and raised in Detroit, Franklin grew up singing in the New Bethel Baptist Church, where her father, C. L. Franklin, was the minister. She was inspired by Clara Ward, a premier female gospel singer. By the age of fourteen, Franklin was a spellbinding gospel performer. Inspired by her father, she decided to step into the secular music world. Both she and her father were criticized by the sanctimonious, because, according to those souls, she was singing the sinful "music of the world." In spite of such critics, she became known as the "Queen of Soul." Many fans, especially women, felt she sang with them in mind. "Re-Re" has twenty-one gold records and has won ten Grammy Awards. She has an honorary Doctorate of Law degree from Bethune Cookman College in Daytona Beach, Florida, an American Music Award, and an American Black Achievement Award, was declared a "natural resource" of Michigan, and was inducted into the Rock and Roll Hall of Fame. Some of the many hits recorded by this diva include: "Precious Lord," "I Never Loved a Man (the Way I Love You)," "Do Right Woman, Do Right Man," "Baby I Love You," "Chain of Fools," "Think," "Respect," "Pink Cadillac," and "Freeway of Love." "Respect" became the anthem for many black activists in the 1960s. In 1977, she sang at the inauguration of President Jimmy Carter. In addition, she acted and sang in the movie *The Blues Boys* (mid-1970s). Her appearance at Idlewild contributed greatly to the reputation of the resort.

CLIFFORD FEARS (22 July 1936–September 1988). As a resident of Detroit, Clifford Fears attended Northeastern High School. He was not an exceptional student but his counselor, Ms. Grace Sanford, recognized his dancing ability after observing him tap dancing. He also sang. After graduating, he attended Connecticut College on a School of Dance scholarship. Later he began performing with the Katherine Dunham dancers, and traveled internationally with her dance troupe. When the Dunham dancers returned to the United States, Fears decided to remain in Paris, where he continued to choreograph and dance. He also visited Stockholm, Sweden, where he performed in the production "Raise God and Dance—The Second Sacred Music Concert," written by Duke Ellington. He became fluent in ten languages. After the troupe disbanded in Paris, Fears found work in discos. In the 1970s and 1980s, the dynamic dancer founded and directed the Clifford Fears Dance Company in Detroit, where he taught the Dunham dance techniques.

When not entertaining, Clifford Fears was fond of taking a leisurely stroll on the beach in Idlewild. Courtesy of John English.

STEPIN FETCHIT (30 May 1902–19 November 1985). Named Lincoln Theodore Monroe Andrew Perry, after four U.S. presidents, he was raised in Key West, Florida, where he attended a Catholic boarding school. An interest in show business motivated him to leave home at a very young age, and he later teamed up with an aspiring comic named Ed Lee. Together they developed a vaudeville act entitled "Step 'n' Fetchit: Two Dancing Fools from Dixie," and Perry adopted "Stepin Fetchit" as his own stage name when the team decided to separate. Perry became a successful actor on the black vaudeville circuit, "as a lazy, dim-witted, slow, shuffling black servant. . . ."[14] Though successful at the time, it was this caricature that caused his detractors to become critical of him, though he starred in more than forty films. *Ole Kentucky* (1929) and *Stand Up and Cheer* (1933) are among his best-known films. Bankrupted, Stepin Fetchit left Hollywood and moved to Chicago in the early 1940s, where he began to perform in local nightclubs and in such other venues as Idlewild.

CLINTON "DUSTY" FLETCHER. Clinton Fletcher entertained African American audiences in both the North and the South. With John Mason, he coauthored "Open the Door,

Roy Hamilton and friend. Courtesy of the Ben C. Wilson Collection, Black Americana Studies Department, Western Michigan University.

Richard," which became a popular song and a saying widely used throughout the black community. He was no stranger to theaters and clubs on the black vaudeville circuit, and he also appeared on Broadway in such musical comedy productions as *Bamboola* (1929) and *Fast and Furious* (1931). In addition to such venues as the Alhambra Theater, the Apollo Theater, and the Cotton Club, he was also an honored visitor to the Idlewild stage.

EARL GRANT (20 January 1933–11 June 1970). Born in Oklahoma City but raised in Kansas City. After graduating from the University of Southern California, he studied at conservatories in Kansas City and New Rochelle, New York, and at the DePaul Conservatory in Chicago. He was a renowned performer who entertained his numerous fans as a mellow vocalist and versatile pianist and organist. He is remembered for such hits as "The End," "Tender Is the Night," "Imitation of Life," and "Tokyo Night." His most memorable rhythm and blues hit was "Sweet Sixteen Bars" in 1962. That tune reached the number nine spot on the charts. His career and life were cut short in an automobile accident in New Mexico in 1970, when he was thirty-seven years of age.

LOTTIE "THE BODY" GRAVES. A Chicagoan, known as the Black Gypsy-Rose Lee, and an exotic dancer. A weekend date at Idlewild with Goose Tatum of the Harlem Globetrotters ended in marriage. As an exotic dancer, she was a favorite of both men and women. At this writing, Lottie is working as club hostess in BoMac's Lounge in Detroit.

ROY HAMILTON (16 April 1929–20 July 1969). A song stylist whose voice had tremendous range, Hamilton left memorable impressions on his audiences with such poignant songs as "You'll Never Walk Alone," "If I Loved You," "Ebb Tide," and "Unchained Melody." He started his singing career with the Searchlight Singers. Idlewild was pleased to host this recording star who was beloved in the black community. Unfortunately, Hamilton, a heavyweight Golden Gloves boxer who turned singer, died a premature death at the age of forty after suffering a stroke.

ON STAGE AT IDLEWILD

Lottie "the body" Graves fondly remembered Idlewild as ". . . [Black] Atlantic City, the Boardwalk, Las Vegas. . . . It was like heaven."[15] As a performer at Idlewild, she might also remember that prior to being entertained by the professional performers, the audiences were entertained by the club dancers, who would do fancy choreographed kicks and shakes, reminiscent of the floor dancers at such well-known Southside Chicago clubs as Joe's Deluxe Club, Club Delisa, the Avenue Lounge, El Grotto, the Bee Hive, and the Honey Dipper. In 1955, Myron Wahls remembers

> getting to Idlewild with a big check earned from working overtime at the Lincoln-Mercury factory. That Labor Day some friends and I headed North to have some fun. During that same time period, Della Reese had just recorded "Time after Time." I rented a room at Phil Giles's Hotel and went straight to the patio, set up my record player and proceeded to blast Della's tune to attract folks—especially beautiful ladies—to our environment. . . . Idlewild was in effect "the place to be" and everyone knew it. [The recently deceased Wahls eventually became a judge of the Michigan Court of Appeals in Detroit.][16]

With the presence of many notables and celebrities from the entertainment world, the resort grew and eventually encompassed nearly all of Yates

Township. "It is now understandable," said Dwight McKinney, longtime resident of Saginaw and frequent resorter, "why Creation Avenue, Miracle Avenue, Grandeur Avenue, Celestial Boulevard, Righteous Road, Kindness Avenue, Wisdom Way, Harmony Boulevard and Justice Avenue were busy with traffic."[17]

A typical show in the Fiesta Room at the Paradise Club—with Ziggy Johnson as master of ceremony, choreographer, and dancer—would include Della Reese performing many of her favorites, such as "One for My Baby" and "In the Still of the Night." In addition, James "Casablanca" Stanford booked many acts from the Detroit area, including the Four Tops and Billy Eckstine. Vernon Clark of Battle Creek enjoyed a show where Jackie Wilson sung a few of his classics, including "That's Why," "I'll Be Satisfied," and "Lonely Teardrops." George Kirby also was known for taking the stage at Idlewild, especially after other entertainers had completed their performances. It was not unusual for him to start with "Happy Go Lucky Square," followed by one of his comedic routines and impressions of Ella Fitzgerald's "Lady Be Good," and Louis Armstrong's "Mack the Knife." Electrifying entertainment also came from the likes of:

LIONEL LEO HAMPTON (12 April 1908–). Though born in Louisville, Kentucky, Hampton spent his formative years in Birmingham, Alabama, and Chicago. As a bandleader, he had a stage presence that crackled with energy and enthusiasm and a "hard-driving swing style." His career as a vibraphonist and bandleader, which stretched over more than five decades, produced numerous extraordinary compositions, including "Flying Home," "Down Home Stomp," "Stompology," and many, many more. Though he formed his own group in the mid-1930s (after recording with Louis Armstrong's orchestra), it was with Benny Goodman's Quartet that Hampton first achieved star status as a jazz musician playing the vibraphone. (The vibraphone, as a musical instrument, had not been recognized as a jazz instrument of any consequence until Hampton began to demonstrate its potential.) As jazz's most influential vibraphonist, and with continued commercial success, he was prompted to leave Goodman in 1940 and go his own way in the world of jazz. That sojourn brought Hampton into contact with many aspiring jazz musicians, a number of whom he nurtured and helped launch their careers. Betty Carter was one of those to whom he gave an opportunity, by hiring her for regular engagements with his band, including appearances at Harlem's Apollo Theater. The

Al Hibbler. Courtesy of the Ben C. Wilson Collection, Black Americana Studies Department, Western Michigan University.

swing bandleader's association with Carter began in 1948 and lasted until 1951, when a disagreement caused them to go their separate ways. Others who performed with Hampton's groups include such greats as Quincy Jones, Dinah Washington, Joe Williams, and Nat "King" Cole.

AL HIBBLER (16 August 1915–). Born in Little Rock, Arkansas, he became known for the growling sounds that punctuated his singing. Hibbler was blind at birth, and fine-tuned his singing ability by entering amateur contests and studying at the Conservatory for the Blind in Little Rock, Arkansas. He won many of those contests as a young man, and subsequently got an opportunity to travel and perform with various bands in many southern cities. Hibbler was a featured artist with the Duke Ellington Orchestra for several years. It was during his affiliation with Ellington that he distinguished himself as a national figure in the music world. Hibbler left Ellington's band in the early 1950s to pursue a solo career. He, too, traveled to Idlewild to perform before appreciative audiences. In 1955, he recorded the hit "Unchained Melody." Among his other recordings on the Decca and Atlantic labels are "After the Lights Go Down Low," "He," and

"Pennies from Heaven." He recorded with some of the greatest musicians of his era, including Duke Ellington and Count Basie, to mention only two. *Here's Hibbler, Al Hibbler's Greatest Hits,* and *Starring Al Hibbler* are three of his more successful albums.

EARL "FATHA" HINES (28 December 1903–23 April 1983). Born in Duquesne, Pennsylvania, one might say that Hines's love for music was a legacy that he inherited from his immediate family. Though this son of musicians was born in Pennsylvania, he left his hometown for Chicago, where he thought he stood a better chance of improving and developing his musical career. Not long after his arrival, this jazz pianist joined Louis Armstrong's quintet (known as the Hot Five and later as the Hot Seven) in 1927. It is said that it was under Armstrong's influence that Hines created the "trumpet style" of playing jazz, a technique he developed using his right hand. He was able to produce hornlike sounds on the piano with one hand and carry the harmony with the other. He played with Armstrong's quintet for nearly a year, at the end of which time he formed his own big band. Before venturing out on his own, however, he and Armstrong recorded two memorable tunes, "West End Blues" and "Weather Bird." In addition to making stops at Idlewild, Hines toured this country, Japan, and Paris and other cities in Europe. In the 1930s, his big band played at Chicago's Grand Terrace Ballroom with Charlie Parker and Dizzy Gillespie, who helped to create and popularize a musical genre that became known as be-bop. Hines was given the nickname "Father" by a Chicago disc jockey. Known for representing the piano as an important part of the jazz ensemble, Hines was famous for such compositions as "Rosetta," "Piano Man," and "Boogie Woogie on the St. Louis Blues." Sarah Vaughan also worked in the studio with Earl Hines's big band.

ETTA JAMES (25 January 1938–). Born Jamesetta Hawkins in Los Angeles, California. Although she was born on the West Coast, James eventually found her way to Idlewild, over two thousand miles away from her place of birth. Born to a teenage mother, James's formative years were spent in the care of foster parents, and she did not rejoin her biological mother, Dorothy Hawkins, until after the death of James's foster mother, Lula "Mama Lu" Rogers in 1950. James was only twelve years of age at the time. By that time, however, she had been identified as a child with a gifted voice. Her talent and ability had been demonstrated repeatedly as a young soloist in her church choir, and she had gained some experience singing on the local radio in Los Angeles. Her continued interest in music allowed her to escape the unhappiness of a dysfunctional family life. She formed the Creolettes, an all-girls group, which brought her some notoriety and a sizeable local following. She subsequently was discovered by Johnny Otis and got her first major break, not in her hometown of Los Angeles, but at the Filmore in San Francisco. Otis is credited with reversing "Jamesetta" to her stage name—Etta James—and changing the name of the Creolettes to the Peaches. Her first hit, "Roll with Me Henry" (renamed "The Wallflower"), was with the Peaches in 1955. Other hit singles included "Something's Got a Hold on Me," "At Last," "In the Basement," and such albums as *Call My Name* (a very successful blues album), *Tell Mama, I'd Rather Go Blind, Mystery Lady* (a tribute to one of her idols, Billie Holiday), and *Time After Time*. In addition to her work, she has been recognized for her gallant fight against various forms of addiction, including heroin. To her credit, in spite of ups and downs in her musical career, and in spite of her drug problems, James has managed to survive. In 1993, she was inducted into the Rock and Roll Hall of Fame and received a Grammy Award.

B. B. KING (16 September 1925–). Born Riley B. King on a plantation between Itta Bena and Indianola, Mississippi. King worked on a plantation for the customary low wages in that part of the country. The conditions on the plantation gave birth in King to an authentic feeling for the blues. For a number of years King sang with various gospel groups, including the Famous St. John Gospel Singers, the first group with which he was affiliated for pay. Booker "Bukka" White, a cousin and blues guitarist with whom King went to live in Memphis, is credited with helping King to refine his unique technique as a guitarist in the 1940s. B. B. King also gives credit to Sonny Boy Williamson, who not only was a source of inspiration but gave him his first chance to perform on radio. The great blues guitarist T-Bone Walker also had an influence on him with respect to the electric amplification of the guitar. The influence of these men helped earn him the name "Beale Street Blues Boy" when he became a disc jockey at a black radio station, WDIA, in Memphis. A shortened version of "Beale Street Blues Boy" became "Blues Boy," which was later truncated to "B. B." King. By the time he arrived at Idlewild, few people knew him as anything other than "B. B." King, who was to become arguably the "King of the Blues." Urban blues were taken to a new height when B. B. King came on the scene with his electric guitar, "Lucille." According to the famous story, his Kalamazoo, Michigan Gibson guitar was named "Lucille." King was performing in Twist, Arkansas, when two men started fighting over her and knocked over a heater, which started a fire. The building was evacuated but King remembered that his

Bobbie Lewis. Courtesy of the Ben C. Wilson Collection, Black Americana Studies Department, Western Michigan University.

own guitar was still in the building, and he risked his life by reentering the burning building to recover it. He later named it "Lucille" as a reminder to always be careful and "not do anything that foolish." While in Memphis he cut his first two recordings, "Miss Martha King" and "I've Got the Blues." Yet "Three O'Clock Blues" in 1951 was his first number-one hit of that era. His biggest hit ever came twenty years later in "The Thrill is Gone," for which he received a Grammy Award in 1971. His other hits include: "Live and Well" (with Bobby Bland), "Together for the First Time," and the Grammy-Award-winning "There Must Be a Better World Somewhere." His unique style of playing and performing has earned B. B. King a place in the Blues Hall of Fame (1984) and the Rock and Roll Hall of Fame (1987). He received the coveted Presidential Medal of Freedom from President George Bush, and a star on Hollywood's Walk of Fame in the early 1990s. Over the years, this musical institution has been an inspiration to musicians around the world in the field of blues and jazz.

GEORGE KIRBY (1923–1995). Born in Chicago, Illinois, George Kirby was known for taking the stage at Idlewild, especially after other entertainers had completed their performances. As the emcee, he would introduce entertainers such as Della Reese or

Jackie Wilson. After these performers exited the stage, it was not unusual for Kirby to come out singing "Happy Go Lucky Square," followed by one of his comedic routines and impressions of Ella Fitzgerald's "Lady Be Good," and ending with Louis Armstrong's "Mack the Knife." Kirby was a favorite at Idlewild.

BOBBIE LEWIS (16 February 1927–). Born in Hodgerville, Kentucky, Lewis was raised in an orphanage and ran away from his foster home at the age of fourteen. To support himself, he worked carnivals, small clubs, and theaters. He was one of those talented performers whose recognition was confined to a single hit in the early 1960s, "Tossin' and Turnin,'" written by lyricist Ritchie Adams. The single rode the charts for twenty-three weeks, eventually hitting the number-one spot on the pop and rhythm and blues charts. Lewis, however, had less success with another song, "One-Track Mind." He eventually joined the Leo Hines Orchestra in Indianapolis as a vocalist.

JACKIE "MOMS" MABLEY (19 March 1897–23 April 1975). Born Loretta Mary Aiken in Brevard, North Carolina. A funny, funny lady who made Idlewild one of the places where her social satire demanded "belly-wrenching" laughter from her audiences. Jackie "Moms" Mabley, recognized as the first African American woman to perform as a single act in stand-up comedy, earned her living by playing the "Chitlin Circuit." This rather benevolent woman would transform herself into a toothless, knowledgeable, opinionated seer of the black community who did not draw lines in the sands when it came to race, gender, or any other type of relationships. With her down-home brand of comedy, she would have her audiences in tears, laughing at her jokes and her special philosophy about life. She was noted for her "dirty old lady" routines. "There ain't nothing an old man can do for me but bring me a message from a young one," is one of her famous lines. This great-granddaughter of a slave is alleged to have run away from home at an early age because of a disagreement with her father. Because she could sing and dance as well as tell jokes, she decided to join a traveling minstrel show that played the movie houses and theaters in the black community. As her popularity grew she moved up into the "big league" by playing at the more famous venues, such as Connie's Inn, the Cotton Club, Harlem's Apollo Theater, and Chicago's Regal Theater and sharing the stage with some of the country's greatest musicians. Cab Calloway, Louis Armstrong, Count Basie, and Duke Ellington were among the many entertainers who came to know and share the stage with this outrageously funny "first lady of comedy." "The Funniest Woman Alive" (Chess Records) and "Now Hear This" (Mercury Records) were two of her most successful recordings. In 1974, in spite of health problems, Mabley starred in her only major movie, *Amazing Grace*.

ESCAPE TO WOODLAND PARK FOR REST

In the mid-1960s, Ms. Theresa Allen, a Flint resident, was reminiscing about Idlewild to Rhonda Sanders, who wrote an article in the *Flint Journal* entitled "Idlewild on the Mend?" According to Ms. Allen, when her uncle Peter Perrin owned Club Paradise, ". . . it [was] a top-drawer establishment. There was valet parking, and tuxedo-wearing, white-gloved waiters. . . . The classy atmosphere was enhanced by candle-lit table[s]. . . . An all glass back wall framed a picturesque view of Lake Paradise." In that same article, Sanders further mentioned that "the main clubs offered two shows a night, making it possible to see the early show at one club and the midnight show at another."[18] If hungry after partying, the revelers, and often the entertainers as well, would head for Ms. Hippy Dippy's Place for an excellent fried chicken sandwich or dinner. Others would wind their way to Woodland Park, located between ten and fifteen miles from Idlewild in the rather sedate Newaygo County. This placid place became known as a community where one could go for rest. The black residents there wanted to maintain a quiet retreat without the disruption of show business. They did not mind, however, if the Idlewild entertainers and celebrities visited or even bought property there, as long as they did not perform there. It was here in Woodland Park that world heavyweight boxing champion Joe Louis, the president of Murray's Haircare Company, and countless other celebrities would retreat for a night of restful sleep, away from the club noises and constant parties in Idlewild. These celebrities, like many who partied in Idlewild, owned property in both places.

Mr. Freelon Carter Jr., a Detroiter and native of Woodland Park, frequently remarked that "Idlewild lived up to its name—folks were more 'wild' than 'idle.'"[19] To the youngsters who accompanied them, however, aside from the fun at the roller-skating rink, the place was called Idlewild because at night the children were "idle" and the parents were "wild.'" This was a profound change from the original vision of a place where pioneer black professionals could "idle" a while in the "wild." Nevertheless, Idlewild continued to be a place hustling and bustling with music, such as that performed by:

BIG MAYBELLE (1 May 1924–23 January 1972). Born Maybelle Louis Smith in Jackson, Tennessee, with an enormous vocal talent. Because of her mountainous stature, she was given the moniker "Big Maybelle," a woman before her time who could belt out the blues with such flair and command that audiences were spellbound by her powerful voice, which was refined within the confines of her local church choir. By the time Maybelle was fifteen, she had performed with an all-girls band (the Sweethearts of Rhythm) and had toured with the Christine Chatman Orchestra. Later she was sought after to sing and record with the likes of the Quincy Jones Orchestra, the Danny Mendelsohn Orchestra, and others. Working for a variety of labels, Maybelle recorded numerous songs and had several hits. In addition to working Idlewild, Maybelle frequently worked at the Apollo Theater, the Brevoort Theater in Brooklyn, and many other venues. Allegedly, drug addiction was the cause of the demise of her singing, as well as a contributing factor in her premature death in a diabetic coma in 1972, at the age of forty-seven, in Cleveland, Ohio.

BARBARA MCNAIR (4 March 1939–). Barbara was born in Racine, Wisconsin. She began taking voice lessons at the age of ten and later studied at the Chicago Conservatory of Music. In the late 1950s and early 1960s she appeared on such television shows as *The Jack Paar Show*, *Spencer's Mountain*, and the 1963 musical *No Strings*. She went on to dramatic acting in the television series *Hogan's Heroes*, *Dr. Kildare*, and *I Spy* in the mid-1960s. As a satiny smooth vocalist she released three albums, entitled *I Enjoy Being a Girl* (1964), *Here I Am* (1967), and *The Real Barbara McNair* (1970). In addition, she starred in her own weekly musical variety television show, *The Barbara McNair Show* from 1969 to 1971. As an actress, she had cameo appearances in *A Change of Habit* (1969) and *They Call Me Mister Tibbs* (1970).

ARTHUR PRYSOCK (1929—1997). Arthur Prysock began singing as a featured vocalist with Buddy Johnson and his orchestra in the late 1940s as a youngster. He was signed to a contract with Decca Records and cut the hit "Blue Velvet" in the late 1950s, which brought him immediate national prominence. He continued as a featured vocalist and eventually broke away from the Johnson Orchestra. He had successful engagements at various sites throughout the United States, especially at Bohemian Jazz nightclubs and cabarets. For a number of years, Prysock, with his silky smooth voice, was considered one of the hottest singing sensations in America. Among the songs Idlewild vacationers loved to hear him sing were: "This Guy's in Love with You," "I Didn't Sleep a Wink Last Night," and "The Very Thought of You."

GERTRUDE "MA" RAINEY (26 April 1886–22 December 1939). Born Gertrude Pridgett in Columbus, Georgia. She became one of black vaudeville's stellar stars, with her great voice, penchant for comedy, songwriting ability, and the necessary acumen to operate and manage her own minstrel road show. Such shows typically consisted of beautiful girls in a chorus line, comedians (whose materials focused heavily on sexual relations and other adult themes), outstanding singers, nimble dancers, and men and women who were adept at juggling and acrobatic antics. She married William "Pa" Rainey in 1904, and they performed as a team for many years. It was widely known, however, that Ma Rainey was the star, and she was indeed the manager of the Rabbit Foot Minstrels, a job she performed expertly and profitably for many years. The moniker "Ma" was given to her because she took good care of her younger artists, her performers were paid on time, and she was always there for her troupe. In 1923 she decided to accept a recording contract with Paramount Records, and she went on to become one of the most prolific musicians in the country. She recorded nearly one hundred songs for Paramount within a five-year period, writing more than a third of those tunes herself. Though she was often accompanied by some of the most out-standing jazz musicians in the country—Louis Armstrong and Fletcher Henderson among them—Rainey was more at home performing with a jug or washboard band. Nonetheless, many of her recordings, such as "See, See Rider" and "Prove It On Me," were economic successes (though for each recording session she was paid a flat fee that was far less than what her white counterparts received). Her success prompted Rainey to tour the South and the Midwest, where Idlewild, where she most often per-formed before packed houses, was a beneficiary of her tours. Ma Rainey, a classy lady and one of the first professional female blues singers, retired from show business in 1935 and returned to her native state of Georgia, where she died four years later at the age of fifty-three.

DON REDMOND (29 July 1900–30 November 1964). Redmond is perhaps best remem-bered for his association with Pearl "Hello Dolly" Bailey. He was her music director for many years. Prior to this association, however, Redmond had distinguished himself during the 1920s and 1930s as one of the greatest composers in the history of jazz. His innovative arrangements suited best the big band that featured an outstanding soloist. This feature was keenly demonstrated when Redmond organized his own big band in 1931. His orchestra visited Europe after World War II. Sometime later he became Pearl Bailey's music director and appeared with her on many occasions.

Della Reese. Courtesy of John English.

LULA REED. A longtime associate of pianist/producer Sonny Thompson, Reed recorded for King Records during the mid-1950s. In 1951, she released the moving ballad "I'll Drown in My Tears." It was later released by Ray Charles as "Drown in My Own Tears" (1956). After first serving as Thompson's vocalist, the attractive chanteuse was sufficiently established by 1952 to rate her own King releases. A multifaceted performer, Reed sang urban blues most of the time but temporarily switched to gospel in 1954. She briefly moved to the Chess subsidiary Argo in 1958–59 but returned to the King Records fold in 1961 (as always, under Thompson's direction) on their Federal imprint. While at Federal, she released a series of sassy duets with guitarist Freddy King in March 1962. She recorded with Ray Charles on the Tangerine label between 1962 and 1963, then abruptly disappeared from the rhythm and blues scene. People who watched her perform at Idlewild were always impressed with this electrifying entertainer.

DELLA REESE (6 July 1932–). Born Deloreese Patricia Early in Detroit, Michigan, she began singing in her local church choir at six years of age. By the time she was fourteen she was touring and singing with one of the greatest gospel singers in the country,

Mahalia Jackson. She remained with Jackson's gospel troupe for nearly five years. By the time she was eighteen, Reese had formed her own group, the Meditation Singers, while majoring in psychology at Wayne State University. By the end of 1950, her mother had died and her father had become terminally ill. She dropped out of the university and worked various jobs to support the family. As a gospel singer she made very little money, so she toyed with the idea of singing secular/popular music in nightclubs. This clashed with her religious convictions but she was encouraged by her pastor at New Liberty Baptist Church to put aside her reservations and pursue a career as a secular performer. She took the stage name Pat Ferro and later Della Reese. After a stint with Erskine Hawkins, she struck out on her own as a solo singer and rapidly distinguished herself as a recording star with such hits as "And That Reminds Me," " I Got Love to Keep Me Warm," "Time after Time," "September in the Rain," "In the Still of the Night," "Don't You Know," and "Not One Minute More," followed by such well-received albums as *Della, Special Delivery,* and *Classic Della.* Reese spent a considerable amount of time at Idlewild and has been known to lament the fact that more entertainers did not invest enough of their time and money in making that community a showcase for the world. At Idlewild, Ziggy Johnson—as master of ceremony, choreographer, and dancer—would have Della Reese perform many of the crowd's favorites. Since the late 1950s, Reese has appeared in numerous films and television shows. *The Ed Sullivan Show, The Tonight Show, Chico and the Man, Charlie and Company, The Royal Family, The A-Team,* and *To Tell the Truth* are just a few of her many television credits. More recently, she has been a mainstay on CBS's popular series *Touched by an Angel.* In the 1980s, at the age of forty-eight, while taping a segment for "The Tonight Show," she collapsed with a brain aneurysm. She recovered from this near fatal incident due to her faith and the talents of a Canadian neurosurgeon. Her strong religious convictions prompted Della to pursue ordination in the Universal Foundation of Better Living. The Reverend Della Reese considers this "a glorious development" in her life. She remains an irresistible woman, whether singing or acting.

THE SPINNERS (formed in the mid-1950s). This group started in the Detroit area as the Moonglows and changed its name to the Spinners in the early 1960s. The group distinguished itself with memorable melodies, rich harmonies, and a musical delivery full of spirit and vivaciousness. The original group consisted of tenor Robert Smith, bass Pervis Jackson, baritone Henry Fambrough, tenor-baritone Billy Henderson, and tenor George Dixon. They began their musical career in Detroit when three of the original vocalists graduated from Ferndale High School. Harvey Fuqua organized the group. From time to time, members of the original group left, but Philippe Wynne, John Edwards, Edgar Edwards, and G. C. Cameron replaced them without skipping a beat. Some of their most memorable hits were: "I'll Always Love You," "I'll Be Around," "Could It Be I'm Falling in Love," "The Rubberband Man," and "If you Wanna Do a Dance All Night." Many fans considered their tune "Then Came You" with Dionne Warwick the ultimate upbeat love ballad.

JESS STACY (1 August 1904–5 January 1994). Stacy was largely a self-taught pianist whose style was influenced by jazz musicians Earl Hines and Bix Beiderbecke. He became known for his enormous talent for improvisation, and after displaying his talents on riverboats he was invited to join Benny Goodman's big band. He was the top sideman in the Goodman band from 1935 to 1939. In the 1940s he performed with a number of bands including those of Bob Crosby, Tommy Dorsey, and Horace Heidt, as well as continuing his association with Benny Goodman. Stacy made several attempts to organize his own big band, but success was as elusive in those efforts as it was in his marriage to singer Lee Wiley. Stacy maintained an association with Benny Goodman until he moved to California in the latter part of 1947. By that time, he had recorded with Eddie Condon and had some of his own recordings on the market. Though he essentially retired in 1963, over the years he would still on very special occasions sit in on a session or go into the studio to record his work.

NATURE, SWIMMING, BOATING, AND HORSEBACK RIDING

During the daylight hours, hiking, fishing, boating and horseback riding were available for all at Idlewild, especially for the children.[20] The Idlewild Chamber of Commerce folder mentioned that:

> our lakes are tested annually by the State Department of Public Health to ensure your swimming to be safe from any possible contamination. Should you desire to learn to swim, instructors in swimming are given at each beach daily. Special care is exercised in watching out for the welfare of the tiny tots on these beaches. Here they can play in the shallow water and on the sand with perfect safety and enjoyment. If you enjoy hiking and are a lover of nature, scenically lovely Idlewild presents for your approval and pleasure the surrounding woods with its stands

Vacationers fishing on Lake Idlewild. Courtesy of the Ben C. Wilson Collection, Black Americana Studies Department, Western Michigan University.

of tall, stately pines and mighty oaks, in which you can study shy graceful birds, native to this region; find delicate wildflowers whose beauty and gentle fragrance permeate the air; or pursue with your camera our bounteous supply of wildlife, saucy squirrels of several species, fleet little rabbits, comical looking porcupines, sly raccoon[s] and best of all the elusive, graceful deer. Indeed, nature hikes and picnics coupled with study of wildlife peculiar to our location are perfect ways in which you can forget the hustle and bustle of the city. Boating is another way in which to pass away many a pleasant, carefree hour. Boats may be rented by the hour or day on either of our larger lakes. Perhaps you own a canoe, rowboat or motorboat; if so, bring it up and take advantage of our unusually fine waterways. Many enjoy drifting along at night on a moon-drenched lake listening to the strains of an orchestra being wafted to them on the evening breeze.[21]

Attorney Sam Simpson of Detroit observed that "your parents felt very comfortable about letting youngsters go where they wanted in Idlewild. All the older resorters were very protective. Devilishment would be reported to your parents immediately. But we all knew that everyone there had access to our behinds if our parents could not be reached and informed of our bad behavior."[22] However, since there were numerous activities available for children, many were having too much fun to misbehave on a regular basis.

Before he went blind, the diminutive 5'3" Sergeant Johnson—a veteran of the Spanish-American War—provided horseback riding at the resort. He owned about twenty-one saddle-broken horses, and the Clover Leaf Ranch was in full-scale operation from the late 1920s through the 1960s. In his book, *Blue as the Lake*, Robert B. Stepto said:

> Truly the most exciting thing I did . . . was to ride in Sarge Johnson's horse round-up. Sarge was an Idlewild institution—a wizened old black man . . . who ran a stable from which you could go on horseback rides around the lakes. You couldn't go anywhere else—or at least kids couldn't—and Mrs. Johnson, a brusque woman half Sarge's age, made sure you didn't by driving slowly along behind you in her Oldsmobile. Two honks from her and the horses commenced to trot; one honk later and they fell back into a walk, much to the relief of the tourist folk who didn't know how to post and usually got jostled up pretty bad. Some of them moaned . . . ; I was secretly amused by that, especially when the moaners were adults. I rode the horses . . . every summer of the 1950s, and reveled in advancing from the tottering, ancient mounts to the friskier horses requiring some skill to ride. In the last years, I had a "job" at Sarge's, leading strings of riders and horses on the route around the lake. My pay was that I rode for free, and I rode enough to have Saddle Sores. . . . [23]

Sarge's riding-club pupils had to report to the stable by 10:00 A.M. each morning, and he always remembered, even after he was almost blind, which person should ride which horse. As the horses left the stable, he would bark out instructions, such as: "Squeeze your knees, Geoff," "Let go the saddle, MC, hold the reins," or "Did you adjust your stirrups, Francell?" He would always say, "My horses should break no sweat." Detroiter Walter Sims recalled that "his voice sounded like a drill instructor, but he had a sense of humor and loved the kids who begged to linger after lessons. They diligently helped to clean the stables or rub down the horses hoping for extra rides. . . . Sarge was an unforgettable character."[24]

Horseback riders from Sarge Johnson's stables. Courtesy of Ruth Burton.

Judge Marilyn Atkins (36th District Court, Wayne County) mentioned that "the skating rink was the center of attention for the younger people, but Sarge's horses had to be ridden."[25] With respect to his horses, Sarge had strict rules and was not above using profanity to get his point across when these rules were violated. Robert Stepto provides a striking illustration of Sarge's idiosyncratic behavior:

> I was riding at breathtaking speed, not knowing where in the world I was going. At one point, my buddy caught up and yelled, "hey, cool it, the Johnsons are going crazy, you're running that horse too hard." Then the Oldsmobile pulled along side of me, and Sarge leaned out. "Rein that horse in or I'm going to kick your ass.". . . Sarge cursed me every minute of the way. . . . After I was dropped off at home, the Oldsmobile left with a roar and spewing of gravel. When I approached the kitchen door, tired and forlorn, my father asked, "what was that all about?"[26]

Sarge's idiosyncrasies aside, he nonetheless was an important part of the resort community. Sarge's horses, the music, the celebrities, the dancers, the nightclubs, the lake, the rustic scenery, and more, were among the reasons

Idlewild's population soared. Beatrice Buck, a resorter and a good friend of the now deceased recording artist Dinah Washington, recalls "One day while we were strolling around the resort we became hungry and Dinah told a lady who was barbecuing that she was a good cook even though Dinah had not tasted the food. The cook responded by saying 'Girl you haven't tasted this meat.' Dinah, the witty extrovert, said, 'I'm complimenting you in advance 'cause I know you will set me out a plate, please.'"[27] In addition to music rendered by Dinah Washington, vacationers also enjoyed:

THE TEMPTATIONS (formed in 1962). Thanks to their entertaining dance routines and even finer harmonies, the Temptations became the definitive male vocal group of the 1960s. There were many groups "doo-woping" and harmonizing on the street corners in the black communities during the late 1950s and early 1960s. None, however, truly rivaled this group, which was an amalgam of two separate groups, the Primes and the Distants. The blend came about in 1962 when former Distants (baritones Otis Williams,

John English (middle) and two members of the Four Tops: Levi Stubbs (right) and Abdul "Duke" Fakir. Courtesy of John English.

Elbridge Bryant, and bass Melvin Franklin) and former Primes (tenors Eddie Kendricks, Paul Williams, and Kell Osborne) agreed to join musical forces. Almost overnight, they became the group that others tried to imitate. In particular, their impeccable dress and flawlessly choreographed dance steps were the envy of other groups. The merger of the two groups brought with it a Motown contract and many top-ten hits. Some of their greatest are: "On Cloud Nine," "My Girl," "Ain't too Proud to Beg," "Get Ready," "Fading Away," "Since I Lost My Baby," "Don't Look Back," and "The Girl's Alright with Me." The Temptations are still recording and performing. The group is a veritable institution.

THE FOUR TOPS (formed in the late 1950s). Detroit's Levi Stubbs, Renaldo "Obie" Benson, Abdul "Duke" Fakir, and Lawrence Payton called themselves the Four Ames and found themselves in great demand to sing at parties. Because there was another group known as the Ames Brothers, in 1956 the Four Ames became the Four Tops, to avoid confusion among their fans. As the Four Tops the group became a part of the Motown organization and soon developed into one of the country's most successful singing groups. Between 1964 and 1972, they had numerous hits, which included "Standing in the Shadow of Love," "Baby I Need Your Loving," "Bernadette," "It's the Same Old Song," "I Can't Help Myself," "I'll Be There," "Ain't No Woman Like the One I've Got," and others. When former Supreme Florence Ballard died of a heart attack in 1976, the Four Tops were the honorary pallbearers at her funeral. Lawrence Payton succumbed to liver cancer in 1997, and since then the group has been known simply as the Tops.

SARAH VAUGHAN (27 March 1924–3 April 1990). Born in Newark, New Jersey, Sarah, like many other talented African American singers, was early in life found singing in the church choir. Vaughan's "bebop phraseology" became an integral part of her work, an element that helped rank her as one of this country's most influential female jazz singers. Billy Eckstine heard her sing at an amateur contest at the Apollo Theater and brought her to the attention of his bandleader, "Fatha" Hines, who hired her to perform with his big band. After a significant stint with the Hines organization she accepted an offer to join Eckstine, who, along with several other musicians, had left Hines and formed his own band. It was with Eckstine that Vaughan recorded her first song, "I'll Wait and Pray." It was perhaps this memorable tune that audiences at Idlewild most enthusiastically enjoyed, along with "Tenderly," "If You Could See Me Now," and "A Night in Tunisia." Vaughan's departure from Hines's big band in 1944 did not end her association with Dizzy Gillespie, Charlie Parker, and other musical greats who had also been members of his band. Just the opposite, in fact, as Vaughan continued to team up with those artists to record such cuts as "Signing Off," "Lover Man," "East of the Sun," and others. Besides Gillespie and Parker, this diva's illustrious and unique career brought her into professional association with the likes of Herbie Mann, Quincy Jones, Ray Ellis, Count Basie, Joe Williams, and many other truly great musicians. Her contracts with various record companies (Columbia, Roulette Records, and Mercury among them) helped to enhance both her fame and fortune. Though she was a tremendous success in the musical world, such success eluded her in three marriages. The lady known as "Sassy" died in 1990 at the age of sixty-eight.

T-BONE WALKER (28 April 1910–16 March 1975). Born Aaron Thibeaux Walker in Linden, Cass County, Texas, he grew up in the shadows of his step-dad, Marco Washington, who played bass fiddle with the Dallas String Band. Washington's influence was not lost on his stepson, who had a strong desire to become a blues guitarist. It was in this connection that he played the lead role in the electric amplification of blues guitar. B. B. King is only one of many guitarists who owe a debt of gratitude to T-Bone Walker for his pioneering work, which dates back to the early 1940s, and other contributions to the blues genre. In 1942, T-Bone finally got his first record, entitled "I Got a Break Baby," recorded by Capital Records. His own nephew, guitarist R. S. Rankin, was so taken with his success and popularity that he decided to identify himself as T-Bone Walker Jr. on his song entitled "Midnight Bells Are Ringing," released on the Dot Label. With the passage of the years, T-Bone was recognized as a very versatile performer who was associated with big band jazz, both rural and urban blues, and jives.

THOMAS "FATS" WALLER (21 May 1904–15 December 1943). Born in New York City, Waller became a professional pianist at the age of fifteen and was heard in many bars, cabarets, and theaters during the 1920s. He accompanied many urban blues vocalists, including the legendary Bessie Smith. In 1932, Waller traveled to France, and soon thereafter began a famous series of Victor record sessions with his six-piece group. His biggest hits were "I'm Gonna Sit Right Down and Write Myself a Letter," "Ain't Misbehavin,'" "Honeysuckle Rose," "Keepin' Out of Mischief Now," and "Blue Turning Gray over You." Usually his lyrics were quite satirical.

DINAH WASHINGTON (29 August 1924–14 December 1963). Born Ruth Jones in Tuscaloosa, Alabama, Dinah Washington became one of the pioneers of rhythm and blues. When she was about three or four years old, the family migrated to the south side of Chicago in search of higher-paying jobs and a better life. Pushed by her mother, Dinah started singing gospel in local churches. She was hired as an accompanist to Sallie Martin, Mahalia Jackson, and Sister Roberta Martin. Her secular singing career took off after she sang with Lionel Hampton in the early 1940s. After splitting from Hampton to work as a solo performer she recorded "Blow Top Blues," "I Love You, Yes I Do," and "What a Difference a Day Makes." Her album *Dinah Washington: The Jazz Sides* caused many to tout her as the heir apparent to Bessie Smith. She was also labeled a "wild woman" because she had numerous affairs. Her seven marriages were a testimonial to this wild lifestyle. She eventually moved to Detroit with her last husand, Dick "Night Train" Lane, a defensive back for the Detroit Lions professional football team. On 14 December 1963 Dinah died in the Motor City of an accidental overdose of sleeping and diet pills.

JACKIE WILSON (9 June 1934–21 January 1984). Born and reared in a troubled-plagued neighborhood in Detroit, Michigan, Jack Leroy Wilson fell victim to the self-defeating patterns of life that are typically associated with truancy, gang affiliation, dropping out of school, and various other sorts of misbehavior. His mischief landed him in the Lansing Correctional Institute. It was during his incarceration that Wilson's interest in boxing was enhanced, and he became proficient enough at the sport to become a Golden Gloves boxing champion in Detroit at the age of sixteen. While boxing held his interest, however, it did not compare to his love for singing, an activity that he had enjoyed from an early age. Whether it was gospel or doo-wop, it did not matter, as long as it was singing. In fact, his first earnings as a singer came from singing with the Ever Ready Gospel Singers, a group he formed, in various churches in the Detroit area. Later he sang with such secular groups as the Thrillers and Billy Ward's Dominoes. It was with the Dominoes that Wilson's vocal career began to soar. It reached new heights after he left the Dominoes and went solo. Material written or co-written by Berry Gordy Jr. and Roquel "Billy" Davis proved to be key to his skyrocketing career. "Reet Petite," "That's Why," "I'll Be Satisfied," and "Lonely Teardrops" were among the songs that made Wilson a success in the black community. However, legal trouble followed Wilson into adulthood. He was shot twice by one of his lovers, Juanita Jones, in 1961, costing him a kidney, and he was arrested on moral charges in 1967. He had issues with the Internal Revenue Service over unpaid taxes on earned income, and had marital issues with his first wife, Freda Hood, whom he married when he was seventeen. He had the marriage annulled in 1965. In spite of his problems, Wilson was a consistent hit-maker from the mid-1950s through the early 1970s. His stardom was largely confined to the black community, however; he never became a crossover superstar. A massive coronary brought an end to his career as he was performing at the Latin Casino in New Jersey in 1975. Though he rallied from a coma to a semi-comatose state, Wilson remained hospitalized from 29 September 1975 until his death on 21 January 1984. In all those years, the entertainer never said another word.

STEVIE WONDER (13 May 1950–). Born Steveland Morris in Saginaw, Michigan, he spent his formative years in Detroit, Michigan. Though blind since infancy, Stevie was endowed with an extraordinary musical ability, which manifested itself in various forms early in his life. His growth and musical development were similar to those of another musically gifted child artist, Little Willie John, who became an overnight success with the tune "Fever." As with many African American stars, the black church was among the first places where Stevie expressed his musical talent. Motown's head, Berry Gordy, was very interested in this emergent young talent because he fit perfectly into Gordy's larger plan to nurture black talents who would have a strong appeal to white crossover audiences. Little Stevie Wonder's "Fingertips, Part 2" (from his first album, *12-Year-Old Genius*) was a smash hit, just like Little Willie John's first recording. Stevie stayed with Motown for nearly nine years, touring and performing with many African American artists affiliated with the Gordy stable of stars. He also performed with such white stars as Frankie Avalon, Annette Funicello, and the Rolling Stones. This musical genius left the Gordy stable and formed his own recording studio in the early 1970s, which gave him a chance to experiment widely with the various forms of music, employing a variety of different instruments. Some of his most popular tunes are: "For Once in My Life," "Signed, Sealed, Delivered I'm Yours," "Living for the City," "Black Man," "Isn't She Lovely," "Happy Birthday (for Martin Luther King)," "Sir Duke," "Ribbon in the Sky," and "I Just Called (To Say I Love You)." During a typical stop for Stevie at Idlewild the audience would include both those who had heard him play in their neighborhood church and those who had heard about this child genius, but who still marveled at the "wonder" of his phenomenal musical skills and abilities, especially for one so young and sight-challenged. In addition to his music, Wonder has achieved a world reputation for his humanitarianism, especially his efforts against world hunger and racism.

Some Famous Athletes at Idlewild

In addition to the musical stars we have just discussed, Idlewild's guests also included a number of stars from the world of professional sports. To catch a live performance given by, say, Cab Calloway, and be able sit next to and talk with Satchel Paige or Joe Louis in the Fiesta Room would give visitors something to talk about for a long time, if not for a lifetime. Many today still remember very fondly their encounters with these famous men and women. Of course, many were not so famous at the time. The following athletes left their mark on resorters and the nation, if not the world:

JOE LOUIS (13 May 1914–12 April 1981). Joseph Louis Barrows, the son of sharecroppers, was born in Chambers County, Alabama, near Lafayette. The family left Alabama for Detroit in search of a better way of life and higher-paying jobs. After settling on the east side of Detroit, the young Louis decided to compete as an amateur fighter. Amazed by his raw skill and power, trainers realized his potential and encouraged him to pursue a professional career as a heavyweight fighter. The quiet and reserved Alabamian devoted himself to the development of his pugilistic skills and became known as the "Brown Bomber" because of his knockout power. He trained in the Idlewild area before some of his fights. He was drafted during the Second World War, at the height of his boxing career. During his military stint he gave numerous boxing demonstrations and made personal appearances at benefits on behalf of his country. Some of his most memorable bouts were against such fighters as Primo Cannero, Max Schmelling, and Rocky Marciano. Upon retiring from the boxing ring, he became a professional wrestler and a fight referee. Prior to his death, Joe Louis was a professional greeter for one of the casinos in Las Vegas.

SUGAR RAY ROBINSON (3 May 1921–12 April 1989). Sugar Ray Robinson was born Walker Smith in Detroit, Michigan. He was a six-time middleweight boxing champion. Many boxing analysts consider him the best fighter, pound for pound, in the annals of pugilism. Sugar Ray started his professional career in the 1940s, and continued to fight until the late 1960s. In 201 professional bouts, he had 109 knockouts and suffered only 19 defeats. Most of those losses occurred after he passed forty years of age. He retired from the ring several times. During one hiatus, he entertained audiences throughout the Midwest, including Idlewild, as a dancer. Not able to earn enough money as a

Heavyweight champion Joe Louis and his manager, Mr. Roxborough, enjoying the scenic beauty of Idlewild. Courtesy of the Ben C. Wilson Collection, Black Americana Studies Department, Western Michigan University.

dancer to pay his bills, Sugar Ray went back into the fighting ring. He finally retired from the sport for good at age forty-four. In addition to doing bit parts in television and movies, he formed a youth foundation in 1969. When Robinson died in Detroit, many celebrated him as one of the best fighters in the annals of boxing. He was a colorful and charismatic athlete and won the hearts of fight fans around the world.

WILT CHAMBERLAIN (21 August 1936–12 October 1999). Born Wilton Norman Chamberlain in Philadelphia, he was one of the eight children of a custodian/handyman father and a housekeeper/laundress mother. Although his parents were of normal height, Wilt grew rapidly during his teenage years, until he reached the height of 7'1". His three years at Overbrook High School were an indicator of his basketball prowess. In his three years there he scored 2,252 points, with 90 being scored in one game. Upon graduation, he was awarded a scholarship to Kansas University and was named All-American in his sophmore and junior years. The Kansas University superstar took his team to the National Collegiate Athletic Association finals in 1957, where they lost to the University of North Carolina as a result of a new strategy, which slowed the game to neutralize Wilt's amazing scoring abilities. Rather than returning to the University of Kansas, he joined the razzle-dazzle comical touring professional team, the Harlem Globetrotters. He joined the Philadelphia Warriors of the National Basketball Association (NBA), with a large bonus incentive, in 1959. Chamberlain was an NBA star from the beginning, leading the league in scoring and rebounding. In his first year in the league he was awarded honors as Rookie of the Year and Most Valuable Player in the League, recognizing his skill as one of the greatest rebounders and scorers in the game. Because of his height and dominating skills around the basket, the game of basketball underwent some significant changes. Wilt was the only player to score one hundred points in a single game, against the New York Knicks. Wilt's nemesis was Bill Russell, center for the Boston Celtics. Upon retiring from the NBA, the "Stilt" coached professionally in San Diego, played professional beach volleyball, and racquetball, and ran track and field. His controversial autobiography, A View from Above, caused a commotion and sold well due to Wilt's ludicrous claim that he had slept with over twenty thousand women over the course of his life as a "player/womanizer."

James Thomas "Cool Papa" Bell (17 May 1903–7 March 1991). Born in Starkville, Mississippi, he began as a pitcher for the St. Louis Stars in the Negro National Baseball League at the young age of nineteen. He earned the nickname "Cool" when he struck out the legendary Oscar Charleston. Later his manager added "Papa" to his moniker. He went on to become a center fielder for the Pittsburgh Crawfords and the Homestead Grays, and player-manager for the Kansas City Monarchs. In the 1930s he batted .391 over a five-year period. According to the legend, he was so fleet of foot that he could turn a light off and be in bed before the room became dark. Even sprinter Jesse Owens declined to compete against Bell in a foot race exhibition. He was elected to the Baseball Hall of Fame in 1974.

Leroy Robert "Satchel" Paige (7 July 1906–8 June 1982). Born in Mobile, Alabama, he was one of the greatest pitchers in the history of baseball. When he was about seven years old he earned money by carrying bags and satchels at the local railroad station. He sometimes dangled several satchels at a time from a long stick, causing other kids to nickname him "Satchel Tree." Eventually, the name was shortened to "Satchel." Paige was the first African American to pitch in the American League, as well as the first African American to pitch in a World Series game. He was known for his famous hesitation pitch and had the ability to throw so fast that many hitters claimed that once the ball reached the plate it became the size of a BB, virtually invisible. He was one of the best known players in the black baseball leagues and became the first black elected to the Baseball Hall of Fame. During five seasons in the American League, from 1948 to 1953, Paige won twenty-eight games and lost thirty-two. At age fifty-nine, he was the oldest man ever to pitch in the majors. He was not a stranger at Idlewild, and his presence, along with those of many other celebrities, prompted other African Americans to visit there.

JOSH GIBSON (21 December 1911–20 January 1947). Born in Buena Vista, Georgia, Gibson was known as the greatest slugger and defensive catcher in the Negro Baseball League. His legend includes a long home run during a game in Monessen, Pennsylvania. The mayor of that city stopped the game to measure the distance of the hit—512 feet. His record of eighty-five home runs in one season is still standing. (This record is separate from the Major League record because this feat occurred in the Negro Baseball League in the United States during the Jim Crow years.) He is often called the "Black Babe Ruth." Gibson played for the Pittsburgh Crawfords from 1927 to 1929 and the Homestead (Pennyslvania) Grays from 1930 to 1931 and 1937 to 1946. He led the Negro National League in home runs for ten consecutive seasons. His career batting average was .347. His exploits on the baseball field got him elected into the Baseball Hall of Fame in 1972. Gibson died of alcoholism in 1947. Many attributed his drinking problem to depression over the fact that he was overlooked by the major leagues.

JOHN "BUCK" O'NEIL (1911–6 October 2006). Born in Carabelle, Florida, he was a smooth-fielding first baseman for the Kansas City Monarchs of the Negro Baseball League when that team won four consecutive Negro American League pennants. In 1946, after a three-year stretch in the military, O'Neil won the Negro American League batting title with an average of .353. He joined the Chicago Cubs as a scout in the mid-1950s and became the first black coach in major league history in 1962. O'Neil is best known today as the driving force behind the Negro League Baseball Museum in Kansas City, Missouri, an important destination for anyone interested in the history of Negro baseball in this country.

REESE "GOOSE" TATUM (3 May 1921–8 January 1967). Born in Calion, Arkansas, he signed with the Harlem Globetrotters during the post–World War II era. He quickly established himself as a basketball prodigy and an inspired comedic genius on the basketball court. Tatum's arms were so long that his hands reached below his knees, an attribute that added enormously to his ball-handling ability. He also was a star baseball player for the Birmingham Black Barons before signing a contract with the Globetrotters. In the mid-1950s, Tatum started his own basketball team called the Harlem Road Kings. The team was modeled after the original Harlem Globetrotters, but it did not have the same audience appeal or staying power.

In sum, the professional entertainers and athletes who frequented Idlewild helped guarantee good times for the resorters. Because Idlewild became the showcase for black entertainment between 1940 and 1960, many clubs and organizations from Chicago, Detroit, and Columbus, as well as many other cities, decided to hold their retreats at the resort. Among the numerous clubs that held retreats at the resort were: The Jolly Old Timers, the Gracious Grannies (Chicago), the Swell Elegants Club (Columbus), and the Mid-Michigan and Chicago Idlewilders. In addition, members of the various secret societies—the Prince Hall Masons and black fraternities and sororities among them—took advantage of the facilities and activities at the resort for many years. Its popularity also drew the pure party animals and those with a penchant for golf, especially the Idlewild Duffers. The Briar Hills Country Club, in White Cloud, was more than a challenge for their Fifth Annual Golf Tournament. The 1961 defending golf champ, Dr. Cortez English of Grand Rapids, encouraged the Duffers to hang out all night. He and his son, John, were awestruck when they played with gambler "Saginaw Pete," who carried buckets of money with him at all times but would never bet more than ten cents per hole.[28]

With the passage of the Public Accommodations Act in the 1960s (discussed in the next chapter), Idlewild found itself facing certain severe challenges. With the passage of time, this once vibrant community experienced some drastic changes that not only crippled its economic base but had profound consequences for virtually every aspect of the community. The next chapter provides a more in-depth discussion of these changes and their implications for the future of Idlewild.

SOCIOLOGICAL ILLUMINATIONS

Two separate entertainment circuits—one for African American performers and one for Jewish-American performers—were created as a direct response to the segregated social system in the United States. Racial and ethnic bigotry made it impossible for entertainers and performers who belonged to these two groups to display their talents in the larger society. Hence, behind the walls of segregation, the "Chitlin Circuit" (for blacks) and the "Borscht Circuit" (for Jews) provided venues where they could earn some money, if not a persistent and sustainable living wage, as professional entertainers. Moreover, those same venues were often the only stages for the young amateurs to showcase their talents and where they could gain insights for further improvement. As historian Harry Reed has suggested, "these young performers served a considerable period of their apprenticeships in such venues. While there, the young players learned acceptable professional standards."[29] The performers on these circuits worked to improve their instruments or voices, and internalized a positive attitude toward improvisation or ad-libbing.

For the black entertainer, Idlewild was only one of many stops on the Chitlin Circuit. Making a living on that circuit was not an easy task. Those who made it had to "pay some dues," which—translated—meant long, arduous road trips (often by bus), living out of one's suitcase, inadequate (or no) dressing rooms, sparse accommodations in the black community, and performing in "dives," "juke joints," or "chicken shacks" for low pay. "Paying dues" resulted, for some, in the opportunity to play in the bigger or more luxurious venues in the larger cities such as New York, Detroit, Chicago, and Birmingham (Alabama). It also meant a recording contract for those black performers who survived and were superbly talented. Receiving a recording contract, however, was no guarantee that one's records would be sold to the general public or played on white radio stations. For decades black music was strongly criticized, especially rhythm and blues, as decadent and unfit for consumption in the white community. The black community was not unanimous on this matter, either; when it came to different types of music, there were some divisions.

The entertainers who performed at Idlewild appealed to these divisions. For example, Arthur Prysock, Lionel Hampton, Duke Ellington, Count Basie,

Dancers in the Purple Palace. Courtesy of Florence Powell Washington.

Cannon Ball Adderley, and Barbara McNair appealed to the entertainment needs of those African Americans who had more education and considered themselves to be more sophisticated than those with a lesser education. On the other hand, Jackie "Moms" Mabley, B. B. King, Jackie Wilson, T. Bone Walker, and Betty "Be-Bop" Carter performed largely before an audience that came from a more grassroots background. At the same time, however, it was not unusual to see Idlewilders from across all divisions "jammin'" to the sounds of Dinah Washington, Al Hibbler, or the Four Tops. In spite of the pretenses and the efforts made by some Idlewilders to maintain social distance from certain elements, music often brought all African Americans together, if only temporarily.

A similar observation can be made about the impact of Mel Torme, Joey Bishop, Sophie Tucker, Jerry Lewis, Milton Berle, and other entertainers who frequented the Catskills resorts. Though social divisions persisted in both the black and Jewish communities because of the artificial barriers created to maintain social boundaries and social distance, segregation often forced people to share a commonality that transcended those barriers. Victimized by the evils of ethnic bigotry and racism, Jews and African Americans found it necessary to spend their leisure time where they were most comfortable, without worrying about racial and ethnic proscriptions upon their fun time. In Michigan, Idlewild became the most popular venue for blacks, while Fiddleman's Resort, near South Haven, tried to become part of the Borscht Circuit.

In sum, when considering racial and ethnic segregation, one usually thinks about its impact on the political, economical, social, and educational well-being of people. Rarely does one think about how such a system might affect how the segregated minorities spend their leisure time. What are some consequences on the talents and expressions of a minority group that is forced to live behind the walls of segregation, knowing that their talents will not be accepted in the general society? Idlewild and the Catskills resorts—microcosms of America—are two separate but similar responses to the need for these groups to find a satisfactory place to enjoy themselves and to serve as an outlet for their talents. Without a doubt, both Idlewild and the Catskills resorts provided a sanctuary, however temporary, for the entertainers and vacationers who sought an escape from the evils of racism and bigotry, which were ubiquitous in the larger society.

5

Some Intended and Unintended Consequences in the Black Community During the Civil Rights Era

LIVING IN A CASTE SYSTEM IN THE UNITED STATES

From its very beginning, the United States has been a country replete with contradictions, a place with incredibly wide discrepancies between its preachings and its practices, especially when it comes to racial minorities. A universal tenet in the United States asserts that all citizens will be treated equally, and their rights to the pursuit of freedom and happiness will not be hampered because of skin color or other such characteristics. Just the opposite, however, has been the practice. The United States has allowed a virulent form of racism to exist for centuries, and it is within this historical context that Idlewild was formed into a recognizable community during the early part of the twentieth century. Moreover, it was precisely because America had established a racial caste system that a small group of white men was able to purchase a large parcel of land in Michigan, develop it, and vigorously market it as a place for "the best coloreds" in the country. That same group had no compunctions or misgivings whatsoever about establishing another resort for whites, where it was generally understood that even their black maids and chauffeurs were not welcome overnight.

Racial segregation and discrimination were the twin evils that contributed to the emergence and persistence of a caste system in this country, a system that allowed a stratification order to be formed for both blacks and whites, in the sense that there were distinct social classes within each caste. At the same time, there was a rigid geographical and social caste line that separated the two races. The caste line, of necessity, meant that the black community had to have its own set of social institutions, similar to those found in the white community, to meet the needs of its people, including churches, schools, boarding houses, barber shops, carpenters, doctors, teachers, and many others.

In short, differential opportunities gave rise to the social classes found among both whites and blacks. The main difference, however, between the two communities was seen in the fact that blacks in general had far fewer opportunities than whites, a fact that was due primarily to the racial discrimination that held sway in all communities, whether rural or urban, northern or southern. That the United States was a "white man's country" meant that no minority group escaped unscathed from the hostilities and prejudicial attitudes of the majority of the whites. Jews, for example, had been the victims of centuries of persecution throughout various parts of the world. Unfortunately, upon arrival in the United States they did not find themselves in a place filled with ethnic tolerance. Instead, like African Americans, Jews found themselves unwanted and unaccepted at many public and private restaurants, boarding houses, hotels, hospitals, beaches, and so forth. Hence, they, too, found it necessary to establish their own places, where they could interact with kindred souls from their own ethnic group, and where they could escape some of the anti-Semitic hostilities. Thus, it was within the context of this caste system that many blacks and Jews became involved with resorts—Idlewild for the black community and a number of Catskills resorts for the Jews—that were established specifically for them.

The Catskill Mountains resort community in upstate New York is just one example of a place where the Jews created a haven for themselves, away from the hostilities of Gentiles. Though accessible by railroad, a trip to the Catskills resorts most often meant long hours traveling by car over unfriendly roads, unpleasant even when making the trip in a chauffeur-driven limousine. Jewish resorters, like their black counterparts at Idlewild, did not mind making the trip, because these resorts were the only places open to them.

These places came into existence at a time when the workweek was being defined, and a one- or two-week annual vacation became an integral part of the work world. The affordable automobiles coming off the assembly line in Michigan's manufacturing plants added enormously to the ability of American families to travel long distances in pursuit of an enjoyable and pleasant vacation experience, and resorters traveling to Idlewild or the Catskills resorts did not hesitate to take advantage of this opportunity.

The Civil Rights Movement versus the Caste System

The Civil Rights Movement that had its beginning in the 1950s did not emerge out of a social vacuum. There were salient flashpoints and developments throughout the country, events that constantly challenged a caste system that segregated and disadvantaged its minority citizens. A detailed treatment of these developments falls outside the purview of this book, but suffice it to say that the Tulsa riots in Oklahoma in the 1920s, the 1943 riots in Detroit, the Zoot-Suit riots in California in the 1940s, and the Montgomery Bus Boycott in the mid-1950s were among those historical flashpoints. The Civil Rights Movement inspired people to work and hope for a system of justice and fairness in every state and for all people, regardless of their race, religion, color, or sex. To that end, the Public Accommodations Act, a part of the 1964 Civil Rights package, was heralded as an ameliorative action that would move U.S. society dramatically closer to being a just social system.

Specifically, the act stated that all persons would be entitled to the full and equal enjoyment of the goods, services, facilities, privileges, advantages, and accommodations of any place of public accommodation without discrimination or segregation on the basis of race, color, religion, or national origin. It forbade discrimination in any inn, hotel, motel, or other establishment that provided lodging to transient guests. Further, restaurants, cafeterias, lunchrooms, lunch counters, soda fountains, or other facilities principally engaged in selling food for consumption on the premises were required to disband their Jim Crow laws. Motion picture houses, theaters, concert halls, sports arenas, stadiums, and other places of exhibition or entertainment also had to comply. In most situations, the effects were immediate, though in other cases the forced transition was gradual.

Social integration was proclaimed by many civic leaders and politicians as the true American ideal, which is arguably best represented by the late Dr. Martin Luther King Jr. in his "I Have a Dream" speech, where he talked about black boys and white boys holding hands, and America living out the true meaning of its creeds. Though strident separatists' voices could be heard, established leaders in both black and white communities thought that those voices represented a minority opinion. The major focus of the Civil Rights Movement was on integrating the disparate groups into a harmonious social, political, and economic whole. It would seem that, in spite of fierce white resistance, many blacks readily embraced both the enabling legislation and the challenge of going into the various white establishments to purchase a meal, a hotel room, a bus or train ticket, or a seat at the theater, and felt that such action sent an unequivocal message that the United States was no longer just a "white man's country."

On Integration: A New Phase and a New Crisis

Thousands of people literally risked their lives for social justice, to bring down the walls of segregation and discrimination in this country. Thus, pioneers, resorters, and vacationers alike were keenly aware of individual hardships and the collective struggle of black people for equality and freedom. Still fresh in their minds was the fact that, before leaving on a long journey, they had the onerous task of cooking and packing enough food and drink for the entire trip because they knew white establishments would not accommodate them during their travel. Also, many personally remembered the "white only" and "colored only" signs, and the fact that blacks were not allowed to come to the front door in white neighborhoods, a common practice in the southern states. Moreover, many recalled singing protest songs with the words: "no more segregation," "I'll be buried in my grave before I'll be a slave," and "we shall overcome."

Accordingly, the desire for integration and social justice was almost universal among African Americans when the Public Accommodations Act was passed. Many African Americans were inspired to assert actively and boldly their rights as U.S. citizens by patronizing white establishments that had previously barred them. To do otherwise would mean that those people—both black and white—who had risked everything, including life itself, to usher in an era of extraordinary social change was in vain. In essence, African Americans found themselves entering what Daniel Patrick Moynihan called "a new phase, and a new crisis," involving the twin ideals of liberty and equality. According to Moynihan:

> Given the ethnic group structure of American life, equality for Negro Americans means that they will have open to them the full range of American economic, social, and political life, and that within the pattern of endeavor that they choose, having assessed the comparative advantages of time, place, and cultural endowment, they will have a fully comparable share of the successes, no less than of the small winners and of the outright failures. The test of American society will be whether it can work out arrangements so that this happens more or less naturally for Negro Americans, as it has more or less naturally happened for other groups.[1]

Self-Validation, Self-Actualization, and Identity

With the Public Accommodations Act, many blacks felt that the time had come to become self-actualized by doing what they had long been denied. On the one hand, one can only imagine the effect that some twenty-two or twenty-four thousand Idlewild vacationers had in eroding the influence of Jim Crowism on such cities as Indianapolis, Indiana; Jackson, Mississippi; Chicago, Illinois; Detroit, Michigan; Kansas City, Missouri; Cleveland, Ohio; and Grand Rapids, Michigan, as well as numerous other large and small cities and rural areas. On the other hand, the opportunity for self-actualization by those same African Americans and their sisters and brothers throughout the country was a motivating factor to become validated as first-class citizens, just like whites, who had long enjoyed first-class citizenship no mattter their station in life. Though not everyone thought it necessary that self-actualization be expressed in exactly the same way or manner, it is very evident that the decades of the 1960s and 1970s constituted an era very different from any other in the history of black people in this country. To be able to walk into a white establishment and be treated like any other person was important. Hence, self-actualization was paramount for many, who proudly asserted such slogans as "I'm black and I'm proud," and "We shall overcome."

Self-worth and racial pride, often expressed in the popular protest songs of James Brown, Curtis Mayfield, Aretha Franklin, and other artists, were openly expressed by a generation whose ancestors had been forced to acknowledge the "rightness of whiteness." Such an acknowledgement, of necessity, robbed a people of their self-worth, even for those who were fortified by a strong sense of internal dignity.

For many blacks, then, it became important at this time that they behave in a manner whereby their true essence, as a human being, would be self-validated and expressed as they transformed the Public Accommodations Act into a vehicle of social change. The Civil Rights Acts of 1964 and 1965—along with the Supreme Court's decisions, which outlawed separate but equal schooling—were necessary conditions toward the full inclusion of African Americans into what Talcott Parsons, a highly respected sociological theorist, called the "societal community." These conditions, however, were not sufficient unto themselves for the acceptance of African Americans as first-class citizens. That long-sought-after status could be achieved only through each individual doing his or her part to overcome the enormous resistance to black inclusion by the larger white society. Thus, the Public Accommodations Act was simply another event that encouraged and inspired the collective black community to find its rightful place in society by exercising its moral and legal prerogatives. Regarding the importance of black inclusion, Talcott Parsons makes the following assertion:

> This seems to me to constitute a crucially important focus for the future of the collective Negro identity. The Negro community has the opportunity to define itself as the spearhead of one of the most important improvements in the quality of American society in its history—and to do so not only in pursuit of its own obvious self-interest, but in the fulfillment of a moral imperative. It is a change in American society which is deeply consonant with our moral traditions, but also one which could not come about without strong, systematically exerted pressures and strong leadership. The resistances are quite sufficient to explain these necessities.[2]

The fundamental view held by most leaders of the Civil Rights Movement was that federal laws against discrimination, though very necessary, were no guarantee that racial equality or first-class citizenship would be bestowed upon African Americans. William Raspberry, columnist for the *Washington Post*, shared with his readers Dr. Reverend Martin Luther King Jr.'s cautionary view of equality when he said:

Negroes have proceeded from a premise that equality means what it says . . . but most whites in America, including many persons of goodwill, proceed from a premise that equality is a loose expression for improvement. White America is not even psychologically organized to close the gap—essentially it seeks only to make it less painful and less obvious but in most respects to retain it. Most of the abrasions between Negroes and white liberals arise from this fact.[3]

Moreover, according to Raspberry:

King never thought the passage and enforcement of anti-discrimination laws would, by itself, usher in the racial equality he sought. For him, the legislation was a mere threshold condition, "like freeing a man who has been unjustly imprisoned for years and, on discovering his innocence, sending him out with no bus fare to get home, no suit to cover his body, no financial compensation to help him get a footing in society; sending him out with only the assertion, 'Now you are free.'". . . But mostly King saw his role as (in the Quakers' phrase) "speaking truth to power." And for him, the fundamental truth was white America's "schizophrenic personality on the question of race. She has been torn between selves—a self in which she proudly professed the great principles of democracy and a self in which she sadly practiced the antithesis of democracy. There never has been a solid, unified and determined thrust to make justice a reality for Afro-Americans."[4]

THE DUAL CHALLENGE: TRANSFORMING AMERICA THROUGH INTEGRATION VERSUS RACIAL SOLIDARITY

Awareness and Identity

Sociologically, as a people, African Americans had little success dealing with the dual challenges of socially transforming the country while simultaneously maintaining racial solidarity within their own communities. One could argue that Jews, for example, provided an excellent case of a people who not only mounted effective strategies against anti-Semitism but also learned, through their persecution here and abroad, to maintain a strong sense of group solidarity, as reflected in their institutions, organizations, and business acumen.

There is no doubt that thousands of African Americans moved to northern cities to work in the auto industries and later the defense industries during World War II. They also wanted to escape the virulent forms of racism prevalent throughout the southern states. Yet they found that cities like Detroit were not the "Canaan Land" hoped for. Instead, they found an atmosphere charged with racial bigotry. Though Detroit did not have "colored water fountains," the "colored elevator," the "back of the bus" practice, or the other cultural representations of black subjugation found in the South, there were certain counterparts, as expressed in racial covenants to keep neighborhoods segregated and lower wages for blacks doing the same jobs as whites. It was a city where there were frequent clashes over housing and jobs. It is common knowledge that African Americans paid significantly more for the same quality of housing as white Americans in that city. On 20 June 1943, racial riots erupted in Detroit, prompted by whites who attacked and beat blacks in the streets of that city, who then responded in kind. The riots ended with twenty-five blacks and nine whites dead, and thousands of people injured.

The Detroit example is given as an illustration of the life of African Americans in northern cities. These were men and women who knew first-hand the ugliness of American racial bigotry and who felt a deep sense of obligation to rid America of such ugliness. Many black Detroiters left the South in order to carve out a better existence, one that would be relatively free of blatant racism. Hence, their collective memories of past and continual subjugation were too fresh and vivid in their minds to ignore the fact that Idlewild was built behind the invisible and humiliating walls of segregation. A moral and ethical imperative hung in the air like a low-lying fog, which made it impossible for anyone with a memory of subjugation to walk away from an involvement in the dismantling of segregation. Some of these African Americans were lot owners and vacationers at Idlewild who held the resort in high esteem. It had been a haven for them when they had had no other choice but to conform to the dictates of an unjust social system.

The Idlewild Club House was the principal meeting place for the resorters. Waiters dressed in tuxedos and wearing white gloves served lunch and dinner in the Club House dining room. Courtesy of the State Archives of Michigan, Stanley Kufta Collection.

Liberation and Transformation

After they were legally able to do so, the reasons blacks sought out white establishments are multifaceted: the liberation of the inner person; individual self-actualization; personal and social improvement; and social transformation are just a few. Many blacks found themselves caught up in a multiplicity of social and psychological processes that meant the more they were self-actualized, the less they were able to support the vibrancy of Idlewild. In other words, the more they patronized white establishments, the less they were able to continue their patronage of Idlewild. Sociologically, to the extent to which they engaged in one pattern of life they were effectively prevented from participating in the other. Hence, it seems that many blacks were more motivated to deal with the age-old problems associated with the attainment of first-class citizenship than they were to maintain a segregated resort.

Unfortunately for Idlewild, the vision of a self-sufficient black community was not salient or resonant enough to overcome the more powerful proclivities of the thousands upon thousands of blacks who sought to change the very fabric in which this country had wrapped itself. An understanding of those larger forces and those deeply held aspirations makes it easy to arrive at the conclusion that there was no conspiracy or deliberately planned action on the part of most blacks to simply abandon Idlewild as a black resort community. Rather, Idlewild found itself a casualty of a larger movement of blacks toward inclusion in desegregated white society.

Some Shortcomings of the Public Accommodations Act and Integration

The accommodation legislation fell far short of its mark in the eyes of some civil rights leaders and black businessmen. For one thing, the immediate tangible economic benefits of desegregation accrued disproportionately to white businesses. The result of the legislation was the opening of a closed segment of the domestic market, but the economic windfall blew in only one direction. A floodgate was opened and black customers flooded into stores, hotels, restaurants, and resorts where they had formerly been prohibited. In the process, they neglected black businesses in their own neighborhoods. In return, however, whites did not come across the open economic borders to spend their money in black establishments. For them, the segregationist borders had always been open—at least unofficially.

Consequences of Eliminating the Caste Line

With their newly found freedom, many were at loose ends, because they had no idea of the parameters for their behavior. They therefore experimented by traveling into strange territories and seeking out new ventures. Thus, with the passage of the Public Accommodations Act, many African Americans were motivated to test new social waters by turning their attention to establishments in the white society. The caste line began to slowly crumble, with the unforeseen result that many institutions in the black community suffered and many resorts like Idlewild witnessed hard times. Some would argue that African Americans, in their rush to integrate, lost one of their most precious and vital core values—a blend of caring and sharing that had served the group, both individually and collectively, since before emancipation.

When the Public Accommodations Act became law it should be understood that it was a natural development for black citizens to put to a test the efficacy of that act and to seek to participate in transforming the unjust system that had long denied black people the amenities of a rich and prosperous nation that they, too, had played a significant role in building. Accordingly, then, if they were to transform an unjust society, that could occur only if they took full advantage of the existing public accommodations by frequenting inns, motels, hotels, restaurants, cafeterias, lunch counters, motion picture theaters, concert halls, sports arenas or stadiums, entertainment halls, resorts, and other places that had once been denied them. Thus, on the one hand, the act was a major corrective action in the society; on the other hand, however, it had some rather devastating consequences for a number of components of the black community.

Dr. Mark Foster, historian from the University of Colorado in Denver, has said:

> Affluent blacks, as well as their less fortunate brethren, still face daily "reminders" of their race, however unintended or "subtle" such indications might be. A well dressed young black male might be "carded" at a night spot, while his white friend standing next to him might be admitted without a check; or a black couple dining at an elegant restaurant might notice that a group of whites at a nearby table received service from a waiter before they did, even though they arrived earlier.[5]

These and other discriminatory circumstances made it apparent to the black elites that green money in black hands did not bleach their skin tone.

The results of the Public Accommodations Act were predictable, even foreseen. A major part of the economic backbone of the Idlewild resort, so painfully erected in the face of the protracted struggle against racism and other forms of social injustice, slowly began to collapse with the cancellation of racial exclusivity. As township supervisor Norm Burns phrased it, "First we had segregation, and then integration. Then disintegration."[6] Playwright Beatrice Buck lamented, "Once integration was in, . . . black resorters went elsewhere and that . . . act had a detrimental effect on the resort, especially for black businesses there."[7] Sunnie Wilson reinforced that contention when he mentioned that:

> Desegregation prompted blacks to take their money to white businesses. White nightclub-goers no longer had to go to the black neighborhoods to see a black

A view of the Idlewild business district. Courtesy of the Ben C. Wilson Collection, Black Americana Studies Department, Western Michigan University.

jazz group or stage act. . . . Along with the judges, black businessmen like me thought desegregation would open up a new era. When they introduced integration . . . , I thought it was going to be a two way street for blacks and whites. Black businessmen thought it would strengthen the economic condition of our community. After integration, however, the white people didn't have to go to . . . [black] after-hours spots for entertainment. Instead, they drew the black entertainers into their clubs and lounges. The whites stopped spending money in the black neighborhoods. Although I fought for integration all my life, I never thought it would become a one-way street. . . . [8]

Concerning various aspects of the caste system as they are associated with the future prospects of African American-owned businesses, sociologist Richard T. Schaefer makes the following poignant observation:

Historically, the first Black-owned businesses developed behind the wall of segregation. African Americans provided other African Americans with services that Whites would not provide, such as insurance, hairdressing, legal assistance, and medical help. Although this is less true today, African American entrepreneurs usually cater first to the market demand with their own community in such areas as music and mass media. However, if these new ventures become profitable, the entrepreneur usually faces stiff competition from outside the African American community. A very visible example is the rhythm-and-blues music industry and more recently the rap music business, which began as small black-owned businesses but which, as they became profitable, were often taken into large white-owned corporations.

The future of Black-owned businesses is uncertain. Among the factors creating new obstacles are the following:

1. Continuing backlash against affirmative action programs.
2. Difficulty in obtaining loans and other capital.
3. A changing definition of minority that allows women, veterans, and people with disabilities to qualify for special small-business-assistance programs.
4. A reduction in the number and scope of set-aside programs.[9]

Genessee County resident Dallas McDonald said, "Idlewild has changed but I won't say it's changed for the worse or better. . . . The posh night life is gone but summer regulars manage to entertain themselves with cookouts, golf tournaments and weekend jazz sets. . . . A round of parties and other festivities are hosted . . . by private clubs formed by lot owners from St. Louis, Chicago, Detroit and other places. . . ."[10] Gill Griffin (in a *Lake County Star* article entitled "Idlewild: Welcoming Resort Meant Summer to Black Families") quoted his mother, Gladys Scott-Griffin, who said, "We have places to dance and roller skate and go to nightclubs. . . . You felt like you belonged. Now, we entertain ourselves going from cottage to cottage and playing bridge. We enjoy the tranquility." The writer of the article further mentioned that his mother hosted and played in many games through the years with best friends Edna, Theonita, and Carolyn. "Over the years these women have been like my aunts. That was the joy of spending my early summers there in the 1970s . . . the sense of community and family."[11]

However, "Integration killed the place" is an expression heard in many quarters.[12] A 2 July 1967 story in the *Detroit Free Press* headlined "Idlewild: A Victim of Racial Progress?" predicted that the community would continue its

One of Lela and Herman Wilson's Idlewild businesses, a grocery store, is now in disrepair and boarded up. Courtesy of the Ben C. Wilson Collection, Black Americana Studies, Western Michigan University.

economic slide: "Today Idlewild is fading, and if it dies in the next few years, its Negro owners, businessmen, and residents will be paradoxical victims of their own race's social progress. What is sapping the life out of the area is integration. If nothing changes, Idlewild is on its way to stark Southern-style poverty."[13]

Lack of Economic Correspondence from the White Community

As pointed out by Sunnie Wilson, Idlewild suffered not only from the fact that more and more blacks were going into the white community but also from the fact that whites did not patronize the black community in any significant number. Those who did frequent Idlewild to enjoy the entertainment stopped coming once they found that they could see those same entertainers in the white community. This lack of economic correspondence had long-term consequences for the vitality of Idlewild and served as another instance of unequal relations, a phenomenon that contributes to the continual dominance of the majority group.

The Paradise Club had become an eyesore before it was torn down. Courtesy of the Ben C. Wilson Collection, Black Americana Studies Department, Western Michigan University.

Not only did integration have negative consequences for Idlewild and other black communities, it could be argued that, in terms of the Civil Rights Movement, African Americans were short-changed in the process. By focusing on integration the leaders of the Civil Rights Movement allowed attention to be diverted away from a greater need to (a) abolish racial exploitation and (b) create a society where there was a more equitable distribution of land and wealth. Economically, at the time, people of color had not been able to defend themselves from the residuals of colonialism in this country.

Just as the integration of organized baseball essentially eliminated the Negro Baseball League, integration also had negative consequences for other sectors of the black community. Throughout the South, fear reigned supreme among black educators and administrators, who had no guarantee that there would be a position for them in an integrated public school system. In many instances, their fears were justified, as indeed some fell victim as staunch white resistance to school integration collapsed and black and white children attended the same schools and sat in the same classrooms. When this

Another view of the Paradise Club before it was demolished. Courtesy of the Ben C. Wilson Collection, Black Americana Studies Department, Western Michigan University.

occurred, some black teachers and administrators lost their jobs or were demoted.

Furthermore, the civil rights legislation did not go far enough, because black communities were left unprotected. What is gained by blacks being able to eat at white lunch counters when lunch counters in their own neighborhoods are being closed due to the lack of patronage? Parenthetically, the philosophical argument that those sacrifices should have been anticipated as a normal aspect of social change was accepted by some but bitterly opposed by others as simply another instance of black oppression in a racist society. About the only institution that was untouched by integration was the church, which remains the most segregated institution in society, even today.

DID THE PUBLIC ACCOMMODATIONS ACT ALONE KILL IDLEWILD?

The assertion that "integration killed Idlewild" is something both heard repeatedly from many now in Idlewild and written in many documents about that community. A more critically poignant corollary claims that African

Americans simply abandoned Idlewild; they deserted it for the white world that was once closed to them. To be sure, the Civil Rights Movement and integration had a negative influence on Idlewild and other black resorts in particular and on black institutions in general throughout the United States. However, it would be an egregious error to accept as completely factual the simplistic notion that African Americans abandoned black businesses and institutions erected behind the walls of segregation and, once the walls collapsed, rushed en masse, pell-mell, into the white world. Many factors, in addition to integration, had far-reaching consequences on the black experience, of which Idlewild was a part, in the aftermath of the Civil Rights Acts of 1964 and 1965, especially the Public Accommodations Act of 1964.

Idlewild Will Always Be There!

"We can always go to Idlewild when we can't go anywhere else" was an expression repeated by many blacks after it was legally possible for them to enter white establishments. Yet it was precisely this type of attitude that allowed many blacks to take Idlewild for granted as they experimented with their newly found social prerogatives. Thus it seems that the extent to which they experimented with white establishments limited their ability to continue their support for Idlewild. Indeed, Idlewild would always be there! Although white establishments did not welcome black patronage with open arms, with the passage of time, Idlewild faded in the minds of many blacks as they carried fresh memories about the new places that had been long forbidden to them in the white world. Arguably, those blacks who took Idlewild for granted in essence placed its very existence in peril.

St. Clair Drake and Horace R. Cayton recite a story, as told by a black woman, that points up both the experimental aspects of public accommodation and the accompanying diminished support for black businesses:

> They want to appear important, and many of them go to a white man's place just to make him wait on them. It is like getting revenge for not having had the opportunity of going into some white places in the South. The one sad thing is the Negro does not realize that he is hurting himself in doing this, for his group needs his trade to stay in business.[14]

This statement by an unnamed woman captures both the importance to blacks at the time of taking advantage of the public accommodation legislation and the sad impact this had on Idlewild with respect to the lack of black patronage. What happened to Idlewild in the face of the Public Accommodations Act (and other important acts) was an unintended development that nonetheless had major consequences for black entertainers as well as for those who had decided to make that community their permanent home.

Not everyone was out to get revenge by merely having whites wait on him or her. For many, the enormity of the task of making America live up to the true meaning of a constitutional democracy was not taken frivolously because it literally meant the difference in whether one was treated as a first- or a second-class citizen. Congress passed the laws, but the onus was on the blacks themselves to step forward and integrate the cafeterias, the ballparks, and the theaters. The "separate but equal" doctrine never materialized for black people.

The results of the public accommodation legislation have not been uniformly positive in the larger society. There are still pockets of intolerance, bigotry, and hatred for people of color, regardless of their status in life. For example, in recent years, some national restaurant chains have been sued for practicing racial discrimination. Thus, the words "in many instances the doors are open but their hearts remain tightly closed" are as true today as when they were spoken by an African American in the late 1960s.

Virtually every man and woman who visited Idlewild had a southern connection in some respect. Some were born in the South or had a close relative still residing there, and many had had personal encounters with the brand of racism found only in the South. Memories of the "Colored" signs, of not being allowed to try on hats or shoes in white stores, and of other inhumane treatment were still fresh in their minds. Thus, for many blacks, not to "integrate" would send the wrong message to white America, to the freedom riders, and to those who had marched and died for freedom and justice. So, for some, Idlewild had to wait, so to speak, until the more urgent task of being accommodated had been accomplished. Many assumed, "Idlewild will always be there for us!"

Today, however, given Idlewild's lugubrious status, the question is: Will blacks be there to help revitalize a community built as the result of segregation and discrimination, but whose vibrancy was destroyed in a large measure by integration?

"Greener Pastures"

Though largely confined to the black community, the music of many sensational black entertainers ended up in the hands of white recording companies. As more white artists began to play and sing the music of such black artists as Little Richard, Fats Waller, Chubbie Checker, and others, and as more whites expressed an interest in listening to the records and watching the performances of black artists, aggressive white businessmen began to hire "suitable" blacks to perform in their large auditoriums and theaters. Accordingly, record deals and bookings in white clubs opened new venues for many entertainers who had used Idlewild as one of the stages on which to polish and perfect their craft.

Greater exposure meant more money and prestige for many entertainers who had paid their dues on the grueling entertainment circuit. With the passage of time, though Idlewild occupied a special place in their minds, many of these entertainers found themselves spending less and less time in the black community in the woods of northwest Michigan. As fewer and fewer entertainers played Idlewild, numbers of vacationers and visitors gradually dwindled. Many whites who had frequented Idlewild to take advantage of the black entertainment now found no reason to visit the resort, because those entertainers were now playing in the white communities. Undoubtedly, these music lovers felt more comfortable in the clubs in their own communities than they had, say, in Idlewild's Fiesta Room in the Paradise Club, where white patrons were always in the numerical minority.

Lack of Leadership and Vision

No one doubts the role that integration played in the decline of Idlewild, yet it was not the only factor in the turn of fortunes of the resort. Another contributing factor was a lack of vision among the community's leaders that did not speak to the changes necessary to maintain the vitality of the resort. Very few posed the question, "What will the community do if the entertainers desert Idlewild for greener pastures?" Many Idlewilders idealistically saw the place as staying the same forever, never declining but forever remaining a popular place with overflowing crowds and top quality black entertainers. In time, however, it became clear that the resort could not compete with white resorts.

A leadership crisis also contributed to the decline of the community and the concomitant flight of blacks to other vacation spots. Between 1960 and 1990, internal bickering and the transference of leadership at the resort exacerbated an already troublesome set of relationships. Personality difficulties proved to be a major problem, with many people unwilling to run for township offices, yet always ready to criticize. As often seems to be the case, those most critical of the system lacked political skills, while those with political skills lacked the vision needed to succeed. Township administrators began to lose their power base due to abrasive personalities and conflicting visions of the future.

This lack of effective leadership was compounded by a dwindling tax base. The infrastructure of the resort went into disrepair, and on one occasion the state threatened to turn the lights off due to delinquent bills. Other bills also went unpaid because, quite frankly, there was a lack of economic resources.

AN INCOMPLETE INFRASTRUCTURE: ANOTHER FACTOR

The number of blacks who owned homes, cottages, or land at Idlewild was significantly smaller than the number of black vacationers who did not have any possessions whatsoever at the resort. It was reported that during its heyday Idlewild on a national holiday could expect between twenty-two and twenty-four thousand black vacationers. While good times may have been had by many, crowds of that magnitude could not be favorably accommodated by the community. Thus, when white establishments were legally mandated to accommodate citizens regardless of race, many blacks began to patronize those places. If Idlewild could have comfortably accommodated the swelling multitude, would the Public Accommodations Act have been as devastating to the resort? Perhaps not. The absence of both an adequate physical infrastructure and a social infrastructure played havoc in Idlewild, once blacks could avail themselves of erstwhile forbidden places, especially those closer to home.

Some view the decline in popularity as an admission that Idewild was not physically up to the challenge presented by the accommodation legislation. Audrey Bullett, a resident and former township supervisor, once said, "If you hear people talk about this place, they call it the black Las Vegas, but it was always [a] burned out nickel and dime place. It's romanticized."[15] It therefore seems that those who clamor about integration killing Idlewild might be oblivious to the existence of other factors that acted in tandem to erode the vibrancy of that community.

THE PASSING OF THE GREAT ONES

The splendor and grandeur Idlewild reached during its heyday slowly disappeared with the deaths of its significant movers and shakers. Their passing failed to galvanize others in the community who had the resources and expertise to fill the void. Each death of an Idlewild luminary thus advanced the growing poverty and despair now permeating the community.

The final days of June 1962 were drab for Idlewilders across the country, and especially in the Midwest, after they learned of the death of Judge Joseph Craigen of Detroit. The native of British Guiana had served with distinction as the commissioner of labor and as a referee in the courts of Michigan.[16] Then in August 1963, Mrs. Sulee A. Stinson, for many years president of the Idlewild Lot Owners Association, was memorialized in Detroit, where more than one hundred thousand persons viewed the body at the wake. The service in Detroit was followed by memorial rites held in Idlewild, where the remains lay in state for a day. Mrs. Stinson, director of the funeral home that carried her name in Detroit, had been active in social clubs and youth work. Moreover, she had been the chairperson of the State Board of Mortuary Science—the first woman and the first black to be so honored. Stinson and Craigen had been visionaries with the expertise and business acumen needed to sustain the development of the resort. They had often spoken about improving the sewer system, bringing in natural gas lines, improving the bridges, installing streetlights, and paving more roads. They had also believed that beautiful landscaping would make the resort more attractive.

Also during August 1963, Phil Giles, owner of the Flamingo Club and the Giles Hotel, died of a heart attack at Harper Hospital in Detroit. Aside from his business interests, Giles had served as Yates Township supervisor, resigning during his eighth year in office. Two or three weeks after Giles's death, Andy DeLuc, talented and popular member of original Chicago Idlewilders, also died of a heart attack. The memorial service in Chicago attracted a large number of Idlewilders who came to honor DeLuc's memory and give comfort and solace to his family.[17]

Despite the importance of the aforementioned people, however, arguably the greatest loss to the Idlewild community was the passing of Herman Wilson. A general contractor for ten years, he had spurred building and been a prime mover behind the development of the resort, especially the Paradise Lake area. He had been supervisor of Yates Township for four years, had been a member of the school board, and had operated a grocery store there for countless years. Four years after his death, Lela Wilson, his widow, was unable to continue administering her many businesses due to poor health. Consequently, she sold her estate in Idlewild, which included the Paradise Club, Wilson's Grocery, and other large property holdings.[18]

The deaths of these Idlewild pioneers created important gaps in the leadership and economic structure of the community, and those gaps turned into major chasms when they were not filled by dynamic and innovative young black leaders. This crippling phenomenon, then, is another reason for the rapid decline of the vibrancy of Idlewild, and an indication that the demise of the resort may have been due less to integration than has been claimed. That not enough care was given to mentoring and training younger family members as entrepreneurs and leaders who were capable of taking over and running a small family business is a fact that has far-reaching implications and cannot be ignored.

An unwillingness on the part of potential stakeholders to pursue their fortunes in a rural setting was undoubtedly another factor in the resort's decline, especially for those family members who were enamored with big-city life. For many, it was paramount that they escape the rural, agricultural way of life, which was associated with hard work, low wages, backwardness, and poverty, especially in the southern states. It was not uncommon for a black farmhand to make as little as five to ten dollars a week during the 1950s and early 1960s in states like Alabama and Mississippi. Thus, poverty and virulent forms of racism were ample motivation for many blacks to seek to escape the confines of the rural environment. Generally speaking, in 1963, the incidence of poverty was approximately three-and-a-half times as great among black families as among white families in the United States.[19] Thus, Idlewild, though beautiful, peaceful, and rustic, did not represent the type of environment where many ambitious young people wanted to "cast down their buckets."

IDLEWILD: A QUESTION OF SURVIVAL

In the mid-1960s a new breed of younger blacks began to learn about the history and significance of Idlewild. Cable access productions helped inform many potential youthful investors from the western Michigan area about the resort. Black nationalism resonated widely among this new element, which did not want to see the resort die. Consequently, Mid-Michigan, St. Louis, Cleveland, and Chicago-based Idlewild clubs were reinvigorated by an infusion of younger members. Additionally, the Idlewild Lot Owners Association (ILOA) was rejuvenated, with the old-time resorters forming the nucleus of the membership. The old-timers came from various Midwest cities but mostly from the Chicago and Detroit areas. As mentioned by John Meeks, owner of Morton's Motel and a member of the Lake County Chamber of Commerce, they were hopeful of rebuilding "the lost civilization."[20] For two weeks every summer, usually in mid-August, members of Idlewild clubs and associations poured into the resort to discuss its future. Specifically, realizing that Idlewild had not been prepared to meet the integration challenge, the ILOA annual conventions addressed the issue of the possible renaissance of the resort.

Now-deceased Idlewild real estate agent John Reynolds captured the spirit of these meetings when he said, ". . . we have not even addressed the notion of blacks supporting black businesses economically. Our people can certainly be a strange lot. We are the only ethnic group that refuses to support our own."[21] Many, like Reynolds, continued to invest in the vacation land with the hope that the black crowds would eventually return.

While no one can relive the past, it seems natural that contemporaries might have built on the foundations developed by the early pioneers, in spite of any federal legislation. It seems that those who could afford to do so might have invested in the resort in order to allow it to continue attracting black vacationers. However, many were not interested. The gamblers, teachers, lawyers, and—most importantly—the entertainers moved on to greener pastures, quickly forgetting the Black Eden and disregarding its history, its significance, and its survival for future generations. They exploited Idlewild, just as the early lumbermen had exploited the land. They made their profits when entertainers' names appeared on the marquees of the clubs in Idlewild. Once those names were gone, so was the resort's base of support. In the 1960s, actress and singer Della Reese noted that "we did not invest in the place and the consequences will eventually be ours."[22]

This notion was succinctly reinforced by Robert B. Stepto in his *Callaloo Magazine* article entitled "From Idlewild and Other Seasons." In this piece he mentioned that

> ... celebrities, including athletes and stars of the stage and music world, made investments as well, though to my knowledge, they rarely built summer or retirement homes on their land, even when they owned coveted lake front properties. This often vexed the people owning adjoining land who had cottages, and who naturally were anxious about whether another cottage suddenly was going to go up, sometimes just a stone's thrown away. My parents, for example, after buying a house of their own in Idlewild, near my grandparents and on the lake, tried repeatedly to protect their privacy by purchasing the lot just north of them, owned by Lil Armstrong, Louis Armstrong's former wife. She refused their offers, and they had to settle into the hope that she would neither sell to someone else nor crowd a cottage in between us and the elderly woman presently next door.[23]

On a more positive note, some contemporaries still hold the belief that an infusion of youthful "go-getters" can revitalize the resort. Bill McClure, a retiree from Indianapolis and owner of the Red Rooster Tavern, is one who subscribes to that notion. He notes:

> We want to encourage young African-American men and women between twenty and forty to bring their families to Idlewild. Idlewild needs some young blood. The future of Idlewild is with these children. . . . [They] need to see black people

Vacationers on the beach at Idlewild. Courtesy of the State Archives of Michigan, Stanley Kufta Collection.

living in beautiful lakefront homes, water skiing, jet skiing and paddle boating. They need to take the children on nature walks through Idlewild. The village is rich in decades-old history. The land is plentiful and ready for development. Affordable lakefront property is available for purchase, as well as weekend cottage rentals. There are Idlewilders waiting with open arms to welcome you to this quaint community. As a people, we owe it to ourselves and our ancestors to preserve our history. We have a responsibility to refurbish those old buildings and reopen businesses.[24]

If Idlewild is to be rejuvenated, it will take hard work and commitment. If the current trend of new interest in the resort continues, however, this precious monument to the spirit, vision, and abilities of the pioneers may be preserved.

Presently, on many weekends, the buzzing sounds of saws and the pounding of hammers reverberate throughout the forest.[25] Ron Stodghill, in his article entitled "Letter from Michigan Return to the Black Eden," mentioned that

We are part of a new generation rediscovering Idlewild. Houses that fell into disrepair in the 1970s are being refurbished. Vacationers my age [thirty-two] are
returning for clear air and nostalgia. Retirees are moving from Detroit and
Chicago to the country. Lake County, Idlewild's home, has the third highest percentage of blacks in the state and the highest population over sixty-five in
Michigan's Lower Peninsula. Many of the Idlewild's three hundred [permanent]
residents welcome redevelopment. Over the past two years, shuttered hotels and
motels including the famed Beach Front Morton Motel, have reopened. Some
twenty [or more] shacks have been razed, and refuse cleared from public lots. A
few Michigan politicians are pushing a state bill to make Idlewild an
"Empowerment Zone," with tax breaks and incentives to jump-start tourism.[26]

Admittedly, it's easy to paint the past with bright, garish colors, but in the
case of Idlewild there may be something worth romanticizing, certainly worth
preserving. The old-timers talked of the 1930s, 1940s and 1950s with a zeal
and luster that can be seducing. They talked of dancing in the streets, literally, and of gala picnics on Idlewild shores. They talked of the famous and
not-so-famous who spent their summer weekends there. They talked about,
and perhaps yearned for, the unusual camaraderie and companionship of
those days. In this instance, the old "in-crowds" and the new "out-crowds"
were of one accord—the resort must survive, and its history and significance
must be preserved.

SOCIOLOGICAL ILLUMINATIONS

The caste system in the United States made it possible for a group of white
developers to use the race factor for purposes of self-aggrandizement at a
time when rural land was plentiful and extremely cheap at the turn of the
twentieth century in Michigan. History suggests that it would have been
highly unlikely that a bank would have advanced a loan to a black group to
buy a huge tract of land to start a resort on the scale envisioned by Idlewild's
white developers. With the ownership of land comes power, and white bank
owners have had a long history of denying loans to blacks to acquire land. On
the other hand, it would have been difficult to find a black person with the
ready cash to purchase the nearly 2,700 acres needed to start the resort. Even

had the cash been available, there was no guarantee that the sellers would have sold to a black person or group.

Though efforts to eliminate the racial caste system must be seen as a factor in the unforeseen changes that took place at Idlewild, it is quite clear that this does not provide a total and complete explanation of the eventual decline of that community. It was the convergence of a plethora of factors, rather than any single factor, that was responsible for the unfavorable consequences experienced by Idlewild from the mid-1960s onward.

One of those factors was the struggle for freedom and the integration of black people into the mainstream of American society as first-class citizens. With the passage of significant pieces of legislation in the 1960s, the circumstances seemed right for black people to introduce themselves to those white places that had been heretofore forbidden to them. At the same time, however, whites made no attempts to integrate formerly all-black sites. Clearly, integration was a one-way street, with black traffic and cash flowing to white facilities, not vice versa. This process of integration was clearly associated with the dramatic decline in Idlewild's fortunes. To an unfortunate extent, the struggle for freedom reduced the ability of many African Americans to continue their contribution to the vibrancy of Idlewild as a resort community.

A corollary factor in the community's decline was the fact that, as a community built behind the walls of segregation, Idlewild was unprepared to compete with other institutions in the larger society, once those walls started tumbling down in the 1960s. A partial explanation for this unpreparedness, it seems, was the common notion that Idlewild would always be a haven for black people because there always would be segregation. Such thinking prevented the resort from being able to adequately meet the awesome challenges presented by integration. Though Idlewild had been in existence for over fifty years by 1964, the economic structure of the community still depended primarily on vacationers or resorters. There had been little or no effort made to economically diversify the community in order to build strong social institutions on a year-round basis. Though it would have greatly strengthened the community, no attempts were made to open banks, build schools, establish a college, or use the dollars brought into the resort, especially during the summer months, to create a self-sufficient, year-round community. Furthermore, those facilities and activities that did exist had not been created on a scale that would enable Idlewild to compete with other resorts once the walls of segregation were torn down. In short, lack of vision and leadership were primary factors in the decline of the resort. Once African Americans started going to other places, the process simply accelerated until it became a runaway train, going away from Idlewild and toward Las Vegas, Disneyland, Atlantic City, and Fountain Bleu. Today, that same train takes African Americans to other vacation sites, resorts, and casinos in Michigan such as: Soaring Eagle Casino and Resort in Mount Pleasant, Little River Casino in Manistee, casinos in Detroit and St. Ignace, Mackinac Island, Grand Traverse Resort in Traverse City, and McClure's Resort in Cadillac.

6

A Snapshot of Idlewild's
Contemporary Social Status

As a geographical area in Michigan, Idlewild is not politically either a city, a township, or a village. The concept of "unincorporated community" or "district" more nearly describes it as an entity within Yates Township. In fact, Idlewild as a "district" extends beyond Yates Township into Pleasant Plain Township. However, the terms "community," "district," and "area" will be used interchangeably in this discussion of Idlewild. It was placed on the National Register of Historic Sites in 1979.

A major problem that the district of Idlewild faces is the fact that it does not have the critical mass (population) or the economic base to deal aggressively with any obstacle of a significant nature. Consequently, the district has to work with other agencies and organizations, both public and private, to deal with its social and physical difficulties. Because of the desire by some residents to see Idlewild regain a greater measure of vibrancy, progress has been made in this respect in some areas, yet little noticeable improvement has been made in others. This chapter attempts to paint a balanced picture of the social issues and problems that currently exist in the Idlewild district in particular, and in Lake County in general.

Social Structure of Idlewild

Due to the tiny size of the district, it would be misleading to talk about a social structure of Idlewild in a strict sociological sense. However, several categories can be identified, which allow a categorization of residents in terms of their social standing in the community. They are:

1. *Resorters:* People who come to Idlewild primarily between Memorial Day (May) and Labor Day (September) or late October each year. These African Americans, many with a longstanding relationship with the community, come largely from Midwestern cities, and many have professional backgrounds and careers. They also have property and standing in their respective home communities. During the spring and summer months, they help to swell the population of Idlewild from six hundred to between three and four thousand. Some of these people are retired but do not spend the entire year at Idlewild. For many, if not most, in this category, the relevancy of skin color has disappeared, with economic status now being the primary category of differentiation between people.

2. *Year-Round Retired Resorters:* People who are living primarily on their social security and pensions. These people tend to live rather comfortably year-round at Idlewild. Their homes or cottages are well maintained and they are able to leave the community for visits to friends or relatives in other cities. Moreover, some of the retirees in this category are active members of the community. They participate in the various organizations and in the affairs of their church and local government. The community's senior citizen facilities include a housing unit and a community center.

3. *Idlewild Commuters:* People who live year-round in Idlewild but who work outside the community in the manufacturing and service industries in such cities as Grand Rapids, Reed City, Ludington, and Manistee. They must commute because Idlewild does not have the economic sufficiency to offer employment to more than a few of the local residents. Lake County itself has only four industrial employers, who combined employ about one hundred workers. Hence, adequate transportation and the willingness to spend time commuting from home to the job are necessary elements for those who want to work yet continue to live at Idlewild.

4. *Idlewild Underclass Residents:* People who are on general assistance and live at Idlewild on a year-round basis, receiving their income from state and federal welfare programs. In Lake County, approximately 26 percent of the households live below the poverty level, and 18 percent of the households receive some form of public assistance.[1] There are some in this category who eke out an existence through participation in illegal activities within this tiny community. Prostitution, drug trafficking, and various forms of theft are patterns of conduct commonly found among those, typically youngsters, in this category. Though damaging to individual victims in particular and the community in general, resorting to illegitimate means of obtaining money is often perceived as the only way to survive in an environment with limited economic opportunities.

SOME SOCIAL DEMOGRAPHICS

In Lake County, there were approximately 1,309 black residents during the 1960s; there were 1,274 in the 1970s; 1,291 in the 1980s; and 1,136 in the 1990s. Although there was no precipitous drop in the black population during those four decades, there was a slight decline overall from the 1960s to the 1990s. During the 1990s, the majority of the black residents were either members of or nearing the senior citizen category, since once early resorters retired many decided to permanently settle in Idlewild. The percentage of Idlewild's population over age sixty-five is the highest for any township in Michigan's Lower Peninsula. Presently, it is one of the poorest areas in the state.

According to 2 August 1999 "Lake County (Idlewild Area) Demographic Study," there are fewer than ten thousand people in the county. It is ranked near the bottom of the poverty scale, with only two Michigan counties ranked lower with respect to income. The per capita income of Lake County is 40 percent of the state average (an average of $12,201 for the county, as compared to a state average of $19,586).[2] Of the 9,631 people in Lake County in 1990, 4,367 (50.9 percent) were females and 4,216 (49.1 percent) were males. More than 45 percent (3,866) of the residents were over the age of forty-five. These figures indeed suggest an aging population, not just for Idlewild but for Lake County in general. On the other hand, however, 2,525 residents (29.4

percent of the population) are between the ages of eighteen and forty-four, with an additional 1,577 (18.4 percent) between the ages of five and seventeen. Whites make up the vast majority of the population in Lake County, with a count of 7,279 (85 percent), while black citizens make up the largest minority, with a count of 1,142 (13.3 percent). In addition, there are a negligible number (1.7 percent) of Hispanics, Native Americans, and other racial groups represented in the county.

During 1990, the population count in Yates Township (Idlewild district) was 645. That is to say, only 6.9 percent of the total population of Lake County lived in the Idlewild district at that time. Racially, Idlewild's 425 (65.8 percent) African Americans make up the largest racial group, with 216 (33.5 percent) being white and 4 (0.7 percent) coming from other racial groups. Of the 645 residents, there were 303 (47.0 percent) males and 342 (53.0 percent) females. Fifty percent (323) of the residents in the township were over forty-five years of age and there were 177 (27.4 percent) residents 65 and over. Like the county as a whole, Yates Township has an aging citizenry.[3]

THE BUSINESS PICTURE IN IDLEWILD

The business picture in Idlewild is rather dismal. It has been on a steady decline since the enactment of the Public Accommodations Act, which had a direct negative impact on the community's employment picture. Though they might not have had large staffs, the demise of the Paradise Club, the El Morocco, the Eagle's Nest, the Polk Skating Rink, the Sweetheart Motel, the Oakmere Hotel, the Purple Palace, and others meant that significant employment opportunities left the community. According to one current citizen, the Red Rooster Tavern is the only establishment that has been opened or reopened in the district in the last five years. The property, bought from the Roxborough family, was refurbished and renamed, as the former B. S. Club or Rosanna's Tavern was in desperate need of repair. The current logo is a red rooster attired with a top hat, walking cane, and spats. Across the paved street from this tavern is a renovated Idlewild Party Store, stocked with necessary goods for weekenders who forget to bring their party favorites. The Road Runner, Moniques's Market, and Sharon's Beauty Shop also offer their services.[4] Other updated business facilities are the Morton Motel (owned by John

Meeks) and the Holiday House (owned by Joe and Fredna Lindsey). Though not plush facilities, they are the most readily available and centrally located accommodations in the immediate area.

Just before the turn of the decade, in 1989, Jaye Truesdale Bagley, a former resident of Detroit, purchased the former Flamingo Club, which was scheduled for demolition, renaming it Nana Jaye's Vineyard. "I saved it," she said. "Nana Jaye's is going to be a coffee shop, a nature center and a tour service."[5] As of this writing, Bagley's vision has not been realized for that building. The structure is now owned by the Department of Natural Resources.

"The remoteness of Yates Township and lack of facilities and a skilled labor force makes it difficult to attract industrial development. Currently Yates does not have any industrial employers. Manufacturing employment in Lake County is almost nonexistent, comprising less than 2 percent of total employment."[6] Those words were written about Idlewild in 1987 and they are as true today as they were then. Poor job opportunities aside, it is not unusual to see young, single-parent female head-of-households (16.7 percent of Lake County's population) working in the few available manufacturing, construction, professional, public administration, and service industry jobs in the area. The number of single-parent families in the area rose from 5.6 percent of households in 1980 to 9.2 percent in 1990. Single-parent families represent 31.3 percent of all families with children in the township.[7]

The few entrepreneurs who have invested in businesses in the district are confronted with a persistent issue—the quality of employees, especially the first-time employable young. Many who are employable have developed a dependency on general assistance as fast money. Consequently, some have not developed an acceptable work ethic and they lack reliability, dependability, loyalty, trustworthiness, and competency. Without a doubt, this is a concern for entrepreneurs who have invested their capital in the community. It is not unusual to read about break-ins, drug activity, vandalism, assaults, and homicide in the area. These activities make it difficult for any businessperson to consider investing new capital, when safety is also a pressing concern.

People who have already established businesses in the area frequently complain that it is difficult to get good help, especially males. For this and other reasons, few who have successfully found work at the nearby so-called Punk Prison (Wackenhut, opened in 1999 as the Michigan Youth

Correctional Facility and now privately operated by the Wackenhut Corrections Corporation of Florida) as hourly personnel are residents of Idlewild.[8] This facility was built in Baldwin at a cost of $39 million and rented to the Michigan Youth Correctional Facility for $5.6 million per year, plus $67.50 per day per inmate. It has not been a big boon to Idlewild, though recently the youth prison reached an agreement with the Lot Owners Association to use the ILOA building as a site to train correction officers. Several classes have completed training sessions there. In addition, Wackenhut has established a program to award $5,000 scholarships to Baldwin High School graduates interested in majoring in criminal justice in state universities and colleges.

Business-wise, it appears that from the very beginning, exploitation and self-aggrandizement were among the prime motivations for many who were involved in the development of the resort. Consequently, it has been said that very few, including the professional entertainers who performed there, seriously sought to position the resort community to deal with the enormous challenges of the comprehensive Civil Rights Act of 1964. In spite of such pessimism, however, and thanks to some initiatives implemented by FiveCAP (a private, nonprofit community action program), there is some hope that the business picture will change in a favorable direction for Idlewild.

THE EMPLOYMENT AND INCOME SITUATION

Idlewild had a median household income of $9,116 and a per capita income of $7,475 in 1997. Comparative state figures were $31,030 and $14,154, respectively. Interestingly, in 1960, four years before the Public Accommodations Act, the percentage of black employment was zero at Idlewild; in 1970, it was 15.9 percent; in 1980, 5 percent; and in 1990, 13.2 percent. Many young people living there commute to Grand Rapids, Ludington, Muskegon, or Big Rapids to work in light industries.

The current sad state of employment in the area may be traced back to enormous economic setbacks which began in the mid-1960s. The situation was precipitated by a dramatic decline in the number of small businesses associated with the resort—canning, construction, family stores, restaurants, hotels, and so forth. Unfortunately, Idlewild has continued to experience difficulties, even during the 1990s, a decade in which the United States experienced tremendous economic growth. The Clinton administration will be remembered as a time of low unemployment rates, low inflation rates, tremendous growth in business and industry and some of the best years ever for the stock market—a time of unprecedented economic growth. For Idlewild, unfortunately, this was a time when the enthusiasm for revitalization and a return to its glorious past was not matched by actual economic programming and development on any significant scale. Consequently, the community has been unable to provide jobs except on a very limited basis for its residents, either young or old. The Morton Motel, the Red Rooster Tavern, the Idlewild Party Store, the Road Runner Variety Store, and a few other small businesses provide the only employment possibilities in the community. Also, as noted previously, there are only four industrial employers in the entire county, employing a total of only 105 employees. This means that jobs even outside the Idlewild community were not plentiful, and it must be reiterated that the county is one of the poorest in the state. Thus, residents of Idlewild have had to look outside the county for employment.[9]

In addition to their contributions to the economic base of the community through payment of taxes and assessments, those vacationers who own property in Idlewild add to the economic picture by hiring some of the locals to do a variety of small, part-time jobs on their property during the vacation season. When they are in residence they help to brighten the economic and employment picture for some year-rounders. The income earned from this source, however, is only supplemental, and may be seen as an impediment to the formulation and implementation of a plan to address the employment problems of the district, which would include job training and education.

In an interview with a property owner, who echoed some of the same concerns found among the business owners, he noted that he had had trouble finding people who were willing to work. The young people, according to this man's statement, had a poor work ethic. They were either lazy or felt they were too good to work for minimum wages, a condition found in rural and urban neighborhoods alike. Young black men in economically depressed areas are especially likely to have this attitude. It must be pointed out, however, that while this may be true of some, it is certainly not true of all. There are some young black men who have a deep appreciation for those who are trying to help them to succeed, and they readily acknowledge that fact. In the words of one young man: "You have to crawl before you can walk," and he does not expect to earn a high salary on his first or second job while in high school. His minimum-wage job goes a long way toward relieving some of the financial burden on his family. This young man hopes to complete high school and go on to college.

While it is true that many resorters over the years have worked hard, employed thrift, and achieved a middle-class or upper-class status, the opposite has been the fate of many year-round residents, who face on a daily basis a plethora of staggering problems. Over 43 percent of the year-round residents in Idlewild or Yates Township are below the poverty level on the socioeconomic ladder. The state average is 13.1 percent. Because of the employment situation, many residents, especially the young people, feel trapped. Despite momentous and dramatic economic changes nationwide, for these people economic equality never became a realistic goal.

During a recent five-year period in Lake County, the figures show average unemployment rates for men and women to be 13.2 percent in 1991, 13.2 percent in 1992, 11.9 percent in 1993, 12.1 percent in 1994, and 12.7 percent in 1995. These relatively high unemployment figures are just the opposite of the employment trend in the rest of the state and the nation. Again, it is important to note that this pattern existed at a time when the U.S. economy was robust and the national and state unemployment rates were at their lowest points in decades.

Perhaps the employment picture in Idlewild would be brighter if it were not for the illegal drug use among some of the youth. Many young people currently could not pass employers' drug tests, especially in those places of employment stressing a "drug-free environment." A related issue is the fact that many young people are not motivated to work, because there is the perception that one can make as much, if not more, on public assistance.

CRIME AND DELINQUENCY IN THE TOWNSHIP

Upon graduating from the local public school system, most youngsters have limited options. There is general agreement that "there is nothing for young people to do here except drink, smoke dope, and make babies." Those who go on to institutions of higher learning have no desire to return to the community, and consequently there is no infusion of new ideas or enthusiasm for civic and economic growth from the district's native born. If young people abandon a village, the vibrancy of the community begins to dissipate and the more undesirable elements tend to flourish. Then, according to Bobby Austin in *Repairing The Breach*, "The combination of joblessness, drugs, and crime [vandalism] overwhelms the neighborhood."[10]

Property crimes—breaking and entering, vandalism, malicious destruction of property—tend to occur after the resorters have closed their cabins and cottages for the winter. Other crimes occur either as a result of opportunism or as a result of efforts to acquire money through drug deals or the fencing of stolen goods. Thus, even in this small rural community, the major features of black crime still persist: the black homicide rate continues to be higher than that for whites; it is the black householder whose property is lost through theft; and it is the black youth, mostly, who are markedly demoralized by drugs.

For the last ten years, the rate of delinquency in Lake County has steadily risen. At the same time, adolescents are encountering divorce rates 40 to 50 percent higher than in the previous generation, spending half as much time with family as the previous generation, and living without the basic guidance and support enjoyed by the previous generation. These familial factors are disturbing, since there is a proven positive relationship between parental/familial affection and adolescent self-esteem. In regard to family characteristics in Yates Township in the 1990s, 45 percent of all juveniles listed their mother as the sole household provider. Nearly two-thirds of juveniles (63 percent) were from families who were on government assistance. In comparison to whites, higher percentages of African American youth were from families where the mother was sole provider (56 percent) and were on government assistance (77 percent). One-quarter (24 percent) of youth were reported to have had a psychiatric diagnosis, and a similar percentage (26 percent) of youth had a father with a criminal record. Furthermore, the negative impact that drugs and juvenile lawlessness have on the moral fiber of the person and the family and, in turn, the associated social and financial costs of these factors on the entire community definitely has hurt Idlewild.[11]

The small and poorly organized Yates Township Police Department, established in 1955 primarily for crowd and traffic control, needs restructuring to adequately deal with the aforementioned problems. The national standard for police officers on duty in 1987 was one per three thousand residents, but Yates Township has only about one-sixth of that figure in year-round residents. Thus, the cost per person for police services in the township is substantially higher. The cost of meeting state requirements for one full-time officer would probably exceed $30,000 per year, while the existing township's budget for that position is only $20,000. For that reason and others, the township has incurred difficulties in recruiting and retaining trained and qualified officers.

As of this writing, patrols by the Lake County Sheriff's Department are limited. The county has fewer than fifteen officers and no more than seven or eight vehicles on the road, which often results in poor response time to calls. The response time becomes even longer on weekends, when tourists increase the summer population. Because they had the highest crime rate in the county, concerned citizens of Idlewild organized a volunteer crime patrol group to nip in the bud many property crimes, including vandalism, break-ins, and thefts. The Neighborhood Watch program has considered hiring an undeputized monitor to periodically patrol selected areas and report suspicious activity directly to the county sheriff or Yates Township constable.

Though people in the community do not express any intense anxiety about walking the streets at night, there is a growing uneasiness with the recent murders of several young men, thought to be drug related. Similar to many other communities, the crime pattern in Idlewild is one where black people are victimized at a much higher rate than their counterparts in the white community.

THE HOUSING DILEMMA IN IDLEWILD

A drive through the Idlewild community exposes one to a number of nondescript dwellings. Many are substandard dwellings or Section Eight housing (subsidized housing), or mobile homes. There are many eyesores in the district, including abandoned structures, structures in disrepair, and old vehicles that are no longer operable. The township, together with the county, has made some progress in removing such eyesores from the district in an effort to beautify and enhance the community's curb appeal. More demolition work is necessary.

Concerning occupancy and tenure, about 279 housing units were occupied and there were some 841 vacant housing units being used seasonally, recreationally, or on an occasional basis. This means that approximately 75 percent of all housing is seasonal, or that these units are occupied during only the spring and summer vacation months. It should be noted that, though slightly more prevalent in Idlewild, this occupancy pattern is consistent with that of Lake County as a whole, where 60 percent of all housing is seasonal.[12] Of the total 1,120 housing units in Yates Township in 1990, 219 (19.6 percent) were trailers or mobile homes. Again, this is consistent with the housing pattern for the entire county. Nearly one-third of all year-round housing is in the form of a mobile home or a trailer.[13]

The median value of owner-occupied units in Yates Township was $25,000, an amount that reflects the fact that the district is indeed a poor one. Approximately 109 units (84 percent) were valued at less than $50,000; another 20 units (15.3 percent) had a value between $50,000 and $99,999. Only one owner-occupied unit was listed between $100,000 and $149,000 in 1990. Regarding renter-occupied units paying cash rent, units in the district carried a median rental charge of $185 per month. The overwhelming majority (73 percent, or 57) of the renter-occupied units went for less than $250 per month, while another 20 (26 percent) went for between $250 and $499 per month.[14]

Since blacks represent the majority of the population in Yates Township, it only makes sense that they would also occupy most of the housing units: blacks occupied 193 (69.2 percent) units while whites occupied 83 (29.7 percent). Thus, together blacks and whites occupied 98.9 percent of all housing units in the township.[15]

The preceding information is a good indication that the housing stock in the district leaves much to be desired. Many teachers do not live in the area, but commute in from other nearby areas. Furthermore, many workers at the relatively new prison—Governor John Engler's so-called punk prison—were unable to find suitable housing in the area; they also commute in. Accordingly, then, there appears to be a need not only for low-income housing but also for accommodations for those who can afford the more moderately price dwellings.

In this connection, it is reported that the number of housing permits have increased in the last few years in the district. A number of these permits are for the placement of prefabricated or trailer housing on lots scattered throughout Idlewild. Most, if not all, units will be owner-occupied and will not have a major impact on the renter situation, which is rather deplorable both in Idlewild and the county as a whole, where, according to "The Plan":

> One out of six Lake County families lives in rental housing. Such units have a relatively large proportion and variety of structural defects. Periodic inspections need to be carried out by two to three newly hired and trained members of the county and/or township staff with enforcement powers to assure that deficiencies are detected and corrected. Ongoing inspection with enforcement powers should prevent the recurrence of blight. The number of abandoned housings units is not known but is believed to be large (probably exceeding 500) and scattered throughout the county. The number and location can be determined through the proposed housing inventory.[16]

The lack of affordable new housing hurts Idlewild's ability to attract either new residents or new businesses or companies.

FAMILY CONCERNS

With respect to family households, there were 94 (32.2 percent) married-couple families in Yates Township in 1990, with another 148 (53 percent) non-married-family households. Households averaged about two persons per household for the district. Interestingly, in 1997, 32.2 percent of the houses in the area were occupied by married couples, and 16.7 percent were occupied by female householders. That same year, 40.2 percent were occupied by householders living alone (18.6 percent occupied by householders age sixty-five and older living alone). There were 20 people living in group or institutionalized quarters in the area during this period.[17]

Idlewild, like the rest of Michigan, has seen an increase in the number of black families headed by single females who live in poverty. Statewide, approximately half of all African American families with children are headed by women. Unfortunately, a significant number are among the poorest of the poor families in Yates Township, as well as elsewhere in the state of Michigan. Babies having babies is a pervasive concern, along with the likelihood of babies being born to mothers on drugs. Too frequently, mothers in this category are not mature enough and do not have the financial support to give their children a chance at a decent life in our highly technical society. A corollary of this observation is the fact that many fathers cannot contribute in any substantial way to the welfare of these children because they themselves are dependent on their parents. It should be noted, however, that many single female parents do a commendable job of raising their children even in the face of overwhelming odds.

EDUCATIONAL STATUS AND PROBLEMS

Many public school systems, in both rural and urban areas, are in a state of crisis in Michigan, New Jersey, California, and elsewhere in the nation. Minority children, especially blacks and Latinos, continue to drop out at an alarming rate and gross deficits are frequently found in the reading, writing, and computing levels of many who do manage to graduate. Consequently, education is no longer seen as an elevator for those students in these school systems who want to raise themselves out of poverty and despair. Dr. Diether H. Haenicke, president emeritus of Western Michigan University, paints a dismal picture in his weekly newspaper column of some schools charged with teaching youngsters. He writes:

> A brief look at some truly shocking statistics gives a perspective of the dilemma we are facing in some public school districts. Detroit, Flint, Pontiac and Benton Harbor, large population centers in our state, graduate less than two-thirds of their students. In Detroit, by far the largest city in Michigan, the school system appears beyond repair—unless truly revolutionary changes are made, which is unlikely to happen in a highly organized and entrenched National Education Association union environment.[18]

Even more appalling are the almost unbelievable statistics for some of the elementary schools in Detroit. Haenicke writes:

All statistics suggest that students score higher on tests in the early grades. But even there the Detroit picture is distressing. According to reports in the Detroit papers evaluating the 1999 MEAP test results, only 36.5 percent of the pupils in fourth grade in Joyce Elementary passed the math test, and an unbelievably low 26 percent passed the reading portion in fourth grade in Birney Elementary. But it gets worse. In Drew Middle School, only 4 percent scored proficient on the seventh-grade math portion, while not a single eighth-grader passed the science section of the test. At Cody High, only 10 percent of the eleventh grade passed the math portion.[19]

Is the situation the same in rural areas like Idlewild? Fortunately, there are not many, if any other, situations like Drew Middle School in this state. Recent test results and graduation rates for Idlewild students were unavailable, since those students attend the public schools in Baldwin, Michigan. Yet one can only hope that the results are not as woeful as those reported for the students in the Detroit public schools. At any rate, the strategic plan for Lake County, where only 6.6 percent of the population over twenty-five has a bachelor's degree, evinces some concerns about education. The county anticipates upgrading the curriculum, providing vocational and high-tech education, and making other changes in order to bring education in the area into the twenty-first century and enhance its citizens' employment skills.[20]

In addition to an adequate education, Idlewild's school-age kids need appropriate adult role models, who can mentor, guide, and advise them with respect to vocations, avocations, and other matters. The type of education that kids get from adult role models in their community can be as valuable as the formal education they get from the classroom. Unfortunately for many children in Idlewild, most of their potential role models leave the community for their respective homes in Chicago, Detroit, Indianapolis, and the like once the cabins and cottages are closed for the season. Most of those who are left are the year-rounders who are on public assistance, working at minimum-wage jobs in the service industry, or surviving on a day-to-day basis on a limited income.

Environmental Issues

In contemporary society, it is not surprising to see environmental concerns occupy front-page news. There is the ever-present concern over water pollution, a major concern throughout the country as more and more water sources are being contaminated by industrial waste and farmland runoffs. Though nestled in the countryside in northwest Michigan, far away from an industrial environment, Idlewild is not free of environmental concerns. For example, in the 1990s a residential water well in Idlewild was placed on the Michigan Department of Environmental Quality list for being contaminated with benzene, toluene, and xylene.[21] Moreover, major environmental concerns go back at least to 1978, when the officials in Yates Township thought it necessary to document the quality of the water in the lakes and wells. It was in that year that the township:

> . . . commissioned Richard H. Kraft Engineering to prepare a Facilities Plan for wastewater management. That plan adequately addressed the need for a coordinated wastewater collection and treatment program to protect groundwater for human consumption, and to preserve water quality in Paradise Lake, Tank Lake, and Lake Idlewild. Considerable documentation was provided to illustrate that wastewater contamination had affected not only lake water, but also groundwater and several private wells. The proposed management plan involved a combination of collection and treatment strategies including gravity sewers, pumping stations and force mains, cluster septic systems, a package treatment plant, upgrading of isolated septic systems, and an overall watershed management program. As a long-term objective, wastewater collection and treatment by the methods recommended in the Facilities Plan would effectively protect ground and surface waters in Yates Township.[22]

The concern with protecting the groundwater and surface waters is exacerbated by the fact that second septic fields in some residential areas are not feasible, due to the age of the septic tanks, which make them "susceptible to failure," and by the fact that

Most of the lakefront lots were laid out prior to the adoption of the Plat Act. As a result they are too small for a replacement septic field in case of failure. Thus the same septic area is used repeatedly and becomes so overloaded that wastes are improperly treated before they run into the lakes.[23]

Thus, a sewer and treatment system has long been needed in the Idlewild community to solve the contamination problem, which has serious health implications. To this end, however, there is an initiative in the works to have at least part of Idlewild covered by a sewer system out of Baldwin, Michigan. Unfortunately, at this writing, the plan does not involve connecting all of the houses and cottages in the community to the system. Many houses located away from the lake area are not slated to be hooked up; only those houses on the lake are targeted to be connected. While this makes sense, given their proximity to the lakes, it is regrettable that the entire community cannot be the beneficiary of the proposed sewer and treatment system, because:

The most probable sources of wastewater pollution are private septic systems installed prior to development of minimum state standards for soil absorption systems. Common problems encountered in these older systems include poor soil drainage, undersized drainfield or lack of drainfield, high groundwater table, location too close to surface waters, plugging with solids, and lack of separation from wells. Left unattended, failed septic systems may ultimately lead to such dilemmas as unsafe wells, closed swimming beaches, or even transmission of disease. It is therefore important to develop and implement a long-term strategy for wastewater management before acute problems arise.[24]

Though not as serious in magnitude as the water contamination problem, the disposal of solid waste is another environmental issue that has plagued the community for decades. The township provides for the collection and disposal of waste via private haulers, but the residents must pay a subscription fee, which is subsidized by the township. Unfortunately, some residents elect not to subscribe to the service, and instead,

they often allow trash accumulation on their property, or illegally dump in secluded areas in the Township. Persons from outside Yates Township also commonly use the community's remote areas to dump trash. This practice not only detracts from the community's natural tourism atmosphere, but presents health hazards as well.[25]

Improving the physical appearance of the community is an ongoing concern, and there has been some progress in recent years. However, it is not uncommon to find debris, undoubtedly thrown from moving vehicles, in the form of empty bottles and cans, discarded food wrappers, and the like, on the streets and off roads. Hence, the community has a ways to go before it can be satisfied with its general physical appearance, though getting more citizens to take advantage of the subsidized waste collection service would undoubtedly remove some of the temptation to dump solid waste in remote areas of the community.

THE TRANSPORTATION SYSTEM

The major highways leading to Idlewild are in rather good condition, but once the traveler leaves u.s. 10, for example, there are still few paved roads in the district, and street lights are definitely in short supply in various sections of the community. Most roads in the district are unpaved and narrow, contributing to what some refer to as the quaintness of the area because they are generally navigable and in good order. However, what is quaint and attractive to one person is ordinary and unattractive to another. Thus, comments made by some visitors to the district make it apparent that they find the unpaved roads not an asset but a liability to the revitalization efforts. (This issue is one that "The Plan" addresses in Lake County and thus has some implications for the Idlewild district. More on this issue in chapter 8.)

HOPE AND ANXIETY FOR THE FUTURE OF IDLEWILD

A comprehensive blueprint for the revitalization of Idlewild does not exist, primarily because there is a lack of consensus among residents, who are at odds—often bitterly so—as to the nature of their problems, their causes, and their solutions. Among the different voices, there are those who think the community's problems can be solved by: (1) a massive dosage of government intervention, (2) more local private initiatives, (3) identifying and mobilizing the community's own resources for black self-help programs, (4) greater collaboration among and between pertinent private and public partners, or (5) some combination of the above.

As an economically depressed community, Idlewild's problems are rather ominous, yet there appear to be some hopeful signs on the horizon, which will be discussed in the forthcoming chapters, where discussions will include some recent efforts and ameliorative strategies. Suffice it to say here, however, that "The Plan" for Lake County is a source that provides the people of Idlewild with some hope for the future. On the other hand, that same plan is a source of anxiety for those who criticize it for not containing enough specifics with respect to the problems discussed in this chapter.

There are also anxieties over the perception that perhaps Idlewild does not have the will or determination to marshal its local resources to change dramatically the general nature of the community. Or that perhaps the community does not have requisite resources to take full advantage of the opportunities articulated in the county's plan. "The Plan" does not resonant well because, it seems, not enough people are thoroughly familiar with the content of that document, even as various aspects of it are being implemented in Lake County, and particularly in Yates Township.

SOCIOLOGICAL ILLUMINATIONS

As noted in chapter 1, Idlewild came into existence in 1912—over eighty-eight years ago—and flourished steadily from about 1930 to roughly 1965. It began to languish in the late 1960s, however, and thereafter for the next thirty years, which is a lengthy period of time, making recovery very difficult. During the interim, in very simple terms, the world changed dramatically. Race and intergroup relations have taken on new and different dynamics today, especially with the changes in demographics that are reshaping the racial and ethnic landscapes throughout the United States. When one looks at the current social structure of Black America (and the way black people behave within and outside of that structure), it is very different from what it was during the early part of the twentieth century and by the time it entered the decade of the 1960s. It is obvious, then, that just as the social structure has changed significantly, so, too, have the African American people who live in that structure. Idlewild is no exception. Unfortunately, however, many changes there have been on the negative side of the ledger.

Today, Idlewild is in the unenviable position of becoming what some social scientists would call a "client community." As more residents become powerless to affect their lives and that of the community, they, ironically, tend to fall victim to the very institutions established to help them become self-sufficient and responsible citizens. An argument can be made that a social environment that allows a significant segment of its people to remain dependent on welfare agencies and governmental programs for survival is an environment that robs its people of dignity and purpose. Moreover, the community suffers as a result of this dependency. Consequently, Idlewild—as a community—must seek alternative routes if the problems of poverty, unemployment, welfare dependency, crime and violence, drugs, and other social ills are to be addressed any time soon.

Sociologically, it seems imperative that social policies, programs, and activities be developed to aggressively address those problems. At the same time, it is also imperative that the community's assets, capabilities, and abilities be identified and mobilized to attack those problems. Not to do so would be to ignore the fact that there are resources even in poor communities that can be utilized, especially in conjunction with outside resources, to mount a more effective defense against poverty and its attendant problems.

So, the question "Why go to Idlewild?" is indeed an important and relevant query, especially given the fact that there is so much talk about the revitalization of the place, and the fact that some efforts have already been made to improve the infrastructure of the district. Nostalgia and historical memories are fine but they do not take the place of economic investments, which the area certainly needs. Also pertinent to this question is the relatively new strategic initiative (called "The Plan") formulated by Lake County, which addresses three key areas: economic development, human services, and housing. (More on "The Plan" can be found in chapters 7 and 8.)

Revitalization: 1960–2000 Activities

Mid-Sixties: The Shadies and the Saints

When the black middle-class professionals began deserting the resort, many white hunters and fishermen, gamblers, and black pimps and their stables of prostitutes did just the opposite. They pumped a few dollars into the resort.[1] However, most of the dollars ended in the hands of pimps and prostitutes from Detroit, Indianapolis, Battle Creek, Chicago, and other places. In the late 1960s and 1970s, it was not unusual to see ladies in red working deer-crossing areas, tributaries of the Manistee River, and many inland lakes. During the height of the deer season, some panderers bought or rented mobile homes to be used as brothels on wheels, especially if the beds were already occupied at the Eagle's Nest. Many ladies were on a first-name basis with their customers. One of the females, desiring to remain anonymous, stated that, "Once some of those white Johns went black, they never wanted to go back. They wanted to have fun, sex, and coke."[2] Furthermore, some white customers felt that they had been initiated into true manhood after being with a black woman. Occasionally, such fellows would carry more than wild game home.

Gradually, a few of these sportsmen began to recognize the pristine beauty of the resort. Some of the properties deserted by the descendants of the pioneer resorters were acquired by whites. The black character of the resort gradually began to change, much to the lament of the old guard. Many realized, as did John Reynolds, that, "Land is made by God. Unlike cash, it is not man made. Furthermore, how can Black folks talk about Nationalism if they have no land base?"[3] To their credit, some descendants did hang on to their land and refuse to be lured by the Madison Avenue-style advertisements of the recently desegregated resorts, which were hoping to gain favor among those who were once victims of Jim Crowism.

A New Breed Brings Hope to Old-Timers

After learning of the resort's history from the old-timers, many nationalistic blacks did not want the resort to die. Every summer for two weeks in July and August, members of the ILOA and the various Idlewild clubs would pour into the resort to discuss its future, the intoxicatingly seductive zeal and luster of Idlewild in its heyday between 1930 and 1960, and the new investors and investments. Perhaps a renaissance could be initiated by new blood from the outside. Overhearing those reminiscing about the good old days, the young bloods knew that the resort was a vital cog in the black heritage. The idea of a "connection" between the old and the young, through the clubs and the associations, led to knowledge of heritage and a continuation of the Idlewild experience.

Before his death, longtime Idlewilder John Reynolds insisted that "Idlewild will continue to grow, it won't die."[4] Yet the former realtor knew property sales were not good in the area. He wondered how the town would survive beyond his generation. He often said, "I wonder why there's so much interest in the past rather than the future. . . . We need some new ideas."[5] In this same connection, Audrey Bullett, former county administrator, lectures, "When you write about all those people who came up here and drank, about the glamour of the past, you forget those of us who have stayed around here and tried to make something of this place."[6]

ACTIVITIES TO STOP THE DOWNWARD SPIRAL

Aside from the efforts of the ILOA and Idlewild clubs as articulated in their bylaws,[7] in the mid-1970s, attempts by various individuals to revitalize Idlewild had begun. Some who had inherited property decided that they did not want to lose their land because of delinquent taxes. By paying the assessments, they reinforced their commitment. As a matter of fact, some decided to increase their holdings by taking advantage of tax sales. The lots of those who had defaulted were sold at tax auctions in Detroit, Lansing, or Baldwin. As in the past, some who attended the public sales bought the property sight unseen. The motivation for the new acquisitions was an unwillingness to see what was once theirs become the property of "the man."

Interestingly, a few whites, who in years past had had no interest in owning property near that of blacks, could not pass up the incredibly cheap land. Land prices in predominantly white resorts were skyrocketing, land was becoming scarce, and some lakes were polluted. The cheap land and cleaner, deeper lakes in Idlewild were attractive and available. A few lots were sold to white buyers.

ACTIVITIES TO REMOVE SQUATTERS AND IMPROVE THE COMMUNITY

Slowly, most individuals did their part in rebuilding their holdings in the resort. Occasionally, however, property owners found it necessary to evict a few squatters before improvements and repairs could be made. Squatters not withstanding, Viola and Johnny Phillips, the former owners of Colors Lounge in Battle Creek, are prime examples of property holders working to maintain their lots in Idlewild. At least twice a month during the summer and early fall, they journey north to do needed repairs on their summer home. "Old furniture that I am moving out of my home in this city," said Viola, "is carried north to our Idlewild place. . . ."[8] Ruth Burton is doing her part in continuing to build or improve Idlewild. She believes the peaceful, quiet resting place should be improved each year. "It certainly is better than it was two years ago. You know the state is matching some funds received from the federal government."[9] John Meeks is the perfect example of the optimist. He

Morton's Motel, located on beautiful Paradise Lake, before renovations. Courtesy of the John Meeks collection.

purchased and refurbished an abandoned Idlewild motel.[10] As Gill Griffin explained in the *Lake County Star,*

> [Meeks] bought Morton's Motel [in 1989], closed it in 1992, remodeled and eventually reopened the 17-room inn in 1994. "Everybody thought I was crazy," said Meeks, who rents rooms for $34 and $45 a night. It had no value, it was antiquated, and the electrical wiring was insufficient. "I wouldn't refer to it as a loss, but I'll never make a return on it while I'm alive." Meeks bought it, he said, because he loves the community. He hopes his purchase will spur others to reinvest in Idlewild. . . . "Someone had to step up to the plate," Meeks said. "I love this place more than my birth place."[11]

According to Harry Solomon, a former township supervisor, seventy abandoned and dilapidated buildings had already been demolished as of January 1978. He further stated in his report that:

> A rehabilitation program [has] been activated by [the] township under a H.U.D. grant. Twenty [additional] units have been surveyed for interior and exterior

Morton's Motel after renovation. Courtesy of the John Meeks collection.

rehabilitation. We have plans of continuing this project for several years. . . . Sometime in the near future we hope to consider some new or recondition[ed] roads. . . . Also a bridge high enough for boats to proceed into the north section of Idlewild Lake is required to activate these waters to keep this section of the lake from dying. . . . Idlewild is on the move; Idlewild lives with pride and dignity. . . .[12]

Activities from the Yates Township Board: A Time for Action

A review of the 1970 list of needed improvements in Idlewild, articulated by the Yates Township Board, revealed that that list is essentially the same today as then. In other words, the current list of needed improvements has not changed substantially from the 1970s list, which included the following:

- Improve access to the business district and Williams Island from U.S. 10. The present access is indirect and draws traffic through residential areas.
- Resurface North Idlewild Lake parkway to allow for the seasonal closing of the road across Williams Island.

PROJECT NO. PH·1 AND 26·00632 4 26 77
PH·2 AND 26·00925 6 2 77

WILLIAMS ISLAND
COMMUNITY IMPROVEMENT
PROJECT
IDLEWILD · YATES TOWNSHIP · MICH.
IN COOPERATION WITH
UPPER GREAT LAKES COMMISSION
THE MICHIGAN DEPARTMENT OF NATURAL RESOURCES
THE UNITED STATES DEPARTMENT OF THE INTERIOR
BUREAU OF OUTDOOR RECREATION
TOTAL PROJECT COSTS $174,000
FEDERAL SHARE $99,200
LOCAL SHARE $34,800

SWIM AT YOUR OWN RISK
YATES TWP BOARD

LITTER INCREASES TAXES

A community improvement project. Courtesy of the Ben C. Wilson Collection, Black Americana Studies Department, Western Michigan University.

- Continue development of Williams Island.
- Initiate a community water supply and sewer systems starting in the central area (including water supply for fire protection).
- Draft an Initial Feasibility Study for the Performing and Fine Arts Center (including the theater) and of the potential economic benefits and spin-offs (e.g., privately supplied associated housing, meals, supplies, maintenance services, and construction work and materials).
- Expand the day care center (operated by FiveCAP) to include a modern kitchen and storage space.
- Write a Feasibility Study of a resource/energy management and production oriented industrial area.
- Conduct an analysis of the resource base (50 percent of Township owned by the U.S. Forest Service and Michigan Department of Natural Resources) for recreational and tourist-related improvement and use.
- Reevaluate the business district reinvestment potential, coupled with the Arts Center, industrial area, and recreational/tourism evaluations.

- Construct a community building, especially for the use by the aged.
- Start neighborhood improvements, including road paving, playgrounds, and in selected areas of adequate density, water and sewer services.
- Do a public lands inventory and analysis. Particularly with the high public ownership, careful plans should be set forth for the effective utilization/improvement of needed public lands (federal, state, and local) and the disposition of excess lands, most importantly, for critical private reinvestment projects.
- Investigate the need for private reinvestment in the area of essential convenience goods and services. The community presently has to travel to Baldwin, Reed City, Big Rapids, or Ludington for goods and services (ten to seventy miles round-trip). These services and the tax base and jobs that attend will require a year-round population equivalent of three to five thousand persons.[13]

More Recent Efforts to Revitalize Idlewild

An initiative with great potential was undertaken In 1989 by the Idlewild Civic Investment Corporation, another group interested in the revitalization emphasis. This group was very much concerned about developing a resort facility on Williams Island. To that end, the members of the group hired Perspectives Consulting Group to investigate the potential of a resort facility venture. A report was submitted to Mr. James Patterson (Westland, Michigan) in December 1989, and it gave, among other elements, a brief description of the five forces (demographics, finance, legal changes, labor, and technology) that actively influence the lodging business. Accordingly:

> Recent indications lead to providing outlooks for resorts. Developers, managers and industry analysts agree that resorts can thrive—but the secret is knowing your market segment and tailoring your marketing and amenities to it. The biggest trend in resort development presently is the development of "megas" (short for mega resort) and "boutiques." These terms refer to two extremes of the resort market. Megas go after the convention and incentive markets that the small boutique resorts do not have the capability to service. The boutiques serve

a highly specialized clientele, those desiring specific services such as a golf or tennis clinic. Boutiques are generally smaller, with 100 to 150 rooms, while the megas may have several hundred rooms. Additionally, the mega resorts are usually affiliated with a major chain, while the boutiques generally are not affiliated with any hotel chain.[14]

Regarding Idlewild itself, the report made some interesting observations and recommendations:

1. *Proceed with the development of the Idlewild project.* This study has scratched the surface on some of the factors surrounding the development of a resort at Idlewild. However, the demand and interest in a resort at Idlewild has not materialized and people would use the resort, whether or not people would pay resort prices in Idlewild, etc. [*sic*] These are questions that need to be answered before developing a resort.

2. *Complete a Feasibility Study on the development of a boutique resort project.* Based on the information in this report, a Feasibility Study on the Idlewild project could be conducted. Many of the questions regarding use and development could be answered by the study.

3. *Evaluate the property for other uses than a resort.* All of the emphasis so far has been on the development of a resort project at Idlewild. Resorts are not the only option available for development of the property. Other alternatives include retirement condos, time-share units, membership vacation clubs, cottages and the like. A decision needs to be made as to the intent and goals of the investment group, and then consideration [made] as to the best vehicle to attain these goals.

4. *Discontinue all further action on the Idlewild project.* The project can be stopped, tabled or discontinued fairly easily at this time before a major investment is made in resort development.

It is our opinion that if the investment group wishes to continue at a minimum a Feasibility Study should be completed before any development continues on the resort project. We believe, based on the information in this report, and our experience, that the Idlewild resort project will need to attract a specific segment of the resort market. This segment could be Idlewilders or

some other segment, however, due to the location of Idlewild, we do not antic-
ipate that segment being business travelers, or convention services.

There are several opportunities and problems that have been identified so
far:

- OPPORTUNITIES
  - Potential summer "boutiques" resort market.
  - Idlewild history and reputation.
  - Potential labor force available.
  - Demographics—a retirement community.
- PROBLEMS
  - Lack of natural attractions (especially if the resort is not located on Lake
    Idlewild).
  - Distance to golf, skiing.
  - Financing—changes in tax laws.
  - These are just a few of the opportunities and problems, and there proba-
    bly [are] many more that will need to be considered.

In conclusion, we question the viability of a hotel/motel complex unless it
is developed along the specialized lines of a boutique resort. Such a resort
would need to be financial[ly] viable based on its connection to Idlewild. The
Feasibility Study Plan could focus on such a specialized resort.[15]

The Feasibility Study, as recommended by the writers of the consulting
firm's report, would include: market area characteristics, project site and area
evaluation, competition analysis, demand analysis, recommended facilities
and services, operations estimates, and more.[16]

AN ACCELERATION OF ACTIVITIES TO TURN THE COMMUNITY AROUND

At the beginning of the 1990s, Thomas DeVier, a reporter for the *Detroit News
and Free Press,* wrote an article that highlighted the optimistic views of Audrey
Bullett, who had been the supervisor of Yates Township, which includes
Idlewild, for seven years at the time of the writing. Bullett had an intimate

knowledge of the people, the community and its myriad problems, and DeVier described her as "a woman of irrepressible optimism and pragmatic purpose, . . . leading a new effort to rescue this historic black resort community from the decline that threatens as the memories begin to fade."[17] Among other things, he quoted her as saying: "We have a new agenda. It's to attract at least 40 new retirement households in the next three or four years. People always think of us as we used to be, when there were nightclubs and famous entertainers. . . . People don't go to nightclubs anymore. The times have changed, and we have to change if we're going to survive."[18]

Bullett, whose experience went back to the heyday of the resort community, was pictured as viewing retirees as the savior because they had a stable income and would bring with them much-needed expertise useful in guiding the future of the community. Further, she viewed Idlewild as a community that had a lot to offer retirees who were looking for a quiet, stable community with its own volunteer fire department, law enforcement, senior citizen center, senior citizen housing, street lights, and garbage pickup. Idlewild was a place in which it was relatively inexpensive for retirees to live. Bullett said that there would be an aggressive effort to attract retirees.

By 1998, it was estimated that the year-round population of the community was up to nearly six hundred, with at least 15 percent being white residents. This increase in year-round population is a source of encouragement, and, according to Betty DeRamus, "Idlewild's glory days are long gone, but some residents believe the community is on the verge of creating a new identity as a place to retire, run a small business, rediscover one's roots or even listen to poets."[19]

Of course, not everyone agrees that retirees are the missing piece to the revitalization puzzle at Idlewild, especially since there are still many vexatious and unresolved problems in the community, which may be easily exacerbated by relying primarily on a community of senior citizens. To be sure, the potential exists for senior citizens to add enormously to the stability and vitality of any community, but the potential also exists that these citizens will have special needs that could drain resources away from other important initiatives. Any broad-ranging, call-to-arms efforts against poverty, for example, could be seriously jeopardized if those initiatives have to compete with the need to provide an adequate health care system for the elderly. This latter item is likely to become a paramount factor, as people are now expected to live longer and many will undoubtedly live on a very limited income, especially in a community where the average household income in 1989 was $9,116 (as compared to a state average of $31,080) and the average age of residents in that same year was 52.6.

There is also the argument that a community made up primarily of senior citizens could very well further endanger the general welfare of the community as older people pass on and their properties are neglected because their heirs are not interested in living in a rural community or in spending money on the upkeep of the property. Today, this fact is very much in evidence: as one travels about the neighborhood, some residences and cottages are adequately maintained but many others stand out as eyesores that tarnish the image of the community as a whole.

Still, some property owners are doing their best to increase the beauty and value of the area. Dallas McDonald of Mt. Morris, a retired General Motors employee, noted in an article by Rhonda Sanders in the *Flint Journal* that "new owners are renovating run down cottages or building new ones." He went on to say that a Detroit dentist had done an especially outstanding renovation job, as:

He took a place with no trees, no lawn, nothing, rebuilt the house and put steps down to the lake. . . . That lakefront house is next door to one once owned by Elsie Pratt Seay of Flint. She sold it last July to a Southfield couple. The 1½-story house received a historic designation about 10 years ago, Seay said. She inherited it from her godmother in 1972 but rented it more than she used it. But Seay, 76, is holding onto one of five vacant parcels she and her sisters inherited from their parents. If Idlewild's resort business continues to pick up, they're thinking about putting mobile homes on the lots to rent. . . . [20]

In this same context, William and Bettie McClure should be singled out for their contribution toward the enhancement of the community. Their remodeled Red Rooster Tavern is an outstanding example of what can be done with some imagination and funds. They reopened the property formerly owned by the Roxborough family around the Memorial Day weekend of 1994. Across the paved street from the Red Rooster Tavern is a refurbished party store stocked with necessary goods for weekenders who forget to bring their

A scene at the annual Idlewild Lot Owners Association Convention in Chicago during the mid-1970s. Courtesy of the Ben C. Wilson Collection, Black Americana Studies Department, Western Michigan University.

party favorites. With all of the goodies available, the weekenders run out only of party time. Moreover, Ron Stodghill II, in his article on Idlewild, states that:

> We are part of a new generation rediscovering Idlewild. Houses that fell into disrepair in the 1970s are being refurbished. Vacationers my age [thirty-two] are returning for clear air and nostalgia. Retirees are moving from Detroit and Chicago to the country. Lake County, Idlewild's home, has the third highest percentage of blacks in the state and the highest population over 65 in Michigan's Lower Peninsula. Many of the Idlewild's 300 [permanent] residents welcome redevelopment. Over the past two years, shuttered hotels and motels including the famed Beach Front Morton Motel, have reopened.[21]

Their status as a designated rural Enterprise Community is another reason for optimism about the future for residents and community leaders at Idlewild. Now that federal help is available, according to Eric Freedman, "the goal is to turn around a county economy that keeps one out of four residents

A temporary meeting place for the Mid-Michigan Idlewilders Club. They now meet at other sites. Courtesy of the Ben C. Wilson Collection, Black Americana Studies Department, Western Michigan University.

below the poverty level. Because they envision tremendous growth and development with respect to small factories, restaurants, motels, tourism and more, some believe it will be like the old days when Idlewild was a resort and entertainment magnet for African Americans before and after World War II, an era when black vacationers were unwelcome elsewhere."[22]

During the 1990s, several new organizations were formed and some of the older ones were reenergized in an effort to ameliorate some of the less desirable conditions at Idlewild. Some took a multifaceted approach to the problems and endeavored to promote charitable and recreational events as well as social events. Others were less ambitious, and their orientation assumed a more narrow focus. Those organizations that covered a wide range of activities included:

- *The Mid-Michigan Idlewilders Club Incorporated,* a nonprofit organization in Lake County, was formed in 1997 for the expressed purpose of keeping Idlewild alive, and "to support and promote charitable, civic

Ossie Davis and Ruby Dee during a book signing September 1999 visit to Idlewild's Riffe Youth Center. Courtesy of the Ben C. Wilson Collection, Black Americana Studies Department, Western Michigan University.

endeavors, recreational and social events for the prosperity of Idlewild."[23] At the time the club's constitution and the bylaws were written and adopted, on 5 April 1997, John D. Meek was president and Bettie L. McClure was the secretary of the organization. This organization, among other efforts, brought renowned actor Ossie Davis and his wife Ruby Dee to Idlewild for a book signing session on 18 September 1999 that was held in the Idlewild Lot Owners Club and attended by over three hundred people, who heard Mr. Davis give an eloquent and inspirational speech about being black in America and how the existence of Idlewild made him even more proud as an African American. Buck VanderMeer, journalist for the *Lake County Star*, wrote: "Toward the end of his speech he said, 'When I look around this room and think of what it must have been like when Duke Ellington and Errol Gardner were playing here, it must have been something. The grass must have been doing the lindy.'"[24]

- *The Posse, Inc.* is an organization that teamed up with the Idlewild Lot Owners Association to build a modern playground facility. In the mid-1990s, the two organizations opened a joint account in the Lake Osceola State Bank. According to Buck VanderMeer, "They have raised about $2,000 for the playground that will not only serve to meet the recreational needs of the children in the Idlewild community but also entertain the children who vacation in Idlewild. They are turning the old playground into a modern recreation center."[25] Moreover, Posse president Luke Lockett of Chicago said the playground is part of the general rebuilding of Idlewild. A ground-breaking celebration for the new playground facility occurred during the Idlewild Week in August 1999. No date has been established for the completion of the project, because fundraising is still ongoing at the time of this writing.

The physical infrastructure of Idlewild has never been completed with respect to an adequate sewage system and other modern conveniences. In addition to addressing those matters in recent years, several organizations and agencies have sought to help revitalize the community by the creation or establishment of new business ventures and the implementation of major civic projects. Included in this category are:

- *Nana Jaye's Vineyard* was the dream of Jaye Truesdale Bagley, whose association with Idlewild dates back to the 1950s. As a permanent resident of Idlewild, after leaving Detroit in 1989, she was intent on becoming an entrepreneur once she purchased the old Flamingo Club. Her dream was to place a coffee shop, a nature center, and a tour service in that building. Unfortunately, at this writing, Nana Jaye's Vineyard has not been actualized as envisioned and the old Flamingo Club is being considered for other purposes.
- *Lake County Merry Makers, Inc.*, has an address at the Idlewild Historical Museum because this nonprofit organization, according to its president, Mabel R. Williams, has assumed the responsibility for planning and developing the Idlewild Historic Museum and Cultural Center. The members of this organization have a portfolio of their plans for Idlewild and Lake County, which, among other things, includes the

Friends of Historic Idlewild. The latter is an affiliated group of the Merry Makers, whose minimum five-dollar member contributions will be used to further enhance the efforts of the African American Museum/ Cultural/Convention Center.[26]

- *Yates Township's Waste Treatment Agreement with the Village of Baldwin:* Movement to bring a sewage system to Yates Township made some progress with the signing of an agreement between the two governmental bodies on 9 August 1999. Funded by a 75 percent loan from the USDA Rural Development Fund, which is forgivable, and approximately $300,000 from Yates Township, coupled with a $200,000 grant from the Enterprise Community, the sewer system was expected to be completed in the spring of 2000. Because hookup is mandatory for those who live along the sewer line, some residents have been resentful of that very fact and have unsuccessfully sought relief from township officials, who have maintained that the guidelines were properly followed throughout the entire process.[27] It should be noted, however, that the August 1999 agreement provides sewer service to only a portion of the Idlewild community. Recently, claims have been made that raw sewage has been found in the lake, and reference has been made to the fact that there is still a long way to go before this matter will be satisfactorily resolved. Raw human waste is not a laughing matter and could pose a serious health risk to the people of the community, if allowed to persist. Yet, on a more positive note, the agreement is another reason for the people of Idlewild to be encouraged about their community and to feel that it is on the threshold of making a comeback as a vital and dynamic area.

- *The Idlewild Historic and Cultural Center,* located in the original Yates Township Hall, held its open house in August 1999 as the newest element to be added to the community. On hand for the opening of the center was Dr. Ronald Jemal Stephens, who, in collaboration with Mabel Williams and the Friends of Historic Idlewild, received a grant from the Michigan Humanities Council. Dr. Stephens's traveling Idlewild photographic exhibit is expected to be on display at the museum in the spring or summer of 2002. Buck VanderMeer quotes Stephens as saying: "What I envision is that this will be the first of

ABOVE: Idlewild Historic and Cultural Center that has as its mission the preservation of the history and significance of the resort. Courtesy of the Ben C. Wilson Collection, Black Americana Studies Department, Western Michigan University. RIGHT: Sign advertising the Historic and Cultural Center. Courtesy of Ben C. Wilson Collection.

many contributions to the development of the museum. It is my hope that this will garner support for the museum. Once people become aware of its significance, they will want to become a part of this worthwhile project."[28]

The importance of community solidarity, community unity, and the inculcation of traditional U.S. and African values is paramount for several organizations at Idlewild. The erosion of a sense of community as reflected in the dysfunctional behavior of some residents, especially among the young, is a constant concern, and any revitalization efforts must take this aspect into consideration. Activities and organizations aimed at correcting this situation are:

- *An Annual Community Kwanzaa Celebration*, which runs from 26 December through 1 January of each year. Kwanzaa is a seven-day non-religious African American celebration with an emphasis on strengthening the individual as well as the larger black community. The annual event is viewed as a way of strengthening the community by bringing its members together each year to stress the seven principles (the Nguzo Saba) of Kwanzaa: *umoja* (oo-MOH-jah), or unity; *kujichagulia* (koo-jee-cha-goo-lee-ah), or self-determination; *ujima* (oo-JEE-mah), or collective work and responsibility; *ujamaa* (oo-JAH-mah), or cooperative economics; *nia* (nee-AH), or purpose; *kuumba* (koo-OOM-bah), or creativity; and *imani* (ee-MAH-nee), or faith.

- *The Idlewild Lot Owners Association, Inc.* is an organization that has as its primary goal and mission the task of strengthening families and serving the needs of the local community. According to Audrey K. Bullett, past national financial secretary, "We, along with the Mid-Michigan Idlewilders, the Lake County Merry Makers, the First Baptist Church of Idlewild, and the Tabernacle AME Church, have made a commitment to bringing unity to this community through collaboration and dedicated service to the community."[29]

- *The Idlewild Lake Association, Inc.* is an organization that was started in 1979 by two visionary and tireless men, Arthur R. Parks and William C. Smith, who are credited with establishing a vitally important organization concerned with the general welfare of the community. These two men initially served as the president and vice president, respectively, of the organization. In addition to establishing water safety classes and having the water analyzed in the Idlewild Lake, the organization has identified dredging a part of the lake as a serious priority. According to Ruth Burton of Battle Creek, "We need to dredge the lake on the other side of the island. We are losing the island. It would take a lot of money and probably four or five years to do it but we should dredge the lake and restore it to its original beauty."[30]

Encouraging people to come together at Idlewild and socialize with the residents is seen by some organizations as an important way of adding a spark to help ignite and energize the community, thus helping to revitalize it.

Arranging events on an annual basis is seen by many to be a good approach, because, it is hoped, people will get into a habit of attending and participating in those events year after year, thus assuring the continuance of Idlewild. Such thinking has prompted the following events:

- *An Annual Community Christmas Tree Festival* was started in 1998 by a group of local sponsors (Larry's Landscaping and Nursery, Red Rooster Lounge, Blue Ribbon Cleaners, Idlewild Men's Club, Idlewild Party Store, Coalition of Concerned Citizens, Yates Township Fire Department, Idlewild Lot Owners Association, BMG Sporties, Magic, Dawn's Light Center, First Baptist Church of Idlewild, Foote Tree Service, and others) in an effort to add to the vitality and quality of life of their community.

- *An Annual Poetry in the Woods Festival* is another initiative designed to bring hope and encouragement to the community. Assisted by Gloria Fikes, Jaye Bagley, Audrey Bullett, and other long-time residents, Pharaoh, a poet who is also an auto assembly line worker in Detroit, is the primary driving force behind this effort. According to Desiree Cooper, the Second Annual Poetry in the Woods Festival featured "such notables as Dick Gregory and the Last Poets." Pharaoh told Cooper that: "We want African Americans to fall in love again with the idea of having their own resort. Five years from now, we want people in Nevada to be saying, 'Mark your calendar off for a week this summer, because we're going to Idlewild.'"[31] Cooper further writes: "And the township supervisor, Norm Burns, is helping Pharaoh clear a lot once owned by the African separatist Marcus Garvey. Pharaoh hopes to turn it into a memorial park to host future poetry events. . . . But there was something about Pharaoh's enthusiasm that made him dedicate his precious spare time to the project. Together, the young men [Pharaoh and Clint Evans, his business partner and friend] have sunk countless hours and invested their own money into a venture they hope will mushroom into a national event."[32]

- *An Annual Idlewild Week* brings visitors from big cities such as Cleveland, Toledo, St. Louis, Indianapolis, Detroit, and Chicago, as well as from smaller Midwestern cities and towns such as Saginaw,

Flint, and Kalamazoo, for a weeklong festival celebrating the resort's famed heritage. This event, first sponsored in 1999 by John Meeks, owner of the Morton's Motel, and the Mid-Michigan Idlewilders, seeks to demonstrate to the larger community that Idlewild is far from being a ghost town. In fact, according to Buck VanderMeer, a reporter who covered the event in 1999, "Idlewild Week got off to a great start at the Morton's Motel Saturday as 425 people showed up for the Kick Off Party. A cloudy sky and occasional rain could not stop the enthusiasm of the group as old friends gathered again for the annual occasion."[33]

- *Annual Cabin Closing Party*, sponsored by the Mid-Michigan Idle-wilders Club. The winterization of cabins and cottages is an essential ritual each year in order to prevent the water pipes, the hot-water tanks, and other items sensitive to below-zero temperatures from freezing and requiring expensive repairs and replacements. A special time has thus been designated for owners to combine the winterizing of their properties with one last fling before saying goodbye for the season to their summer neighbors and friends.

FiveCAP: A Major Piece
of the Revitalization Puzzle

In addition to the revitalization efforts of the several aforementioned groups, FiveCAP continues to occupy a central place in the aspirations of the Idlewild community. FiveCAP is a multimillion-dollar private, nonprofit, community action program. In fact, FiveCAP was the fifth (hence the "Five" in its name) community action program started in Michigan under Title II of the Economic Opportunity Act of 1964 for the expressed purpose of assisting low-income families and individuals to become self-sufficient with the aid of federal, state, and private resources. After more than thirty-five years of service, FiveCap has six major areas of focus:[34]

1. *Housing:* FiveCAP provides low-interest home improvement loans, home ownership counseling, home weatherization, a low-income heating energy program, and other services that benefit low-income renters and owners.

2. *Nutrition:* FiveCAP sponsors a food preservation (seed and plants gardening) program; an emergency food assistance program; a summer feeding program for low-income youth; a foodbuying club; a food pantry program, which provides up to thirty days of food to individuals or families; and more.

3. *Emergency Services:* FiveCAP provides a homeless program (FEMA), which helps pay energy bills and provides food and shelter.

4. *Head Start/Child Care:* This FiveCAP program, in addition to focusing on the "social, emotional, physical and intellectual development of low income children ages three to five," provides hearing and vision screenings, immunizations, meals, transportation, and physical and dental examinations.

5. *Community Support Services:* FiveCAP provides a wide array of services, providing for all of Lake County, which include direct services as well as referral services such as legal aid, consumer protection information, employment information, social security information, and much more.

6. *Economic Development:* FiveCAP is a major player in the economic development of Lake County in general and Idlewild in particular.

Many who are knowledgeable about FiveCAP see the agency as a major partner in Idlewild's future growth and development. It has been the prime mover behind the successful push to have a section of Lake County designated as a federal Enterprise Community (EC), the first such rural area to be so designated by the federal government in Michigan. (Clair County has also been designated as an Enterprise Community, but it is not as fully funded as Lake County is.) In this effort, the FiveCAP board, led by executive director Mary Trucks, realizing the potential of the area, pushed to have the area federally recognized as a rural Enterprise Zone. This coveted designation was won as the result of a highly competitive process that involved the submission of a comprehensive strategic plan for the area. Lake County earned the special federal status only after successfully completing a competitive yearlong process involving large group meetings and small work groups.

The award was announced in December 1994.[35] In August 1995, Alvin Brown, national director of the United States Department of Agriculture

Enterprise Zone/Enterprise Community (USDA EZ/EC), and Donald L. Hare, state director for USDA Rural Development operations in Michigan, attended the ceremony formally acknowledging the signing of the Lake County Enterprise Community Memorandum of Agreement. The State of Michigan signed its memorandum of agreement in 1996, meaning that state and federal funds could then be released for the various initiatives, according to the Economic Community (EC) strategic plan.[36]

According to a FiveCAP/Lake County, Michigan, Enterprise Community pamphlet, Lake County Enterprise is: "a federally designated Enterprise Community which covers approximately the southern one-third of Lake County. . . . This designation increases the availability of federal, state and local dollars to the area for economic development, housing and human services. The Enterprise Community benchmarks have established several loan programs."[37] In an effort to increase the number of businesses providing jobs with a livable wage and benefits, EC has created a "revolving loan program" with the following components:

- *Micro Supplemental Income Loan Program* ($1,500 maximum loan) For those low-income residents who want to develop a secondary source (e.g., part-time business) of income to supplement their primary wages.
- *Macro Self-Employment Loan Program* ($1,000 to $10,000 loan) For those residents who are interested in establishing a primary business that will support the owner and his or her family.
- *Small Business Loan Program* ($40,000 maximum loan) For those who want to establish a business that will employ the owner plus four or more people.
- *Direct Loan Participation Program* (DLP) (a 40% FiveCAP, 50% lending institution, 10% applicant formula) For those who are involved in a low-equity business and who wish to have FiveCAP become directly involved with them and a conventional institution regarding a loan package.
- *Intermediary Relending Program* (IRP) (maximum is 75% of total up to $150,000) For those who cannot get a conventional business loan. "The focus of the IRP is to assist in the development of retail and other commercial establishments and assist in the creation of new small businesses or in the expansion of existing businesses."

These five loan programs have the potential of helping to create a sustainable economic base throughout the Enterprise Community, of which Idlewild is a part. These programs are designed to assist and encourage low-equity residents who want to enhance their economic condition by starting a new business, or by developing or expanding an existing one.

An assessment of the Idlewild community suggests that these programs, though they exist and have the potential of creating a sustainable economic base in the community, have not thus far contributed substantially to the economic vitality of Idlewild, especially with respect to the creation of new businesses or the expansion of old ones. This is not to imply, however, that the Enterprise Community initiative has been of no benefit to Idlewild since its inception in 1995. Just the opposite is true. It has enabled Idlewild to address a number of its major infrastructural problems, namely: the installation of natural gas lines to the residents, the resurfacing of some roads, and the installation of at least the first phase of a sewer system.

After calling together a cross-section of its populations, in the mid-1990s Lake County formulated a ten-year plan, which included goals, strategies, and funding sources. Succinctly,

> by restating the vision for the Lake County EZ/EC, it is possible to focus on the primary tasks required. The vision is to "create a community which is economically viable"; a community which stimulates business opportunities, creates jobs, enables residents to live above the poverty line and provides educational and vocational systems that direct and prepare children and adults for careers, employment opportunities and life. The vision includes a countywide transportation system, accessible, quality health care, and decent and affordable housing. Lake County will gain the respect and recognition as the best example of a socially and economically advanced community. This vision will be achieved through economic development and stimulated by cooperation, innovation, racial and ethnic diversity, and a celebration of our shared history.[38]

Though a more detailed summary of "The Plan" will be provided in chapter 8, it is mentioned in this section for several reasons: First, it was formulated during the 1990s; second, it was responsible for the Idlewild district being included in the designated Enterprise Community, which made Lake

County eligible for special financial consideration by both the federal and state governments; and third, it contains items that addressed specifically and directly some of Idlewild's problems. A perusal of "The Plan" leaves one with the impression that Lake County is the beneficiary of visionary leaders who want to position the county to become a model for other economically depressed counties in the states. At the very least, it wants to "gain . . . respect and recognition as the best example of a socially and economically advanced community." If that laudable goal is achieved for Lake County as a whole, then one can hypothesize that Idlewild also will be a direct beneficiary, since it is a component part of that county.

Sociological Illuminations

The formation and proliferation of organizations with an expressed interest in the welfare of Idlewild during the last decade of the twentieth century, along with the renewed interest of the media in Idlewild, may be seen as a vigorous trend toward the revitalization of the area. On the other hand, however, it may also be seen as a trend that only contributes to the contentiousness among the various groups vying for influence in the community. One might be inclined to ask: "Why so many organizations in such a small, sleepy enclave?" The same proliferation of activity that some interpret as a sign of revitalization may to others be a signal that the community is fractious, lacking in solidarity, and thus unable to achieve important initiatives in a timely manner. Regardless of how one interprets these signs, however, it is quite clear that, with the exception of the FiveCAP initiatives, revitalization at Idlewild is not occurring at a galloping pace. This does not mean that those efforts currently being pursued or sponsored by the existing organizations are not worthwhile; some may indeed be adding to the vitality of the community. However, with the exception of the FiveCAP initiatives, there do not appear to be any current substantial developments to enhance the economic structure of Idlewild.

Without combining initiatives to significantly strengthen the community economically, the success of a few organizations with an annual poetry festival, Idlewild week, or closing party will not be enough to turn the sleepy enclave into an economically healthy community. Though useful in drawing visitors to the area, it is unlikely that these events will contribute to the creation of new job opportunities or improve the general welfare of the citizens with respect to poverty, education, and so forth. In sum, these activities are unlikely to cause new businesses to be created or existing ones to expand. Thus, it seems that Idlewild's leaders still have the enormous challenge ahead of developing plans and resources that will genuinely address the issues of revitalization. In this effort, plans that include, not exclude, the activities and efforts of the numerous currently existing organizations should be given top priority in the minds of the planners. Granted, this will not be an easy undertaking. There will be disagreements and heated discussions. Yet, a summit-like meeting, allowing all opinions to be voiced, is a necessary first step in the revitalization effort. Perhaps an outside mediator can be used, so that a consensus can be reached on which efforts are to be initiated first. This does not mean that majority decisions are the only options, or that they are necessarily correct. All proposals that are well thought out should be evaluated by the independent mediator, and decisions should be made based on the merits of each proposal for the entire community. In this connection, the next chapter will explore some important considerations and issues involved in combining the various cultural events currently existing with aggressive economic planning for the future.

A Need for a Comprehensive Strategic Plan: Some Suggestions

THOUGH THE RESORT HAS AN ENORMOUSLY RICH MUSICAL HISTORY, PLANNING for Idlewild's future will not be well served by any great improvisational jazz session, where things are made up as one goes along. Leaders must think long term; patching things together on a piecemeal basis will not serve the interest of the community in the end. Continued piecework will only ensure the stagnation and perhaps even the ultimate demise of Idlewild as it is known today. The discussions in this chapter, then, should be of interest to anyone interested in the revitalization of Idlewild.

Chapter 6 was a narrative "snapshot" of the current community, and it is abundantly clear that a specifically formulated companion plan for Idlewild is needed to go hand-in-hand with the current Lake County "Plan." This complementary plan for Idlewild should take into consideration five important aspects: (1) a need for definitional clarity of the community, (2) the importance of a paradigm shift and transformative leaders, (3) current and future challenges, (4) the companion plan for Idlewild vis-à-vis "The Plan," and (5) sociological illuminations.

A Need for Definitional Clarity
of the Community

When the land that would become Idlewild was purchased back in 1912, the buyers came together and arduously hammered out their strategic plans for the area. Simply put, they wanted to create a resort for "colored men and women" of high status. To transform their vision into a reality, they very deliberately crafted a master plan that had all the essential ingredients of a viable and vital community, one that would be the pride of the black race. Today, however, Idlewild seems to be at a crossroads. It is a community in the midst of an identity crisis, a situation that must be resolved if there is to be any significant progress in the near future. To this end, then, definitional clarity is an important issue as Idlewild wrestles with its physical and social infrastructures—two essential components in any plan to revitalize the community. Conceptually, those interested in revitalization should consider the following remarks as an excellent starting point toward a clearer definition of Idlewild as a community:

A good community, at its core, is a place of peace and safety that provides opportunity for full human development. The well-being of a community is the sum of its physical, economic, and social natures. It is easy to see a community as a place: homes, schools, streets, parks, churches, shops. These make up the physical infrastructure of community; their soundness and attractiveness is essential for a good community. Community also includes economic infrastructures: jobs, businesses, education, sources of capital and investment. Without economic life and opportunity, a community cannot meet its material needs and a good quality of life cannot be enjoyed. Most important, perhaps, community is a social and political organization which embodies elements necessary for getting (or keeping) its physical and economic life. These less tangible elements make up a social infrastructure which creates the polis, a place where people strive to meet their needs, have cultural and historic bonds, and which is characterized by a sense of community. Social infrastructure is built on public kinship and civic storytelling, which give people a place in their society; and on an understanding of a common good expressed through a civic and civil dialogue in which all members of the community can participate.[1]

To become "a good community," Idlewild must accept the definitional challenge and decide what it is that it wants to become. Will it be primarily a retirement community? A black resort? A black historic community? A combination of these? Answers to these questions will not come easily, and it might be helpful if the citizens of Idlewild would acknowledge a need for a paradigm shift before they attempt to engage in any type of strategic planning.

THE IMPORTANCE OF A PARADIGM SHIFT
AND TRANSFORMATIVE LEADERS

A paradigm shift is desperately needed among the leaders of the Idlewild community. This shift should straightforwardly allow the leaders—both men and women—an opportunity to create a political environment within which they all can come together under a common cause. Such an environment would encourage participants to intensify their efforts as authentic and credible men and women who are dedicated to the transformation of the community, while maximizing all of the community's strengths, both real and potential. At the core of this paradigmatic shift should be a sincere desire among the community's leaders to acknowledge their differences and rivalries. At the same time, however, it is very necessary for these leaders to venture beyond the past and focus on the present and the future prize: a revitalized Idlewild community. This shift undoubtedly can occur only if the men and women in the community have the courage to accept the challenge for change and the willingness to persevere through acrimoniously heated debates, at least initially.

It is evident that, like other communities, Idlewild has its fair share of socioeconomic and political issues that cause its leaders to manifest dispositions and behaviors that are far from perfect. Yet, if Idlewild is to become something other than what it is today, its future is arguably dependent on the ability of its leaders to overcome and overlook the shortcomings of the individual as well as the collective whole.

It is within a consensual framework that an opportunity exists for the leaders to transcend their current station by freeing themselves of unnecessary contentious and contemptuous baggage. To chronicle the litany of such issues is not the purpose of this volume, nor would it serve any functional purpose. To do so just might exacerbate a situation in search of consensus. Suffice it to say, however, that those in leadership positions—both private and public—are keenly aware that bickering and backbiting do occur, and that people are sometimes disliked simply because of the color of their eyes or skin, their age, their socioeconomic status, or their sexual preferences and orientation. Therefore, freedom from and clarification of some of these issues will certainly help fashion an environment in which dedicated men and women can come together to hammer out a comprehensive plan for a viable and dynamic community.

Idlewild is fortunate in that it has a small cadre of men and women who are dedicated to its revitalization and have the civic leadership ability to guide the community out of its socioeconomic and political doldrums and into a state that matches their optimism and exuberance. Edward J. Annen Jr., attorney and former mayor of Kalamazoo, writing on this topic in the *Kalamazoo Gazette*, states:

> It can justifiably be said that "civic leadership" is the engine that advances a community's life. A community grows in important ways, when certain people demonstrate an ability and a willingness to travel outside the confines of their own lives, and—with their energy, intellect and dedication—reach out and embrace all and everything that surrounds them.[2]

In this same connection, interviews with many current and former residents of Idlewild, as well as a number of vacationers there, revealed a high level of excitement about the prospects of the community. Mary B. Trucks, Audrey Bullett, William and Bettie McClure, Norm Burns, John D. Meek, MaryEllen Wilson, M. Joe and Fredna Lindsey, Ruth Burton, Sandra Joubert, and many others are still optimistic, in spite of the formidable obstacles facing their community. They hold out the hope and faith that they can marshal the necessary forces and resources to transform the community into a place they can be proud to call "Idlewild." This will be a place where people, especially African Americans, will once again flock to as a means of escaping the fast lanes and the hustle and bustle of city life. It will also be a place where people can retire in the knowledge that they will be safe, surrounded by neighbors who have a deep and abiding faith in the general welfare of the community. It will be a place where people can leave after a visit with a deeper sense of self and peoplehood because of their exposure to a black experience that is found only at Idlewild.

There are examples of other communities that have been successfully regenerated under transformative leadership. An outstanding example of this success is found in the neighborhood known as Paradise at Parkside in our nation's capital. It was at one time described as a "murderous, filthy, broken down slum," by the national media.[3] However, under transformative leadership

> . . . the community has been transformed. Its physical infrastructure has been rebuilt; its economy has improved with opportunities for jobs, education, training, new business development; and, most importantly, its social infrastructure has been restored. This was and is being accomplished through the participation of many neighborhood residents and action by neighborhood institutions. Commitment and investment of the larger community has also been forthcoming. The public sector, at both the local and federal levels, committed resources. Members of the private sector, including developers, businesses, and philanthropic organizations have been active participants and investors. The Paradise at Parkside transformation has been brought about through a progressive partnership among the people who live in the community, its organizations, and the public and private sectors of the larger community which participated in an inclusive planning and investment process to bring about change.[4]

Though there is no comprehensive plan at the present that speaks to the future development of the Idlewild community, the resort's leaders have before them the arduous task of creating and implementing such a document. The following discussion deals with the current and future challenges facing Idlewild and may be useful in deliberations about a comprehensive plan.

CURRENT AND FUTURE CHALLENGES

A historical overview of the progress of the community suggests that Idlewild was on the right road but it simply never quite made it to its proper economic destination. Already discussed were select factors responsible for the erosion of that progress, which was sustained until the late 1960s. There is the contention that economic stability is essential to the vitality of any community, and "for that stability to obtain for any race, that race must become a manufacturer of something everybody wants. Idlewild must have a dream!"[5] Bill McClure places great emphasis on the creation of an adequate economic base for the community, something not achieved even during the days when the Flamingo and Paradise Clubs, and other businesses, were flourishing. He, along with several other Idlewilders, speculates that the "good old days" perhaps were not especially "good" for the general community, because with integration many business entrepreneurs left the community with money-lined pockets; top-named entertainers gleefully deserted Idlewild for places that catered primarily to white audiences. There appeared to be little concern among the entrepreneurs or the entertainers with establishing and sustaining a stable economic base in the Idlewild community. Thus, unfortunately, the community's political and social leaders were unable to forestall the erosion of the economic vitality that had once played an important role in the growth and development of Idlewild. The downward drift has had a lasting and devastating impact on the general community. In addition to the plethora of social problems discussed in chapter 4, Idlewild has to face the following challenges within the context of revitalization:

1. Greater Involvement of the Church in Community Revitalization

An investigation of Idlewild reveals a relative lack of involvement of the black church in the ongoing revitalization discussions and initiatives. There has been no recent major project that was initiated or completed by the religious community. According to Audrey K. Bullett, "The First Bapitist Church of Idlewild, and the Tabernacle AME Church, have made a commitment to bringing unity to this community through collaboration and dedicated service to the community."[6] To be sure, the church has long been a stalwart institution in the black community; it has been the social hub of the community, and the ministers have been in the vanguard among leaders in the political arena, the economic realm, the social justice area, and more. It is important that this relative absence of the church in Idlewild's revitalization efforts be pointed out because of the recent role of faith-based ministries in helping to revitalize neighborhoods, especially in inner-city areas. Faith-based ministries are being heralded not only for their role in turning around the lives of many wayward youths but also for their favorable impact on the entire community.

Dr. John Dilulio, a Princeton University criminologist and political scientist, believes that "no welfare reform, no drug policy, no free-enterprise zones or school reforms, no Marshall Plan for the ghetto . . . can do what faith-based ministries are already doing and can do with more resources."[7] Journalist Tim Stafford says that:

> Dilulio is on a mission for America's inner cities. He believes with all his social-scientist heart that the path to effective change in the rotting urban core runs through gospel-centered churches and faith-based ministries. He is preaching this message not only to white evangelicals, but to foundations, corporations, think tanks, parole officers, majors, and anybody else who will stand still to listen.[8]

Capital Christian Center is a ministry in Milwaukee, Wisconsin, under the leadership of a husband-wife team, senior pastors Michael and Andrea Dudley. It includes a sanctuary, a community health center, and a Marva Collins Preparatory School. This ministry has approximately ninety thousand square feet of space for worship, education, counseling, living and sleeping, feeding, athletics, and health care services. It is dedicated to transforming a neighborhood characterized by joblessness, welfare dependency, crime and violence, drugs and gangs, family instability, vacant buildings, and more.

The fact that 91 percent of inner-city congregations in six metropolitan areas throughout the country were actively involved in programs serving the needs of the larger community should be instructive to the cleric leaders in Idlewild.[9] If Dilulio's assessment of what is needed to transform poor communities is correct, then faith-based ministries in Idlewild can be important co-players in the revitalization of that community, even if it shies away from becoming a tourist attraction at the level of its heyday.

Pragmatically, the church leaders can aid Idlewild immensely in the promotion of community revitalization by identifying those areas where they can realistically make a significant difference in the lives of individuals as well as in the general welfare of the overall community. A top priority should be to position the respective congregations so that they will readily accept some responsibility for engaging in a faith-based ministry dedicated to neighborhood regeneration, for working in various volunteer capacities to harness the available local assets, for "begin[ning to connect] . . . them with one another in ways that multiply their power and effectiveness, and [for beginning to harness] . . . those local institutions that are not yet available for local development purposes."[10]

Ostensibly, then, one would envision a faith-based ministry in Idlewild as one that would want, among other things, to:

- transform that depressed area by working to alter the "habits of the heart" of the residents.
- locally identify, organize, and mobilize the internal and external assets and resources through active volunteers who would connect them with one another in ways that would multiply their impact on Idlewild.
- provide value-based programs to support the creation and maintenance of stable and wholesome families.
- change the residents from "clients" to "providers" and "responsible citizens."
- work collaboratively with other institutions and stakeholders (foundations; local, state, and federal governments; human services agencies, etc.) to transform depressed neighborhoods, and more.

There are those who feel the church, especially the black church in poor neighborhoods, must promote the social gospel and justice, and not simply preach original sin and repentance. Sitting back and expecting miracles in an environment that calls for other ameliorative strategies is an archaic approach that will only frustrate the hopes and aspirations of those in poor contemporary communities.

2. The Challenge of Race and Its Role in the Comprehensive Plan

There is no doubt that race was an issue when Idlewild was created, race was an issue in the dramatic decline of Idlewild, and race will continue to be an issue in the revitalization process. For Idlewild to be saved as a black town or community where its black cultural heritage is to be preserved is an important and laudable effort. However, more and more, diversity is heralded as the American way, and in the not-too-distant future there will not be a dominant or majority group in this country. As a matter of fact, Census Bureau director Kenneth Prewit said that the 2000 census survey would show the United States to be a "microcosm of the entire world."

One has to wonder, then, the extent to which race should be considered as a factor in the future plans and development of Idlewild. There are at least two positions on this matter. One position would argue that the cultural and physical heritage of Idlewild should be preserved for future generations. It should stand as both a monument and an inspiration to future generations of African Americans, a place where visitors can get a firsthand glimpse of this slice of their history, its present and its future. On the other hand, however, there are those who would say that Idlewild will not be a vibrant community if it is to be merely a historical reference point in Michigan as a community built by blacks for blacks at a point in time when segregation was legal and discrimination was rampant throughout the land. According to proponents of this viewpoint, this is not necessarily an either/or situation. Idlewild could be both a black historical reference point and a combination of the ingredients alluded to in our preceding definition of a "good community," where the infrastructures are sound, the economy is strong, and the social institutions provide a host of opportunities for the full development of the human spirit and personality, regardless of the accident of one's birth.

3. Competition from Casinos and Other Tourist Attractions

Another challenge facing Idlewild, as a resort community, is the competition brought by the growth and development of casinos throughout the state of Michigan. This means there will be unprecedented competition for the discretionary dollars, and even nondiscretionary dollars, of visitors to the area. Current research shows that a growing number of people are willing to risk their dollars in the casinos and on lottery games, hoping to either strike it rich or dramatically augment their income. One implication of this trend for resorts is that they will have to find and fill a particular niche in states such a Michigan where there already are many casinos and lottery games. At this writing, Michigan has eighteen casinos, most owned and operated by Native American tribes, and the voters have authorized three non-Native American casinos in Detroit—the MGM Grand Detroit Casino, which had its grand opening in the summer of 1999, the MotorCity Casino, and the Greektown Casino.

According to the *Metro Detroit Visitors Guide,* "With the addition of these casinos to the already established Casino Windsor, metro Detroit is well on its way to becoming a Midwest gambling must-stop, with people coming from around the country to get a taste of Detroit-style hospitality. Around the clock, seven days a week, the metro Detroit nightlife has never looked better."[11]

In addition to the casinos, "Detroit blues musicians do capacity business at many local clubs, and techno, alternative and dance music have a strong youth-centered audience that fills clubs throughout the city."[12] Thus, Detroit has much more to offer residents and visitors than just the gambling scenes in that city, which makes it difficult for lesser-known places, with little to offer in terms of restaurants, recreation, entertainment, and so forth, to compete for the tourists' dollars.

While Detroit is approximately 250 miles from Idlewild, there is also a casino in Manistee, Michigan, only about fifty miles to the west of Idlewild. This casino is marketed to attract tourists from the surrounding counties. We hasten to add, however, that the casino is not the only entity being heavily touted to attract tourists to Manistee. Visitors are also encouraged to visit the historic business district, which has received special attention from city officials with respect to installing new sidewalks, streets, planters, and other things to make the area attractive to tourists. Edward Hoogterp, who wrote a journalistic piece on Manistee, agrees that history draws people:

> Most tourists still seem interested in the outdoor activities that have always brought people here: boating on Lake Michigan; fishing the Big and Little Manistee rivers; canoeing the Pine River; hiking the Manistee National Forest; chasing a little white ball around the area's challenging golf courses. But more and more, they've been coming to stroll quiet streets and taste the town's history. A riverfront walkway, new restaurants including a brew pub, and a selection of gift shops have added in recent years to the appeal of the restored nineteenth-century downtown storefronts.[13]

Idlewild has the acreage on which a casino could be built, but there is no talk of partnering with any Native American tribe to locate a casino at Idlewild now that there is a casino approximately forty miles away. (At one time the Little River Band of Ottawas inhabited Lake County.) Simply put, could the area support two casinos? That issue aside, the propinquity of the extant casino could perhaps be used to the benefit of Idlewild if packaged and marketed in such a way that people would want to avail themselves of both places while visiting the area and enjoying the "marvelous amenities" of the Idlewild community.

Though until 1973 casinos were legal only in Nevada, today Michigan is only one of the twenty-four states with officially sanctioned lotteries and casinos. The National Coalition Against Gambling, Taxpayers of Michigan Against Casinos, and other critics notwithstanding, legalized or authorized gambling in the United States at the end of the 1990s grossed more than $50 billion, making gambling a favorite pastime for millions of Americans.

In pure economic terms, casinos pay off big. Garrison Wells, in the *Kalamazoo Gazette*, noted, "Experts say [casinos] provide high paying jobs, revenue to local governments, lots of tourists and business opportunities."[14] In that same article Jake Miklojcik, president of Michigan Consultants in Lansing (the firm that handled the consulting for the Detroit casinos) stated that in terms of pure economic development, "they're wonderful." Carol Emmendorfer, executive director for the Mount Pleasant Area Convention and Visitors Bureau, said, "the impact of the casino—Isabella County's largest employer with 3,000 jobs—has been very positive."[15]

Although there is a lack of consensus, at least a few residents favor locating a casino in Idlewild because they envision citizens finding employment as dealers, hostesses, bar maids, accountants, security guards, beverage managers, groundskeepers, painters, casino cage supervisors, collection agents, and employment directors. Additionally, they contend, the local and state governments would benefit because there is a current agreement to give 2 percent of the gaming income to the local government and 8 percent to the state government. Supporters readily acknowledge that such an initiative would create a major stir in Idlewild, but they also acknowledge that gambling facilities bring quick employment and improved finances. The windfall profits experienced by the formerly economically destitute Tunica, Mississippi, have been cited as an example of what could happen at Idlewild.

In short, regardless of where one stands on the casino matter, the fact remains that Idlewild faces an uphill battle for the tourist dollar as a resort community. Competition brought on by the growth and development of casinos in the state of Michigan will undoubtedly only increase as more and more gaming facilities are built.

4. Challenges from Other Local Facilities

It addition to the casino at Manistee, there are other resort-type facilities throughout the area—some seasonal and others open year-round—that can be expected to compete with Idlewild both now and in the future with respect to the tourist trade. To be sure, most of the tourists attracted to those areas will likely be white and will therefore not necessarily be interested in visiting a historic black resort in any case. To the extent to which this is true, and to the degree to which Idlewild is interested in cross-marketing itself as a resort, then, Idlewild is faced with a marketing issue involving race. A decision should be made as to whether or not the community will market itself, as in the early years, as a "black resort." If it markets itself as a "black resort" and prefers that only black tourists visit, because of its black history, then perhaps the presence of other resort-type facilities owned by whites in the area will not be a challenge of any moment. (Should that be the decision, however, it certainly will raise the issue of the extent to which there has been any racial progress in the area.) Yet the Manistee casino, among others, will remain a competitor for the tourist dollar, because African Americans as well as whites will be encouraged to frequent that establishment.

Parenthetically, the Lake County strategic plan calls for the economic development of the county as a tourist area, and the county plans to assist others in that area to provide the facilities and services necessary to accommodate tourism. Of course, this could be both a blessing and curse for Idlewild. It could be a blessing if it will help change the image of the community and, through aggressive marketing programs, bring or attract a significantly larger number of tourists to the area. Should this happen, then, Idlewild would stand to get some of that business for its black cultural center and museum, motels, taverns, and more. If successful, this could mean that more facilities would be needed to accommodate the increased traffic in tourism. With an increase in tourism, some thought could be given to reviving the musical entertainment industry, at least on special occasions.

Idlewild would be cursed, however, if other resort-type facilities were to achieve a dominance over the tourist trade with assistance from the county.

Accordingly, if new businesses and facilities are built in the county but Idlewild is ignored, then such a development could very well stifle any crossover growth anticipated for the black community, whether resort-related or not. Therefore, it seems imperative that Idlewild residents (at least the leaders) be thoroughly knowledgeable about the contents of the plans for Lake County and how those plans influence both directly and indirectly the revitalization prospects for Idlewild. Moreover, Idlewild planners must determine what will be required of the community if it seeks to be an integral player in the economic and social development of Lake County.

5. Critical Mass and the Companion Plan

Even the most comprehensive plan possible would be virtually worthless without the critical mass necessary to implement that plan. One of Idlewild's major weaknesses is the lack of citizens who can step into the entrepreneurial role. Idlewild's population count was 585 in the 1990 census, up slightly from 552 in 1980. There was no marked increase in the community's population during the 1990s. In 1998, it was estimated that the year-round population of the community was up to nearly 600, with at least 15 percent being white residents.

The critical mass challenge should not be minimized. It should be noted that between 1990 and 1994, the less densely populated townships in Michigan, located far from cities, tended to have the largest growth rates. Yet, this phenomenon had a negligible, if any, effect on the population in Yates Township. It is also interesting to note that, during this same period, the highest growth rates in Lake County were in Eden Township (47 percent), Peacock Township (35 percent), and Elk Township (30 percent).[16] The fact that Yates Township was not among those townships experiencing an appreciable increase in population has some serious implications for the future of Idlewild. With a robust economy in Michigan, and with its citizens, in unprecedented numbers, literally rushing into townships and unincorporated areas far away from the cities, why is Idlewild being virtually bypassed in this rush? This fundamental question begs to be answered.

Again, the low year-round population in the community should be a source of serious concern, especially when senior citizens make up a significant proportion of the existing "critical mass" in Yates Township. Therefore, it is essential that keen attention be dedicated to finding people external to the community who can be sufficiently motivated to become a part of its economic development. A number of men and women who are capable of playing a variety of entrepreneurial and leadership roles are desperately needed. Perhaps the Idlewilders Lot Owners Association or the Idlewilders Club members could assist in identifying and recruiting some of these men and women. (Acceptance of outsiders by local residents and power brokers might be a problem. Sociologically, it is well known that outsiders are often looked upon as interlopers, and insiders are often most reluctant to accept their leadership, regardless of their intentions.)

While Idlewild can ignore concerns about its critical mass only at its own peril, a warning statement about some of the consequences of the dramatic population growth in Michigan's townships is worth repeating in this context. Specifically:

In the past 24 years, Michigan gained 614,700 people, while cities lost 500,000 and townships as a whole gained 1,056,000 people. The increase of more than one million people in Michigan's townships has put a pressure on rural communities with regard to the environment, services, and other needs. As people continue to move away from city areas, the percent population in townships will continue to increase. If the current rate continues, a majority of Michigan's population will reside in townships and villages after 15 years. The services that these local units of government provide to their residents will become increasingly important. Environmental concerns, expansion of employment and business, and provision of services will be a great challenge to these communities.[17]

This great challenge notwithstanding, if the current population distribution trend continues, and if Michigan's African Americans are part of that trend, then the goal of increasing the population count at Idlewild could very well be met in part by an aggressive marketing program. Hence, a marketing strategy should be an integral component of the comprehensive companion plan. (The drafters of the companion plan could take a page from the brilliant script written by the original founders and developers of Idlewild, who, with their unique vision, launched an aggressive marketing scheme that ultimately brought thousands upon thousands of African Americans to the resort area, which resulted in numerous cottages and homes being built, and many entrepreneurs—both black and white—establishing riding stables, grocery stores, lumber companies, dance halls, restaurants, and other businesses in the community. All of these elements came about because the Idlewild resort was fiercely and aggressively promoted and marketed in the black communities in such cities as Chicago, Detroit, and Cleveland.)

A Companion Plan for Idlewild
Vis-à-Vis the County Plan

In order to understand the suggestion that Idlewild formulate a companion plan to the extant Lake County plan, a rather detailed summary of "The Plan" is provided, followed by suggestions for a comprehensive companion plan. This format is necessary because "The Plan" is connected in several specific ways to the revitalization of Idlewild, in addition to the fact that virtually the entire plan has some relevancy to the future prospects of that community. Therefore, it is logical that there be a companion plan if Idlewild is to take full advantage of the resources available to it as a part of the Enterprise Community in Lake County.

While the companion plan for Idlewild should be comprehensive in scope and nature, it also should be sufficiently flexible to embrace simultaneously both internal and external initiatives. All interested individuals and organizations should have an opportunity to be involved in a meaningful way. An analysis of the situation raises a potential problem regarding the extent to which an established mechanism exists whereby everyone with an expressed interest in helping in the revitalization process can actually do so. This concern is coupled with the fact that there appears to be no readily available means of identifying and mobilizing people who have a genuine interest—and perhaps some resources to contribute—in helping to regenerate the community.

A plan that would allow for various levels of participation on several different types of initiatives seems to be one way of maximizing and utilizing the human and material resources of the community. For example, the plan should carefully consider the potential benefits that could come to the community from economic enterprises that are established on the cooperative principle (i.e., an independent, nongovernmental association that is established to benefit, represent, and serve its members by offering them discounts on a variety of services and products). Under a cooperative umbrella, many services and products could be delivered to the people of the community, especially the senior citizens and others of limited economic means. This would also be a means of keeping more dollars in the community, because jobs would be created and dollars generated would be exchanged within and among the businesses in the area.

Background and Summary of Lake County's "Plan"

The continual deterioration of communities throughout the United States prompted the Department of Housing and Urban Development to address this situation through the creation of Empowerment Zones. In 1993, Congress passed the necessary legislation to authorize the creation of such zones. The Empowerment Zones were

> intended to focus attention on distressed urban and rural communities and to engage communities in the development of comprehensive strategic plans to link economic, physical, and human development reflecting all of the community needs. Hundreds of communities undertook this grassroots planning effort involving wide citizen participation to produce strategic plans. The plans were comprehensive in identifying issues, needs, resources, opportunities, short-term and long-term goals, a vision of the community's future, and a timetable and plan for implementation.[18]

As previously stated, Lake County was one of those communities that participated in this process and submitted a ten-year plan, which included goals, strategies, and funding sources. Succinctly, "The Plan" articulates three major strategic goals: an *Economic Development Goal* (8 objectives; 44 strategies); a *Human Services Goal* (9 objectives; 69 strategies); and a *Housing Goal* (4 objectives; 9 strategies). Along with a named responsible party and a list of potential funding sources, "The Plan" provides specific objectives and associated strategies for the implementation of each of the three strategic goals. Listed below are the objectives and a synopsis of the strategies for each of the three strategic goals found in "The Plan":[19]

A. *Economic Development Goal's Objectives*

1. *Transportation:* to upgrade the transportation systems in Lake County "for the orderly flow of people, goods, and services to occur and to best serve its residents and businesses." Upgrading roads and bridges, transporting people to work, and improving the Baldwin Airport are some of the strategic steps in this transportation objective.

2. *Infrastructure:* to improve the infrastructure as a means of providing for economic growth in the county. Providing full utilities to the Industrial Park in Idlewild, expansion of wastewater treatment in Baldwin, natural gas service along u.s. 10 and m-37, and other strategies will be employed to fulfill the infrastructure objective.

3. *Entrepreneurship Development:* to provide programs to assist startup of new businesses and the expansion of those already in existence. On-the-job training, technical assistance for existing businesses, and other strategies will be put into play to help enhance entrepreneurial activities in the county.

4. *Tourism:* to provide for a dramatic increase in the tourist industry in the area. The improvement of public parks, a professional marketing program, promotion of the musical legacy and heritage at Idlewild, development of additional restaurants, and other strategic activities will be encouraged and assisted to attract more tourists into the county.

5. *Facilities, Retail and Commercial:* to provide for the expansion of facilities "that will assist in the development of retail and commercial uses." Strategies to achieve the facilities objective include, among other things, establishing a historical and cultural facility in Idlewild, and formulating and enforcing a countywide zoning ordinance to "promote orderly growth and to maintain residential, commercial, and industrial areas." Also, water and sanitary sewer service is to be provided in Idlewild.

6. *Environmental:* to protect and upgrade the lakes, forests, air, beaches, and water in Lake County. Substandard structures are to be either rehabilitated or demolished; a recycling center is to be added, along with expanded trash/rubbish service; public beaches and parks are to be upgraded; and other steps will be taken to address additional environmental concerns.

7. *School to Work:* to provide assistance to those residents who are transitioning from the school environment to the workplace. Postvocational education for adults, an enhanced curriculum, and upgraded equipment will be among those efforts to ensure that the labor force has the necessary skills to perform competently in the workplace.

8. *Business Development/Job Development:* to provide a program that will assist in the creation of new jobs via existing business expansion and the creation of new businesses. To achieve this ambitious objective, a comprehensive business incentive program will be used to lure new industries, along with providing funds, land, and buildings to establish new businesses and expand old ones in the county so that jobs will be available to the local residents.

B. *Human Services Goal's Objectives*

1. *Education:* to establish an educational system that is appropriate for today's global economy, and to allow for the gathering of the necessary information from the community and parents with respect to fulfilling the educational needs of the citizens. Strategies will address the high dropout rate, substance abuse, counseling, curriculum matters, sex education, the issue of children of board members attending district schools, and other education-related matters.

2. *Law Enforcement and Public Safety:* to establish a comprehensive law enforcement and public safety program that is accessible at the same time that it is both cost effective and efficient. This objective will be achieved by, among other things, enhancing standards and practices of the police, carrying out programs that will improve police-community relations, and establishing a community watch program.

3. *Health:* to provide an effective and cost-efficient comprehensive health care network to the citizens by removing barriers and making the system accessible to all, regardless of race, age, or economic condition. Strategies will provide for a twenty-four-hour health care service, a mobile health care unit, a community-wide sex education program, and an emergency transportation service, and will improve the Baldwin Family Health Center.

4. *Substance Abuse Prevention:* to reduce substance abuse by providing prevention and educational activities and by encouraging the community

to support law enforcement on drug-related matters. A residential treatment program will be among those initiatives to reduce substance abuse among kids and involve police and the judicial system in the prevention and control of substance abuse, as well as a community-wide drug education effort and other strategies.

5. *Child Care:* to provide specific efforts designed to address the special needs of at-risk children, including teenaged parents. strategies include a program to involve at-risk parents and children, helping to develop area-wide daycare centers, a transportation program for children and parents, specific infant and toddler programs, and programs for before and after school care for children.

6. *Recreation Needs:* to provide a program that will enhance and upgrade the recreational facilities and activities of the county, including artistic and cultural activities. The plan calls for this objective to be met by increasing the number of recreational programs and participants in the county. Moreover, the needs of disabled and handicapped residents—both youth and adults—will be addressed by new programs, along with the development of "new trails for hiking, horse back riding, biking and ORVs to be used by residents and tourists."

7. *School to Work:* to use training and educational services to help make local residents less dependent on social services; to help make them more productive and self-reliant citizens as they move from school to the workplace. By using post–high school vocational programs for youths and adults, reducing the dropout rate, upgrading the curriculum, and other programs, they hope to impact their "school to work" objective.

8. *Family Support Services:* to provide the necessary services to troubled families and individuals so that the social cost will ultimately be reduced. Family counseling and services to abused spouses and their children, a male-oriented self-sufficiency program, and an adult literacy program, along with transportation to and from the workplace, are among those strategies they hope to use successfully in the "family support services" objective.

9. *Transportation:* to provide a transportation system that meets the needs of the citizens of Lake County. Upgrading facilities and services at the

airport, expanding the current public transportation system, and helping to finance low-wage earners in the purchase of their own transportation are some of the strategies formulated to help achieve the transportation objective.

c. *Housing Goal's Objectives*

1. *Existing Housing/Rehabilitation/Demolition:* to make sure that the county has an adequate supply of sound housing by demolishing dilapidated structures, rehabilitating existing others, and building new ones. Dealing with substandard housing and providing low-income families an opportunity to obtain a low-interest loan or grant in order to purchase their own homes or repair their existing residences are among the strategies articulated to deal with the housing goal.

2. *New Housing Opportunities:* to provide low-interest loan programs for the low-income home owners who need to repair and/or upgrade their homes, dry wells, or septic systems. Programs to develop public housing and add to the existing senior housing are two of the strategies to be used in obtaining the housing objectives in Lake County.

3. *Accessibility, Affordability (Elderly and Families):* to especially target the elderly and families regarding housing opportunities that are both accessible and affordable. Strategies here will include those that will give relief to residents on limited incomes and promote single-family home ownership and affordable moderate-income housing.

4. *Community Facilities:* to provide residents with adequate community facilities for ambulance and other services. Ambulance service and the modification of the courthouse to make it barrier free will be among the efforts to enhance existing community facilities in the county.

A COMPREHENSIVE COMPANION PLAN
FOR IDLEWILD: SOME SALIENT SUGGESTIONS

Before providing any suggestions for a comprehensive plan for Idlewild, it is first necessary to provide a caveat about comprehensive plans in general. Too frequently, initiatives and programs cloaked in the language of comprehensive planning are used to perpetuate inequality or merely to placate the angry while maintaining the status quo. There is ample evidence that many so-called comprehensive plans are never implemented either in part or in toto. Hence, so-called comprehensive plans can generate much skepticism, disappointment, despair, and frustration, especially among people in economically depressed areas who are tired of "unfulfilled promises." With that caveat out front, efforts put into forging the companion plan for Idlewild should contain sufficient safeguards against the plan gathering shelf dust.

With the matter of definitional clarity behind them, those hammering out the companion piece should accept as their first task the issue of what revitalization means for the Idlewild community. When and how will one know that the community has been revitalized? How will progress toward revitalization be measured? What criteria will be used in the evaluation of progress?

As one might suspect, the formulation of a companion plan for Idlewild falls outside the scope of this volume. In keeping with the intent of the Enterprise Zone initiative, this exciting task correctly falls to the residents themselves and their leaders. In the Enterprise Zone initiative, local residents themselves participated in producing the strategic plans for the several areas that were later designated Enterprise Communities or Enterprise Zones. Thus, the district of Idlewild needs to do this work, and it should be done under the leadership of the recently created Coalition of Concerned Citizens of Idlewild. The following discussion should make it imminently clear why this entity is the organization best fitted for crafting the companion plan.

The *Coalition of Concerned Citizens of Idlewild* (CCCI), a recently formed and incorporated group, has expressed an interest in preparing Idlewild for the new millennium. A review of its nature and scope reveals that this organization is very much in agreement with what is found in "The Plan" of Lake County. Therefore, it is the most logical candidate to accomplish the task of creating a companion plan for Idlewild. Specifically, according to the incorporation papers of the Coalition of Concerned Citizens of Idlewild, the group's purpose is:

> To assist in the revitalization of Idlewild by proposing and initiating appropriate programs and initiatives; also by working collaboratively with other public and private organizations and agencies for the community. To achieve this purpose, a group of dedicated and concerned citizens will be organized for the purpose of

reversing the stagnation of Idlewild, a rural community in Michigan. Specifically, through a grass-roots involvement, the Coalition—a not-for-profit corporation—will endeavor:

1. to ensure that neighborhood associations and grass-root organizations have a greater voice in the decision-making and planning process of the local government.

2. to encourage what is called "deliberative democracy" by helping public officials to involve the community at the earliest stages of any important planning process.

3. to encourage associations and organizations to include the clergy more in their community revitalization efforts.

4. to position the Coalition to be the "umbrella organization" that is dedicated to work toward the amelioration of existing community problems in the areas of education, housing, employment, mobility, recreation, tourism, safety, crime, environment, and others.

5. to enhance the future prospects of our youth and other citizens.

6. to assist in providing a healthy and safe environment for our senior citizens.

Objective number four (immediately above) stipulates that the coalition wants to be the "umbrella organization" dedicated to improving conditions in the areas of education, housing, employment, mobility, recreation, tourism, safety, crime, and so forth. These concerns are virtually identical to those found in "The Plan" for the county, which means that it could be a useful template in helping the coalition identify specific goals, objectives, strategies, responsible parties (partnerships), and possible funding sources. Moreover, as the "umbrella organization," the CCCI would be expected to work with local public boards and commissions, neighborhood associations, and churches. Needless to say, the involvement and collaboration of the CCCI with the Yates Township Board—its township supervisor, treasurer, clerk, and two trustees —are tremendously vital to any proposed deliberations of plans for Idlewild.

This grassroots group appears to include key individuals who possess the skills, intellect, experience, and motivation necessary to put together a comprehensive companion plan for Idlewild, and in the process chart a direction that will take it to a new and dynamic level as a resort community. Already, in an effort to make CCCI a true grassroots initiative, an officer of the coalition has designed a questionnaire so that residents can began to participate by first identifying their most pressing community concerns, such as the importance of police in Baldwin, children's playgrounds, tutorials, after-school activities, jobs, senior citizens' concerns, housing, and so forth. The data from such a questionnaire should be useful to the leadership and members of the coalition as they become the catalyst for planning and community development.

SOCIOLOGICAL ILLUMINATIONS

Meticulous grassroots planning and aggressive activism by civic leaders have produced some outstanding results in some of the most depressed areas in the country. Paradise at Parkside, in the nation's capital, is one such successful scenario. Though variously described as a "murderous, filthy, broken down slum," by the national media, dedicated community leaders rolled up their sleeves and turned that area of Washington, D.C., into a safe and livable environment.

Another promising story is told by Michael H. Shuman, whose comments about pooling resources are especially pertinent for the revitalization of Idlewild. He asserts that:

> The value of neighbors pooling resources and extending one another modest levels of credit has been established again and again in certain religious and ethnic groups. One reason Jewish and Korean communities, for example, have fared relatively well is because of their well-established traditions to pool resources and extend credit to those within the community. In Santa Ana, California, the Civic Center Barrio Corporation has consolidated the resources of Latino families and renters displaced by municipal development to help them finance the purchase or upgrade of more than 1,200 apartments.[20]

An example of a successful venture in a rural community is found in Greenboro, Alabama, where

> This cooperative grew out of the efforts of two committed local residents (former school teachers) with the assistance of a Northeastern garment manufacturer. It

began as a sewing group composed of local African-American women who came together to make and mend clothes for children. It has grown into a sewing cooperative which has provided skills and jobs for more than 3,000 African-American women. . . . The Alabama Council on Human Relations and the Presbyterian Church provided operating capital and the L. V. Myers Company of New York City provided commercial sewing machines, patterns, materials, and negotiated contracts for products. . . . This Cooperative is also exemplary of the economic development projects we support for small black towns. As a Cooperative, it does not need to show a profit. Indeed, profits are reinvested in the Cooperative to expand its productive efficiency. This approach emphasizes humanistic goals rather than purely economic goals. We believe that this type of development affirms and strengthens the communalistic economic practices characteristic of black communities and towns. . . . In short, this organization represents one of the models of economic development we believe to be best for the black communities and small towns.[21]

In the three examples—Washington, D.C., California, and Alabama—it seems that success was achieved because of the grassroots involvement of people who were willing to dedicate their time, energy, intellect, and other resources to a partnership with nonprofit and profit organizations and agencies. The key to community success is planning. Accordingly, if Idlewild is to become a vibrant, rejuvenated rural community, it too must have a dynamic plan created by its people. If the plan is not solely created by the residents themselves, they must at least be encouraged to participate as full partners throughout the planning phase.

Parenthetically, grassroots involvement could very well be in the form of volunteerism, which is currently touted as an important social movement throughout the United States. General Colin Powell, one of its chief advocates, implores all Americans to step up to the plate and do their part in improving the quality of life for everyone. He has said, "Citizen service belongs to no party, no ideology, it is an American idea, which every American should embrace."[22] A careful analysis of this movement points to the salient fact that volunteerism is a way for local citizens to both have their voices heard and contribute dramatically to the revitalization or transformation of their communities.

On the other hand, volunteerism seems to work best when there is at least one paid worker who is accountable to an advisory board (in this case, the *Coalition of Concerned Citizens of Idlewild*). Moreover, the paid worker should be a private citizen, not connected with any governmental unit, and have a proven record of working successfully with a diversity of individuals and groups in bringing closure in a timely manner on important goals and objectives.

Community foundations might be an excellent source from which to seek funding for one or two paid economic development positions, which should be formulated as an integral part of a larger community initiative. In this instance, the revitalization of Idlewild could be the type of effort that one or more community foundations would view as an excellent investment of their donors' dollars. Perhaps the Kellogg Foundation in Battle Creek, Michigan, for example, could be approached to participate in such an initiative as part of its leadership training program. At any rate, without a master plan, the future of Idlewild as a community—whether it is seen as a resort, a retirement village, or something else—will continue to be uncertain. Without such a plan, it is difficult to see how the community can take advantage of the enormous potential already existing in the FiveCAP organization, or the role that FiveCAP and other organizations can play in positioning Idlewild for a bright and shiny future.

An Epilogue for Idlewild

SUCCESS AND FAILURE

As a community, Idlewild did not become an overnight success; neither was it an overnight failure. In time, after many years of hard work, it became an enormously popular resort, especially for African Americans in the Midwest who were unwelcome at white resorts in the North and legally restricted from attending white establishments in the South. Tired of racism in their everyday lives, these men and women and their children looked forward to spending their summer vacation at the black resort, isolated in a rural area that was at first completely devoid of motels, grocery stores, restaurants, barbershops, beauty salons, and other amenities commonly associated with resorts. These voids were gradually filled by business entrepreneurs who moved in and satisfied the desires of the vacationers for food, shelter, entertainment, and leisure. This symbiotic relationship help formed the foundation for a strong economic base in the community.

Though the community had many exciting and joyous years, many felt the area never reached its maximum potential as a crown-jewel resort in Michigan before it had to compete with the area's white resorts. An inablilty to maintain overflowing vacationing crowds, who turned more and more to white establishments after the onset of integration, was an unplanned result of the civil rights era that eroded the economic structure of the community. In addition, when famed black entertainers eagerly accepted opportunities to perform in the white world, Idlewild's ability to hold on to its African American customers was further diminished. In time, these challenges appeared to place insurmountable difficulties in the path of the resort as it moved closer and closer toward becoming a rural ghost town.

For more than a decade, efforts to reposition Idlewild have not been outstanding or distinguished successes. These efforts, however, have served as a source of encouragement and have attracted the attention of others who might become involved in the revitalization process. Many have come to question whether revitalization is achievable without a comprehensive master plan and the necessary human and financial resources. In the minds of some individuals the answer is a resounding "yes." They readily acknowledge that a master plan is desirable, but think much progress can be accomplished even without such a plan.

As a rural community in need of reflation, Idlewild must simultaneously emphasize its unique characteristics while maximizing efforts to mobilize its resources. In this regard, Kim Fendley and James A. Christenson are particularly instructive. They maintain that

> Rural reflation is a term for a small-scale socioeconomic approach to building livable economies in both depressed rural communities and rapid growth areas. Rural areas cannot become mini-metros, but decision-makers can work to reflate their economies through the manipulation of resources and people, and particularly through maximizing the characteristics of their localities. With public participation, informed leadership, and organizational entrepreneurship, leaders can help citizens develop their community's niche in the world economy.[1]

Following the advice of Fendley and Christenson, this epilogue examines some initiatives that leaders and residents in Idlewild could launch independently of, but later incorporate into, an overall master plan. Too frequently momentum is lost when initiatives are postponed or canceled while a plan is hammered out. For that very reason, individuals, groups, or organizations interested in the reflation or revitalization of Idlewild should be encouraged to aggressively pursue any initiative that would enhance the vibrancy of the community.

ENTERTAINMENT AND LEISURE-ORIENTED BUSINESSES

Not everyone is optimistic that Idlewild can recapture the past. To many, it seems like an impossible mission. What might be possible, however, is for the community to shift its focus from a vacation destination for African American families to a summer music camp devoted to the teaching and training of promising young African American talents in those music forms that are deeply rooted in the Black Experience. This model would combine an image based upon the New York School of Performance Arts as popularized in the TV program *Fame* with one based on the longstanding tradition of a more classically focused music summer camp, such as the one at Interlochen, just south of Traverse City, Michigan.

If the music camp idea was successful and a venue built for student performance, a summer concert series similar to the very successful one offered by Interlochen would be possible. Interlochen offers an exceptional series of music and dance, from classical to pop to country and everything in between, for students, parents and the surrounding communities. Even on a small scale, this would be an excellent avenue by which to invite the white community back to Idlewild, not for a "good old days nostalgia ride" but for a new, fresh look at a successful black community in transition.

The directors of such an enterprise might also look at the Interlochen and Blue Lake radio facilities. Although these two successful enterprises offer Public Radio, Idlewild might consider an FM radio station that offers a programming mix not currently available to the immediate surroundings, such as jazz and rhythm and blues.

There are a number of promising factors associated with this possibility. First, and probably most important, is the possibility of developing a financial foundation through grants and tuition. An examination of how Interlochen finances its programs might be extremely helpful in this regard. A second point touches on the question of how to make a rural setting— which was more attractive to previous generations than present ones, who favor the comforts of Holiday Inns—a viable option. The answer may rest in shifting the focus from adults who bought their shares in Idlewild as a sum-mer vacation destination in the bygone years to talented youth in the manner that has been so successful at Interlochen. (One gets the impression that the rural setting and accommodations have helped make Interlochen a special experience for many youngsters who have attended the camp. Moreover, par-ents who come to see the performances seem to also find the rural setting special.) Furthermore, parents coming to see performances and preferring modern motels would be an economic stimulus for the area. Third, Idlewild could attract top-level professional performers who could give concerts and workshops for the youngsters, parents, and others from the surrounding areas. African American music instructors could be recruited from schools in Chicago, Detroit, Flint, Grand Rapids, and elsewhere. Providing accommo-dations for these musicians and their families (even in small cottages) would provide a big draw, and perhaps could even be considered as a part of the compensation for their contributions. These instructors could also serve as a recruiting base for talented kids in their areas.

While this concept shifts the focus of the resort away from its original basis—a showcase for black performing musical talents—it does preserve the musical tradition that came to define the resort's distinctive nature. It also will allow the community to refocus on a musical tradition that helped to make Idlewild one of the most popular performance venues in Michigan, if not the nation. Once this concept has been implemented and has achieved a modicum of success, then it might be feasible to refocus on the idea of Idlewild as a resort community providing entertainment and leisure-oriented pursuits. Under such conditions the community could possibly again be a successful resort venue. This assertion is based on several observations, namely: (1) as the country moves further into the twenty-first century, people will increasingly devote more of their money and time to leisure-time activi-ties, especially those in the senior citizen categories; (2) a significant number of jobs consequently can be created in the leisure-oriented business, thus pro-viding jobs for residents of the community, both young and old alike; (3) thus, the community has the outstanding potential to become a crown jewel in the entertainment and leisure-oriented businesses (Branson, Missouri, is an excellent example); and (4), accordingly, a window of opportunity exists for Idlewild to return, at least in a measure, to its former glory days, when the area attracted many of the top names in the entertainment world. (If done right, they—entertainers and patrons—will come!)

In short, the proposed musical initiative, which involves talented young African Americans, is seen as a springboard for the implementation of other initiatives such as entertainment and leisure-oriented pursuits. The youth musical initiative could be implemented in tandem with the annual Poetry in the Woods Festival, an initiative already started and assisted by several long-time community residents. That notables such as Dick Gregory and the Last Poets have been willing to participate is an encouraging sign that the aspiration for it to become a national event is indeed an achievable goal. The extent that people will come from Nevada, California, New York, Ohio, Illinois, and other states on an annual basis will certainly be a testimonial to the fact that African Americans have fallen "in love again with the idea of having their own resort."

A Short-Term Alternative to Building New Motels and Restaurants

If young talents and their parents came to a music camp at Idlewild, however, at minimum they would need room and board accommodations. Given the state of affairs in the community at this writing, it might be unrealistic to think that entrepreneurs would risk money to build modern motels or hotels and restaurants based on an unproven concept. The lack of facilities to accommodate people who would come to watch the musical performances and hear the poets would be a major impediment to the success of those two initiatives. Consequently, though it might be unrealistic to think about new motels and restaurants immediately, a plan to provide adequate accommodations for the people must be considered, and it calls for cooperation, creativity, and innovation.

To this end, a short-term alternative would be to incorporate the notion of using existing privately owned cottages as accommodations for visitors until a sufficient number of modern motels and restaurants could be built and staffed. For this plan to work, there must be a sufficient number of property owners willing to open their cottages to the paying public. If these could be found, however, the currently available motel rooms plus a number of privately owned cottages could become part of a centralized and computerized accommodations system open to the general public on a paying basis. With a click of the mouse the customer could access information on the number of rooms available, and their locations, prices, and availability during specific months of the year. (In this connection, it should be remembered that Idlewild has some 841 vacant housing units that are being used seasonally, recreationally, or on an occasional basis. This means that approximately 75 percent of all housing is seasonal, or that these units are only occupied during the spring and summer vacation months. If a significant percentage of those units could become part of the proposed short-term accommodation system, then their owners would be able to make an immediate contribution to the revitalization efforts of the community.

Besides providing sleeping accommodations, it is possible that some of these cottages could also offer a breakfast, lunch, and dinner menu, which would essentially mean that those particular cottages would resemble a regular "bed and breakfast" operation.

The advantages of such a short-term accommodation system are obvious:

- It will increase the number of available rooms almost immediately.
- It will increase the number of potential paying jobs immediately for locals, even on a part-time basis.
- It will increase the involvement of a significant number of citizens in the revitalization process of the community.
- It will help to enhance the economic viability of the general community.
- It will create, on the one hand, a level of involvement that is possible even without a comprehensive plan. On the other hand, this is a program that could easily be incorporated into a future master plan for the community.

If this short-term alternative is successful, it could be responsible for the spawning of numerous other small businesses that are very much needed in the community. Success would speak volumes to the residents, allowing them to realize that they can indeed achieve greatness if they will only employ their

creative and innovative skills. Transforming the community would mean bringing Idlewild Lake up to par with other lakes in the county. With the approval
of the Department of Natural Resources, Idlewild Lake should be dredged and
restocked with fish. It would also mean providing a wonderful community that
has walking trails, tennis courts, and a strong lake association.

Empowerment: Making Use of Existing Resources

Even without a comprehensive companion plan, every effort should be made
by the different groups and eligible individuals to capitalize on the existing
economic opportunities offered by the FiveCAP/Lake County Plan. Since
Lake County is a federally designated Enterprise Community, which means
federal, state, and local dollars are available for many undertakings, opportunities do indeed exist for the citizens of the area to aggressively and dramatically inflate the economic picture of their community. Thus, the leaders of
Idlewild should be neither lax, negligent, nor inattentive in the face of these
empowering opportunities.

Just as the EC initiatives have enabled Idlewild to begin to solve some of
its major infrastructural problems, these initiatives can also help—through
the "revolving loan program"—to effectively restore the economic stability of
the community by increasing the number of businesses and jobs with living
wages and benefits. (Again, EC's five loan programs are designed to assist and
encourage low-equity residents wanting to enhance their economic condition
by "starting a new business, or by developing or expanding an existing one."
In short, through EC, the potential is there for creating a sustainable economic base in Idlewild.) To refresh the reader's memory, the five loan programs are:

1. *Micro Supplemental Income Loan Program* ($1,500 maximum loan) for
   low-income residents wanting to develop a secondary source (e.g.,
   part-time business) of income to supplement their primary wages.
2. *Macro Self-Employment Loan Program* ($1,000 to $10,000 loan) for residents interested in establishing a primary business that will support
   the owner and his or her family.

3. *Small Business Loan Program* ($40,000 maximum loan) for those wanting to establish a business that will consist of the owner plus four or more employees.

4. *Direct Loan Participation Program* (DLP) (a 40% FiveCAP, 50% lending institution, 10% applicant formula) for those involved in a low-equity business who wish to have FiveCAP become directly involved with them and a conventional lending institution regarding a loan package.

5. *Intermediary Relending Program* (IRP) (maximum is 75% of total up to $150,000) for those unable to secure a conventional business loan. "The focus of the IRP is to assist in the development of retail and other commercial establishments and assist in the creation of new small businesses or in the expansion of existing businesses."[2]

As noted elsewhere in this volume, the immediate community has only one small motel, a bar and grill, two takeout stores, and a club house. Because there are so few businesses, only a negligible number of job opportunities can be offered to the residents. Furthermore, all businesses do not operate on a year-round basis. A resident desiring to put gasoline in the car must leave the community and travel several miles to the nearest gas station. The same is true if one intends to do any serious shopping for groceries, household furniture, or even hardware items. If a small appliance falls into disrepair, again the resident must travel outside the community to find a replacement. Though Idlewild has several lakes (including Tank Lake, Idlewild Lake, Paradise Lake, and Watermelon Lake), there are no bait shops or places that offer fishing equipment.

The community needs a year-round filling station, a single grocery store, a small-engine repair shop, a hardware store, and a bait shop, and there appear to be resources available to put them in place in rather quick order. If the Community Enterprise's revolving loan programs are genuine in the expressed purpose of helping to create a sustainable economic base in the county, of which Idlewild is a part, then we must wonder why those and other businesses are not open and operating in Idlewild. Does the answer to this question reside in the fact that few, if any, residents are interested in the loan programs? Who have applied for loans? For what purposes? What were the results of these applications?

To read or hear so much talk about the revitalization of Idlewild and yet see so little evidence of an aggressive move to take advantage of the dollars that could be made available through the revolving programs raises the simple question: Why not? On the one hand, could it be that these programs are not well publicized, and hence the people in Idlewild are unfamiliar with them? On the other hand, could there be little interest on the part of the residents in pursuing these opportunities despite the fact that they have been well publicized? Could it be a combination of factors? These are empirical questions, yet their answers are vital to anyone who professes to have an interest in transforming the Idlewild community.

Answers to these questions cannot be ignored if the community is serious about dealing with its widespread problems, and particularly with poverty. This situation can be ameliorated most directly and immediately by the creation of jobs and the expansion of tourism. To reduce the poverty level, enough small businesses must be created to offer a sufficient number of jobs paying a living wage. Simultaneously, local residents must be motivated to accept the jobs with a willingness to be trained, if necessary, in order to do them effectively. If this cannot be accomplished, workers will have to be imported from the outside, which will still be another challenge to the community, and probably will mean that these developments will not have the desired effect on the poverty level in the community.

Those who maintain that important initiatives can be achieved without a master plan could very well be correct. They should be encouraged to pursue any and all initiatives that have the potential of revitalizing the community, yet these initiatives should be implemented in a reasonable and logical manner. It only makes sense that certain things should take precedent over others, which suggests a need for the movers and shakers to come together to share their ideas and come to some agreement about priorities. Prioritizing initiatives does not mean that one has to abandon or postpone personal or private projects while waiting for a comprehensive or master plan to be hammered out. It does mean, however, that serious attention will have to be given to answering the questions which have been posed here.

Prioritizing those initiatives needed to transform the community will not be an easy task. Neither will it be easy for the leaders and grassroots organizations to build the necessary bridges to form strong coalitions based on a consensual model. The degree to which they are able to do this will indicate their level of commitment to helping Idlewild achieve a stronger measure of power parity in comparison to the more favorable rural—and even urban— communities in the state. This situation will force a recognition that the existing fractious relationships, as they relate to process, positions, perceptions, and problems, are largely responsible for many of the disconnects and incompatible orientations espoused about the status and direction of Idlewild. Who is needed to do what, when, where, and why will also be clearer as a result of this process.

Finally, on the one hand, there is certainly some pessimism. Many people are rather cynical about their community's future prospects. They are distrustful and think the intragroup cleavages have damaged the morale and dampened the spirit necessary to fight a courageous battle at this time. Consequently, they are doubtful there are enough people who are willing to work honestly and fairly on behalf of the general community. There are individuals who are not above allowing their egos to supercede the needs and aspirations of the community. Hence "the tribe" continues to suffer. These people are also critical of those who are nostalgic about the place, in that, while sentimentally gratifying, nostalgia offers no assurance that economic revitalization will occur. To the critics, there appears to be a preponderance of words, based on nostalgic expressions, but a paucity of actions and dollars. Consequently, they feel that if this situation continues to persist then Idlewild runs the risk of remaining an economically depressed rural community. On the other hand, however, there continues to be a sense of optimism among both residents and nonresidents alike as Idlewild enters the new millennium. Some residents think that great strides will be made because they sense a greater collaboration in the future between the private sector (developers, business entrepreneurs, and philanthropic organizations, among others) and the public sector (including the local, county, state, and federal governments) with respect to working hand-in-glove with the residents to transform their community.

A Composite Summary
of Sociological Illuminations

It is not known exactly why a small group of white men would take out a loan to purchase a large tract of land and dedicate it as a black resort in Michigan. Undoubtedly, economic profit was among their motives but they could have achieved that by selling to their fellow white citizens. Not unlike the Quakers who conscientiously risked their lives on behalf of blacks, it seems that this group of white entrepreneurs was motivated to help blacks help themselves by initiating a resort for blacks in a segregated society.

The establishment of the resort occurred at a time when blacks were celebrating racial progress in cities with a sizable African American population. In keeping with that general thrust, Idlewild was promoted as the place where one could interact with the "best" in the black race. In time, Idlewild became an example of what black people could accomplish, once given an opportunity. To be part of a development that offered relaxation away from the daily grind and racial bigotry, and also participate in discussions about the affairs of the race, was meaningful to many blacks who purchased lots in Idlewild.

The white entrepeneurs formed the Idlewild Resort Company and the Idlewild Summer Resort Development Company, which rather quickly formulated a marketing strategy that proved to be very successful. The resort aggressively sought out black salespersons, who sold parcels of land to black people in a manner that most people could afford to buy. The association of the resort with racial pride was either a stroke of genius or a fortuitous occurrence because it turned out to be a major reason for the resort's initial success. With the sale of each lot the resort movement increased both in size and momentum. In essence, Idlewild became more than a resort; it was part of a movement of racial pride and development that was also evident elsewhere in the nation, especially in such places as Harlem, Chicago, and Detroit.

Sociologically, a segregated social system usually reserves participation in the social institutions of the larger society as the exclusive rights of the majority group members. Therefore, since they cannot participate, minority group members are left to their own devices to form whatever social arrangements they can in order to survive. At the same time, they are forced to adjust their behavioral patterns to conform to the decrees and dictates imposed by the segregated society.

Established in a state where segregation was a widespread practice, Idlewild had the arduous task of putting together social and economic infrastructures to meet its own special internal needs. Besides adjusting to the dictates of a segregated environment, the resort also had to adjust to internal changes that occurred as a result of its popularity. Specifically, as Idlewild's popularity increased so did its diversity, as reflected in the different waves of black people who frequented the resort, and in the social cleavages that sparked intraracial strife from time to time. This meant that the resort was no longer a homogeneous community of the black bourgeoisie or the black upper class. Though they came from dissimilar backgrounds, a sense of historical identification was the social glue that held Idlewild's black vacationers together in a community of peoplehood which resulted from being an African American in America.

Because of segregation, minority musical artists were not allowed to showcase their talents in the general society. They were forced to perform only within their own communities. Accordingly, Idlewild became a stop on the "Chitlin Circuit" where black performers could showcase their musical, comedic, or dancing abilities. Because of the social divisions among the black vacationers, some expressed a preference for a more sophisticated type of entertainment, while others had a penchant for the more "down home" type of music. Regardless of the type of entertainment, however, the "Chitlin Circuit" was very demanding for the performers, who often found it difficult to make ends meet, economically. Idlewild, as a popular resort, proved to be better than many of the stops on the circuit, as many of the performers there were better paid, and there was usually a special place available for entertainers to stay while in the community. In short, because black talents knew that they would not be accepted in the general society, Idlewild became a place where they could enjoy themselves as well as showcase their talents.

After suffering many generations of indignities and adversity as a result of segregation and discrimination, many African Americans were most eager to play a role in the elimination of these systems. Yet their elimination brought on some very unfavorable changes in Idlewild. A complete explanation for the eventual erosion of the economic vibrancy of the community can be found only in the convergence of a plethora of factors. Among them are: (a) the unpreparedness of Idlewild to compete with other institutions once segregation was legally abolished; (b) the lack of economic diversity in the community necesssary to build strong social institutions that operated on a year-round basis; and (c) the lack of vision and leadership needed to prepare and train young people to operate small family businesses. It is true, however, that many African Americans who vacationed at Idlewild did not return on a regular basis, once they started going to white resorts, and this definitely was a factor in the resort's demise.

Socioeconomically, Idlewild started to languish in the late 1960s, and this trend continued for the next three decades. During that time, race and ethnic relations changed dramatically throughout the United States and the world in general. Idlewild was not an exception, but the changes that occurred in the country had an especially devastating effect on the total character of that community. Problems of poverty, unemployment, welfare dependency, crime and violence, drugs, and joblessness began to manifest themselves as small businesses closed their doors and fewer and fewer vacationers came into the community each summer.

Many hold the view that unless Idlewild can be revitalized or transformed in a substantial manner in the very near future, it runs the risk of becoming a "client community." This is a community where residents are dependent on the welfare agencies and governmental programs for food, clothing, and shelter. Additionally, it is an environment where residents are more nearly powerless to affect their lives and that of their community; lethargy then finds its way into that segment of society. Thus, it is imperative that leaders begin to aggressively formulate and implement those social policies, programs, and activities that have a good chance of transforming the community and thus keeping it alive.

During the last decade, an interest in the renewal of Idlewild has been expressed by many individuals and organizations. However, with the exception of initiatives associated with FiveCAP, it does not appear that either the individuals or the organizations currently active in the community have the necessary wherewithal to affect a revitalization process that would make a difference. By this observation, however, we do not mean to denigrate any efforts being pursued or sponsored by an individual or any of the existing organizations. However, this observation is made in light of the fact that, to date, there is little empirical evidence to suggest that revitalization is going forward in any vigorous manner. If there are individuals or organizations with substantial means, then there are some serious disconnects because important initiatives are not being implemented in a timely manner.

In sum, given its current status, it is apparent that Idlewild's civic and political leaders have an enormous challenge before them. They are faced with putting together a comprehensive (companion) plan and the necessary resources to implement that plan if they are to genuinely address the issues of revitalization. In the process, they would be wise to include the activities and efforts of the numerous existing community organizations. Members of these organizations could form the grassroots component so necessary in any meticulous plan to transform an economically depressed community that is screaming to be reflated.

Conclusion

Since Idlewild has survived for more than eighty-eight years, its current dilemma is not so much a matter of survival as it is a matter of quality and content of its existence. Accordingly, interested people, both resident and nonresident, do not have to sit in the window and watch Idlewild march by; they can play an influential role in helping to determine not only the tune to which it will march but also its speed and direction. The resort came into existence because of an extraordinary act of kindness by a rare group of white men who set themselves apart from the more insensitive and hateful white racists. It became a safe haven for black men and women and their children, many of whom could voice a sad and hurtful story of hardship, degradation, and inordinate suffering because of their skin color. Currently, it is at a stage in its existence where another extraordinary act is needed: a coalescing of disparate community groups and individuals to bring about a renaissance in the community. That act should include finding the funds to hire a renaissance man or woman in the person of an economic developer who is knowledgeable about financial, market, product, people, and resource strategies. This economic developer must also possess the requisite skills and experience to work collaboratively in a partnership with FiveCAP/EC and other organizations, using government funds and contributions from businesses, corporations, and individuals, to plan and implement those initiatives that would dramatically change the community.

Regarding partnering with other organizations, FiveCAP/EC should be acknowledged as already in a position to play a major role in the resurgency of Idlewild because of its resources and resourcefulness. According to Mary Trucks, chief administrator of the county's strategic plan, virtually all of the Enterprise Community's funds were from federal sources in the calendar year 2000. They were in excess of $100 million at this time, a substantial sum that did not include any private investments, which have been very extensive in comparison to the past years. She further revealed that, in Lake County, speculator activities have been extensive, there has been an increase in home ownership, and there has been an increase in business start-ups. In Lake County more businesses have been opened than closed, a reversal of the pattern of recent years.[3]

As one who has insights into the problems and affairs of the county, Ms. Trucks is optimistic about the future of Idlewild. She is keenly aware of the significance of the Enterprise Community designation and the fact that Lake County is the fastest growing county in Michigan, in spite of its pervasive poverty. Her optimism is based on several important developments and observations, specifically:

- The fact that there are more new, year-round jobs in the county.
- The fact that the economic boom in the state is no longer passing over the county. She thinks that "More and more citizens are participating in the blessings experienced by the rest of the state."
- A grant for $87,000 has been secured, which will go to install fiber optics in the Robert F. Williams Center and the Family Health Care facility. This initiative will enable the citizens in the community to take advantage of modern communication technology.
- Installation of natural gas lines at a cost of a half-million dollars was another project that was paid for in whole by the Enterprise Community. Trucks said, "The project did not cost the residents one dime."
- Another grant for $200,000 has been secured for a sewage project. The FiveCAP agency was able to access resources that the government

could not get because the funds were available only to a private non-profit agency. These funds have enabled FiveCAP to give grants to eligible citizens to help defray the costs of connecting to the sewage lines.

- The bank in the area has grown significantly, granting more mortgages.
- Yates Township is viewed by many as a progressive township because it has a part-time officer assigned by the Lake County Sheriff Department.[4]

Ms. Trucks views FiveCAP/EC as a catalyst to help Idlewild, not to turn back the clock but to make Idlewild fit into today's world. She feels that diversity is a good thing and that everyone need not agree as long as everyone is going in the same direction. Accordingly, she thinks more people are going in the same direction today. As a catalyst, FiveCAP/EC can play a vital role in the revitalization of Idlewild, given its organization, its expertise, and its resources. In her words, "Idlewild can go no way but up; it has hit the bottom." She further states, "I think, as a vital community, Idlewild has a future but not in rejoicing and building on its history, not to relive the history, but in bringing it more into the future. Because progress has left it behind. For those who want to 'keep it rustic' . . . [it] does not meet the needs of the residents of today." Trucks, however, is not oblivious to the fact that Yates Township (Idlewild) once had (between 1960 and 1980) twenty-eight commercial establishments, two industrial establishments, twenty-one motels, and two gas and repair stations. Today, one cannot buy a gallon of gas in Yates Township. The area needs a gas station, a convenience store, and a tourist designation. Moreover, there is a need for low-income affordable housing that has access to utilities such as gas and sewage. There is some concern whether Lincoln Park—an area that covers twelve acres, 50 percent of which is natural habitat—should remain a rustic park area or be used as a housing development on U.S. 10. This is the only large parcel of land where multifamily housing could be constructed to meet the needs of the residents. At this writing, according to Trucks, FiveCAP is working to use that land for the greater good of the residents, in the form of housing.[5]

With its many outstanding attributes (including several lakes, scenic beauty, natural gas lines, sewage system, undeveloped land, and others), Idlewild has the enormous potential to once again become an energized, dynamic, and vibrant rural community. For that to happen, however, an economic developer, in addition to fund-raising, will have to assume the chief role in helping Idlewild—the paramount character in this volume—decide on the shape of its future, whether as a thriving retirement community, a designated resort area, or some combination of these and more.

In sum, nostalgia aside, it is unrealistic to think that historical circumstances can be duplicated and Idlewild can be returned to its former self. Its history should never be forgotten, but it should be used as a building block for renewal, growth, transformation, creativity, and future development. Used in that manner, the past will help contemporary leaders position Idlewild to forever be an essential and valuable segment in the rich black heritage of Michigan, capable of reclaiming and sustaining its place in the sun.

Appendices

APPENDIX 1: *Sample Coupons*

Chicago . . . . . . 19 . . . .

Gentlemen:

Kindly reserve for me a lot in Idlewild, Lake County, Michigan, for which I promise to pay $35.00. Herewith $6.00 and the Balance in sums of $1.00 each week hereafter until the full amount of $35.00 is paid. NO INTEREST on DEFERRED PAYMENTS. It is understood that a deed for this lot shall be issued to me when I have made all payments agreed above; also an abstract showing a good, Merchantable title.

Signature . . . .

Address . . . .

Apt . . . .

Chicago . . . . . . 19 . . . .

Gentlemen:

Kindly reserve for me two lots in Idlewild, Lake County, Michigan, for which I promise to pay $75.00. Herewith $6.00 and the Balance in sums of $1.00 each week hereafter until the full amount of $75.00 is paid. NO INTEREST on DEFERRED PAYMENTS. It is understood that a deed for this lot shall be issued to me when I have made all payments agreed above; also an abstract showing a good, Merchantable title.

Signature . . . .

Address . . . .

Apt . . . .

APPENDIX 2: *Scott's Letter of Endorsement*

Gentlemen:

In 1917 I purchased two lots in Idlewild, sight unseen, upon the recommendation of a friend. My impression of Idlewild is expressed forcibly in the Latin phrase "Resnon Verbis." My wife and I spent four of the most delightful and pleasurable weeks of our lives in August 1918 in . . . Idlewild. So pleased were we that upon our return to Cleveland we purchased four more lots and will erect a cottage next year. We intend to spend our 1919 and all subsequent summer vacations in dear old Idlewild. It is unsurpassed as an ideal spot for an enjoyable, recuperative vacation and is just the place to put a professional man on edge after eleven months of nerve-racking duties. "Idlewild must be seen to be appreciated."

Yours very truly,

Dr. Arthur S. Scott
Dentist

3404 Central Avenue
Chicago, Illinois

APPENDIX 3: *Curry's Letter of Endorsement*

January 21, 1919

To all Lovers of Our Race:

I am glad to speak a good word for the Idlewild Resort Company. It is my duty to inform my friends of any good project that I believe will help this race to higher things. I have made a long study of the Idlewild movement and have been convinced that it is worthy of our support. It is a good, safe investment. Idlewild, in Michigan, will, in a few years, be the center of attraction for our educational, fraternal, business and religious meetings in the summer. I have purchased lots in Idlewild and will secure more this Spring. The Curry Institute is planning a Summer Normal for Teachers to be conducted there. The place is ideal in every way and I shall do all I can for the advisement of the Work.

Yours for humanity,

E. W. B. Curry
President
Curry Normal and Industrial Institute

APPENDIX 4: *Some Early Pioneers in Idlewild*

Mr. & Mrs. Oscar Baker (esq.)	Mrs. Nina B. Hill
Mr. & Mrs. Cyril Barrett	Mrs. Willa D. Hudson
Mr. & Mrs. Charles Berry (esq.)	Mrs. Joan Hunt
The Rev. & Mrs. Bradby & family	Mrs. Sarah Jackson
Rev. & Mrs. H. Franklin Bray	Mrs. Laura Johnson
Dr. & Mrs. Browning	Mr. & Mrs. Jessie W. Johnson
Mrs. Buckles	Mrs. Edith Lautier
Mrs. Laura Cannon	Mrs. Minnie Lawnes
Mrs. Evelyn Casey	Mr. & Mrs. Merchant
Mr. & Mrs. Julian Chipchase	Mrs. & Mrs. Dan Raine
Mrs. Clanton	Mrs. Beulah Riddle
Mrs. Bernice Clayton	Mr. & Mrs. Oscar Ridley
Mrs. Mary E. Cox	Mr. & Mrs. Rober Riffe
Mrs. L. A. Davidson	Mrs. Cora Riley
Mrs. Mary Ellis	Mr. & Mrs. Charles Roxborough
Mr. & Mrs. Elsner	Mr. & Mrs. John Simmons
Mrs. Mary Frazier	Mr. & Mrs. A. K. Simpson
Mr. & Mrs. Charles Gaines	The "Stucco" Smiths
Mr. & Mrs. Charlie Gass	Mr. & Mrs. Smith*
Mrs. Ivy Grace	Dr. & Mrs. Thomas
Mr. & Mrs. Gregory	Mrs. Eugenia Vaughn
Mrs. Priscilla Grey	Mrs. Sarah Washington
Mrs. Myrtle Hamilton	Mr. & Mrs. Herman & Lela Wilson
Mr. & Mrs. Buster Henderson	Mr. & Mrs. Wyatt

* Mr. Smith was known as "Bix Six."

APPENDIX 5: *Purchase Agreement Letter*

Chicago . . . . . . 19 . . . .

Gentlemen:

Kindly reserve for me four lots in Idlewild, Lake County, Michigan, for which I promise to pay $140.00. Herewith $10.00 and the balance in sums of $1.50 each week hereafter until the full amount of $140.00 is paid. NO INTEREST ON DEFERRED PAYMENTS. It is understood that a deed for these lots shall be issued to me when I have made all payments agreed above; also an abstract showing a good, merchantable title.

Signature . . . .

Address . . . .

APPENDIX 6: *Sheet Music: "Idlewild"*

APPENDIX 7: *Sheet Music: "(Idlewild) Duett Chorus: Tango Dance"*

Notes

CHAPTER I

1. Rebecca E. Dinsmore, "Archaeological Perspective of the Lumber Industry in Northern Lower Michigan, 1865–1920" (Master's thesis, Western Michigan University, 1985), 1.

2. Lake County Historical Society, *Lake County: A Collection of Historical Writings* (MTM printing and graphics).

3. Rolland H. Maybee, *Michigan's White Pine Era, 1840–1900* (Lansing: Michigan History Division, Michigan Department of State, 1976), 0–29; Barbara E. Benson, *Logs and Lumber: The Development of the Lumber Industry in Michigan's Lower Peninsula, 1837–1870* (Mount Pleasant: Clarke Historical Library, Central Michigan University, 1989), 15–31; William G. Rector, *Log Transportation in the Lake States Lumber Industry, 1840–1918* (Glendale, Calif.: Arthur Clark Company, 1953), 281.

4. Richard Thomas, *The State of Black Detroit: Building from Strength* (Detroit: Detroit Urban League, 1987).

5. Leon Litwack, *Trouble in Mind: Black Southerners in the Age of Jim Crow* (New York: Vintage Books, 1998), 492–93.

6. Ibid.

7. Pehyun Wen, "Idlewild—A Negro Village in Lake County, Michigan" (Master's thesis, University of Chicago, 1972), 70–73. It was not unusual for unscrupulous speculators to dope the soil. They would simply mix cow manure into poor soil and then grow flowers in the area to convince buyers that the soil was fertile.

8. Audrey D. Strophpaul, article in the *Grand Rapids Press*, 15 October 1946, n.p.

9. Idlewild Resort Company paper. Drafted by a member (Fred) of the Branch extended

family and provided by John Meeks of Idlewild.

10. Nicole Christian, "Town Works to Revive Its Image as 'Black Eden,'" *New York Times*, 27 June 2000.

11. Ann Gregory Hawkins and Henry Gregory Jr. papers. "Founding of Idlewild," mimeographed article in vertical files under Idlewild, Michigan, Michigan History Division, Department of State, Lansing, Michigan.

12. "Idlewild Resort Company Articles of Agreement," vertical files, Archives for the State of Michigan, State of Michigan Library, Lansing, Michigan.

13. *Liber 77*, Lake County, Register of Deeds Office, 536, Carole Engelsman, clerk; for other similar descriptions see *Liber 60*, 164.

14. The Lincoln Jubilee was a gathering to commemorate fifty years of black progress in America. It usually occurred on the anniversary of the day that the Thirteenth Amendment to the Constitution was ratified.

15. With the passing of years, the Paradise Lake Resort, though it started as a separate entity, came to be thought of by many as a part of the original Idlewild. It is located roughly three miles from Idlewild Lake.

16. Frances Hill, "Her Middle Name is 'Spunk'–Meet Lela Wilson," *Negro Digest*, November 1963, 66–67.

17. *Liber 77*, Lake County, Michigan, 215.

18. Ibid.

19. Idlewild Chamber of Commerce, "Folder in the interest of Idlewild," n.d., p. 6.

20. *Idlewild Resort Company Brochure*, Chicago, circa 1917–1919, passim.

21. Ibid.

22. Madame C. J. Walker was an African American millionnairess in the early 1900s who made her fortune on hair care and skin products for black women. She also made a profit by selling real estate in the Indianapolis area. The writers found no evidence indicating that a Walker School of Cosmetology was established in Idlewild. However, beauticians trained in the Walker style of hair care were frequently available for demonstrations, especially at the 1926 and 1927 carnivals and chautauquas.

23. *Idlewild: A Place in the Sun*, WDIV (channel 4 in Detroit, Michigan) video documentary, produced by Mr. Ted Talbert.

24. Interview with Ms. Josephine Love. who maintained it was not unusual to see or read about whites, and a few northern blacks, who took advantage of the growing black consumer market, created by the mass migrations from the rural South to northern industrial cities.

25. Interview with Ms. Carol Hogan, Grand Rapids, Michigan, March 1981. The document was a part of the Hogan family papers. Charlie Gass, her great uncle, had the letter, which he carried while selling Idlewild lots in the Kent County area.

26. *Attorney of Idlewild booklet*, n.d., n.p., vertical files, Archives for the State of Michigan, State of Michigan Library, Lansing, Michigan; interview with Ms. Josephine Love, Heritage House, Detroit, Michigan, February 1981. According to Robert Raskins, a former active Garveyite, a branch of the Universal Negro Improvement Association (U.N.I.A.) was located there too.

27. Idlewild Chamber of Commerce "Folder in the interest of Idlewild," n.d., p. 2.

28. W. E. B. Du Bois, "Hopkinsville, Chicago, and Idlewild," *Crisis Magazine*, n.d., vertical files, Archives for the State of Michigan, State of Michigan Library, Lansing, Michigan.

29. *Idlewild: A Place in the Sun.*

CHAPTER 2

1. *A History of Idlewild*, booklet, n.a., n.d., n.p. vertical files, Archives for the State of Michigan, State of Michigan Library, Lansing, Michigan.

2. Letter to Michigan Securities Commission from attorney Charles A. Wilson (30 June 1927); letter to Michigan Securities Commission from attorney Charles A. Wilson (2 July 1927); letter to Michigan Securities Commission from Herbert Kandler (6 July 1927); letter from William Gilmore, deputy charman of Michigan Securities Commission to Idlewild Summer Resort Development Company (11 July 1927); letter to Michigan Securities Commission from John A. Schmidt (13 July 1927); letter to Michigan Securities Commission from J. E. Lindquist (18 July 1927); letter to Michigan Securities Commission from Ohio Iron and Metal Company (19 July 1927); letter to Michigan Securities Commission from Herbert Kandler (22 July 1927); letter to Michigan Securities Commission from Enterprise Steel and Iron company (19 July 1927); letter to Michigan Securities Commission from White and Reber Law Firm of Fremont, Michigan (15 July 1927); letter to Michigan Securities Commission from Wilbur Lemon (15 July, 19 July, 30 July, 18 August, 13 October, 4 November 1927); letter to Michigan Securities Commission from Edward A. Carter, M.D. (23 July 1927); letter to Michigan Securities Commission from Albert Kauffman (6 July 1927); letter to Michigan Securities Commission from W. E. N. Hunter, architect (7 July 1927); letter to Michigan Securities Commission from Ray Trucks, attorney at law for Lake County Abstract Company (21 July 1927); letter to Michigan Securities Commission from W. C. Osby (6 July 1927); letter to Michigan Securities Commission from Frank Wheatland, general manager of Colony Club in New York (12 July 1927); letter to Michigan Securities Commission from John Bland of the Bowery Savings Bank (15 June 1927); letter to Michigan Securities Commission from the president of Eagle Tire and Rubber Company (1 July 1927); letter to Michigan Securities Commission from H. J. Coleman and Company (16 July 1927); letter to Michigan Securities Commission from Edgar Olson, cashier, Franklin Trust and Savings Bank (7 July 1927); and letter to Michigan Securities Commission from M. O. Bousfield, president, Liberty Life Insurance Company (14 July 1927). Available in the vertical files at the Archives of the State of Michigan, State of Michigan Library, Lansing, Michigan.

3. W. C. Osby, Letter to Michigan Securities Commission. For additional data on the Reverend R. L. Bradby, see Francis H. Warren, *Negroes in Michigan History: Michigan Manual of Freedmen's Progress* (Detroit: 1915), passim; Cara L. Shelly, "Bradby's Baptist: Second Baptist Church of Detroit," *Michigan Historical Review* 17 (spring 1991): 1–34.

4. Edgar Olson, Letter to Michigan Securities Commission.

5. *A History of Idlewild.*

6. Ibid.

7. Vertical files, Archives of the State of Michigan, State of Michigan Library, Lansing, Michigan.

8. *A History of Idlewild.*

9. Interview with Ms. Florence Powell Washington and Mr. Robert Washington, Kalamazoo, Michigan, April 1981 and July 1981.

10. *A History of Idlewild.*

11. "Folder in the Interest of Idlewild," n.d., 4.

12. Idlewild Resort Company letter of invitation from Wilbur Lemon, manager, 27 June 1927, Archives of the State of Michigan, State of Michigan Library, Lansing, Michigan. Way too often black historians, and even more so white social scientists, forget the influence and role of black insurers, and especially their agents, in the dissemination of news in the black communities. Agents and Pullman porters helped spread the news about the resort.

13. For a detailed account of lots purchased, see the record of deeds for the Idlewild Resort Company and the deed for Dr. Williams's landholdings. Both were in the possession of Mr. Rollo Branch.

14. Many of the busboys, waiters, housekeepers, and cooks were students from either Fisk, Tuskegee, or Bethune-Cookman. By working at Idlewild during the summer months, many were able to earn tuition money for the academic year at their respective institutions.

15. Helen Buckler, *Daniel Hale Williams: Negro Surgeon* (New York: Pittman Publishing Corp., 1954), passim.

16. *Idlewild Resort Company Brochure,* Chicago, circa 1917–1920.

17. In addition to the editorial in the *Lake County Star* on Dr. Williams, other information can be found in the article entitled "Early Settlers of Idlewild, Michigan," A list, ISF Lansing, State of Michigan Library, and in Helen Buckler's *Daniel Hale Williams—Negro Surgeon* (New York: Pittman Publishing Corporation, 1954). Many African Americans who still have a connection with the hospital claim that the source of the animosity centered around Dr. Dan Williams's notoriety. Because of his pioneer surgery, he was in demand at several black institutions throughout the nation, and was appointed surgeon-in-chief of the two-hundred-bed Freedmen's Hospital and Asylum in Washington, D.C. Dr. Williams served for four years in this position, during which time he elevated the run-down institution to respectable status. Dr. Williams assembled a staff of twenty nonsalaried specialists and systemized the hospital into seven departments: medical, surgical, gynecological, obstetrical, dermatological, genitourinary, and throat and chest. He also set up two modern adjuncts, a pathological and a bacteriological department, and an ambulance system. His next step was to set up a system of internships to supplement the staff of twenty doctors. This move almost completely did away with the need for two former paid assistants and placed within the reach of young black medical students an opportunity for advancement which was accorded them only at Provident. Dr. Williams next turned his attention to establishing a nurses' training program. His big difficulty lay in the prior existence of a so-called Training School for Nurses undertaken by the Howard University less than two years before.

18. Harry Solomon papers, "An Adventure I Remember," ISF, vertical files, State of Michigan Library, Lansing, Michigan.

19. Gill Griffin, "Idlewild: Welcoming Resort Meant Summer to Black Families," *Lake County Star*, 24 June 1999, 12.

CHAPTER 3

1. The film, *A Pictorial History of Idlewild*, was made at the second annual carnival/chautauqua.
2. Norris Ingalls, "Resorting to Idlewild," *Lansing State Journal*, 2 July 1992, 1D–5D.
3. *Idlewild Lot Owners Association booklet*, 1110 Hartford Building, 8 South Dearborn Street, Chicago, Illinois.
4. Sheet music was provided to the authors by Mr. Don Sims, brother of Joe Billingslea, one of the members of the original Contours, a Motown recording group (Southfield, Michigan) of the Mid-Michigan Idlewilders. Michael S. Harper also wrote a lyrical sounding poem "Idlewild" for Julian "Cannonball" Adderley, published in *Black World Magazine*, January 1976.
5. Ingalls, "Resorting to Idlewild."
6. The three major philosophical views on race relations expressed at the resort were those of Booker T. Washington, W. E. B. DuBois, and Marcus Garvey. The pioneers around Paradise and Idlewild Lakes agreed more with the first two, while those who were urban and blue collar tended to be Graveyites.
7. Yates Township Facility and Service Plan, 33.
8. Sunnie Wilson with John Cohassey, *Toast of the Town: The Life and Times of Sunnie Wilson* (Detroit: Wayne State University, 1998), 68. Many numbers men loaned money to professional black entrepreneurs, such as dentists, doctors, morticians, and insurers. When these men were denied bank loans for the construction of offices, numbers men came to their aid, usually without exorbitant interest rates.
9. St. Clair Drake and Horace R. Cayton, *Black Metropolis: A Study of Negro Life in a Northern City* (New York: Harper and Row Publishers, 1962), 2:492–93.
10. Ibid., 499.
11. As a result of the efforts of the Crime Patrol, such problems are becoming a rarity. The group is comparable to a community watch neighborhood association. Prior to creation of the Crime Patrol, break-ins and acts of vandalism were frequently undetected by local law enforcement officials until the return of the summer vacationers.
12. Drake and Cayton, 506.
13. Ibid., 496.
14. Interview with Joe Lindsey, fall 1999, Idlewild, Michigan.
15. Lawrence Otis Graham, *Inside America's Black Upper Class: Our Kind of People* (New York: HarperCollins Publishers, 1999), 4.
16. Pamphlets, handbills, and programs from the Viola Clark Carr Phillips family papers. Interview with Viola Phillips, summer 1998, Battle Creek, Michigan.
17. *A Pictorial View of Idlewild*, a twenty-three-minute silent promotional film.
18. Handbill, "Big Chautauqua to be held at Idlewild," scheduled for 23 August–27 August 1926, and handbill, "Idlewild's Second Big Annual Carnival and Chautauqua," scheduled for 25 July–6 August 1927.

19. Staff writer, "Phil Giles Credited for Present Idlewild Resort Business Boom," *Challenger*, 31 May 1952.

20. Reynolds interview, summer 1982, Idlewild, Michigan.

21. *Idlewild Resort Company brochure.*

22. *Idlewild Lot Owners Association Booklet.*

CHAPTER 4

1. "The Black Tavern in the Making of a Jazz Musician: Bird, Mingus and Stan Hope," in *Perspectives of Black Popular Culture*, ed. Harry B. Shaw (Bowling Green, Ohio: Bowling Green State University Popular Press, 1990), 7.

2. Desiree Cooper, "Living History," *Detroit News and Free Press*, 1B and 2B.

3. Norris Ingalls, "Resorting to Idlewild," *Lansing State Journal*, 2 July 1992, 1D–5D.

4. Original Chicago Idlewilders 13th Annual Amateur Show and Dance at the Flamingo Club.

5. *Chicago Daily News*, 17 August 1963, 18 August 1962, and 14 August 1965; interview with Willie Curtis, George Anderson, Pertenious Box, and Commodore Carr, 20 August 1999, Kalamazoo, Michigan.

6. Liquor menu provided by Ms. Idella Anderson. Interview with Idella Anderson, summer 1999, Kalamazoo, Michigan.

7. Interview with Bob Hayes and William McClure, fall 1999, Idlewild, Michigan.

8. Sunnie Wilson with John Cohassey, *Toast of the Town: The Life and Times of Sunnie Wilson* (Detroit: Wayne State University Press, 1998), 139. According to them, Lake County has always been a very conservative republican stronghold. The law enforcement officers and Baldwin city administrators were known for their warped sentiments on race. Many of the black resorters wanted to stop the flow of their money to bigots who sold liquor and other spirits in nearby Baldwin. Although a small town, Baldwin upheld segregation in several business places. Governor Mennen Williams's wife, Nancy, was a great help in securing liquor licenses for many club owners in Idlewild.

9. "Are We There Yet? America on Vacation," History Channel production, 17 December 1999. Produced by Pam Wolfe.

10. Interview with Willie Curtis, George Anderson, Pertenious Box, and Commodore Carr.

11. Wilson and Cohassey, *Toast of the Town*, 141.

12. Interview with Joe Lindsey, fall 1999 and winter 2000, Kalamazoo, Michigan.

13. Wilson and Cohassey, *Toast of the Town*, 141; see also Kenneth Cole and Elizabeth Atkins, "Idlewild Rocked in its Heyday," *Detroit News*, 31 January 1992, 4F–5F; and Thomas DeVier, "Idlewild Shakes Free of Past," *Detroit News and Free Press*, 3 March 1991.

14. Daniel J. Leab, *From Sambo to Superspade: The Black Experience in Motion Pictures* (Boston, Mass: Houghton Mifflin Company, 1976), passim.

15. *Idlewild: A Place in the Sun*, WDIV (channel 4 in Detroit, Michigan) video documentary, produced by Ted Talbert, narrated by Emory King.

16. Ibid.

17. Rhonda Sanders, "Idlewild on the Mend?" *Flint Journal*, 22 January 1996, B1–B2.

18. Ibid.

19. Interview with Freelon Tim Carter, June 1999, Lansing, Michigan.

20. Fishing Idlewild Lake, especially in the 1950s and 1960s, could prove to be an adventure for those in small, flat-bottom fishing boats. Those who fished had to worry about the constant waves in the water created by the fast boats captained by the "Super Cool." Little Idlewild, Tank, or parts of Paradise Lake were better for fishing due to the lack of heavy boat traffic.

21. Idlewild Chamber of Commerce, "Folder in the interest of Idlewild," n.d., 2.

22. *Idlewild: A Place in the Sun.*

23. Robert Stepto, *Blue as the Lake: A Personal Geography* (Boston: Beacon Press, 1998), 30–31.

24. Walter Sims in *Idlewild: A Place in the Sun.*

25. Judge Atkins in *Idlewild: A Place in the Sun.*

26. Stepto, *Blue as the Lake,* 30–31.

27. Interview with Beatrice Buck, October 1995, Detroit, Michigan.

28. Interview with John English, fall 1999, Idlewild, Michigan. The flyer advertising the golf outing was provided by Mr. English.

29. "The Black Tavern in the Making of a Jazz Musician: Bird, Mingus and Stan Hope," 7.

CHAPTER 5

1. Daniel Patrick Moynihan, "Employment, Income, and the Ordeal of the Negro Family," *Daedalus: Journal of the American Academy of Arts and Sciences* 94, no. 4 (fall 1965): 746.

2. Talcott Parsons, "Full Citizenship for the Negro American?" *Daedalus: Journal of the American Academy of Arts and Sciences* 94, no. 4 (fall 1965): 1048.

3. William Raspberry, "King Had Much More to Teach America Than His Dream," *Kalamazoo Gazette,* 29 February 2000, C2.

4. Ibid.

5. Dr. Mark Foster, "In Spite of 'Jim Crow': Prosperous Blacks and Vacations, Travel and Outdoor Leisure, 1890–1945," unpublished article by historian from the University of Colorado in Denver, 1986.

6. Interview with township supervisor Norm Burns, fall 1999, Idlewild, Michigan.

7. *Idlewild: A Place in the Sun,* WDIV (channel 4 in Detroit, Michigan) video documentary, produced by Ted Talbert, narrated by Emory King.

8. Sunnie Wilson with John Cohassey, *Toast of the Town: The Life and Times of Sunnie Wilson* (Detroit: Wayne State University Press, 1998), 161, 181.

9. Richard T. Schaefer, *Racial and Ethnic Groups* (Upper Saddle River, N.J.: Prentice Hall, 2000), 249.

10. Rhonda Sanders, "Idlewild on the Mend?" *Flint Journal,* 22 January 1996, B1–B2.

11. Gill Griffin, "Idlewild: Welcoming Resort Meant Summer to Black Families," *Lake County Star,* 24 June 1997, 12.

12. Thomas DeVier, "Idlewild Shakes Free of Past," *Detroit News and Free Press,* 3 March 1991; Kenneth Cole and Elizabeth Atkins, "Idlewild Rocked in Its Heyday," *Detroit News,* 31 January 1992.

13. Gary Blonston, "Idlewild: A Victim of Racial Progress?," *Detroit Free Press*, 2 July 1967.

14. St. Clair Drake and Horace R. Cayton, *Black Metropolis: A Study of Negro Life in a Northern City* (New York: Harper and Row, 1962), 440.

15. Alex Kotlowitz, "Idle Awhile in Idlewild," *Magazine of the Detroit News*, 6 May 1984.

16. "Joseph Craigen Hall—Farewell," *Chicago Daily News*, 18 August 1962, 1.

17. "Final Rites Observed for Three Pioneers of Idlewild," *Chicago Daily News*, 17 August 1963, 116; display advertisement, *Lake County Star*, 30 March 1967, 17; and Kotlowitz, "Idle Awhile in Idlewild."

18. Display advertisement, *Lake County Star*, 30 March 1967, 17.

19. United States Department of Labor, Bureau of Labor Statistics, *The Negroes in the United States: Their Economic and Social Situation* (Washington, D.C.: U.S. Government Printing Office, 1963), 160.

20. Griffin, "Idlewild," 12.

21. Interview with John Reynolds, summer 1982, Idlewild, Michigan.

22. Videotape, *Paradise 1958—Idlewild*, Sound Stage Production.

23. Robert B. Stepto "From Idlewild and Other Seasons," *Callaloo* 14, no. 1 (1991): 20–36.

24. Debraha K. Watson, "Renewing the Spirit of . . . Idlewild," *African American Travel Magazine and Planner Guide*, fall 1999, 10.

25. Ron Stodghill, II, "Letter from Michigan: A Return to the Black Eden," *Business Week* insert, 30 October 1995, 18, 20–21.

26. Ibid.

CHAPTER 6

1. "Lake County (Idlewild Area) Demographic Study," 2 August 1999, 1.

2. Ibid.

3. Information taken from Table 1. "Selected Population and Housing Characteristics: 1990, Yates Township, Lake County, Michigan," as reported in *Michigan and Lake County, 1990 Census Data*, duplicated by The Lake County Cooperative Extension Service, Baldwin, Michigan.

4. Buck VanderMeer, "Idlewild Features Full Menu of Summer Fun," *Lake County Star*, 24 June 1999, 12.

5. *The Detroit News*, Saturday, 29 August 1998, 2C.

6. "Yates Township Facility and Services Plan," The WBDC Group, Lake County, Michigan, July 1987, 68.

7. "Lake County (Idlewild Area) Demographic Study," 1.

8. Gill Griffin, passim.

9. *Detroit News and Free Press*, 3 March 1991.

10. Repairing the Breach, 124.

11. "Lake County (Idlewild Area) Demographic Study," 1.

12. *Lake County Overview*, 22 August 1995, unpublished report: contact Mary L. Trucks, FiveCAP, Inc., 302 North Main Street, Scottville, Michigan 49454–03070.

13. Ibid.

14. Information taken from Table 1, "Selected Population and Housing Characteristics."
15. Ibid.
16. Lake County, "The Plan," unpublished government strategic plan document, 134.
17. Information taken from Table 1, "Selected Population and Housing Characteristics."
18. Diether H. Haenicke, "Can the Detroit Public Schools Be Saved?" *Kalamazoo Gazette*, 4 October 2000, C2.
19. Ibid.
20. Lake County, "The Plan," 109.
21. *Lake County Recreation Plan, Project No. N12075*, January 1997, prepared by Gove Associates Inc., Kalamazoo, Michigan, page III-13, 1997.
22. *Yates Township Facility and Service Plan*, July 1987, Lake County, Michigan, 47.
23. Ibid., 49.
24. Ibid., 47.
25. Ibid., 44.

CHAPTER 7

1. Interview with John Reynolds, summer 1982, Idlewild, Michigan.
2. Interview with anonymous female, fall 1999, Red Rooster, Idlewild, Michigan.
3. Interview with John Reynolds.
4. Ibid.
5. Ibid.
6. Interview with Audrey Bullett, summer 1987, Idlewild, Michigan.
7. Bylaws of ILOA and Mid-Michigan Idlewild Club of Southfield.
8. Interview with Viola and Johnny Phillips, summer 1999, in Battle Creek, Michigan.
9. Interview with Ruth Burton, summer and fall 1999, Idlewild, Michigan.
10. Interview with John Meeks, entrepreneur, summer and fall 1999, Idlewild, Michigan.
11. Gill Griffin, "Idlewild: Welcoming Resort Meant Summer to Black Families," *Lake County Star*, 24 June 1999, 3.
12. Report prepared by Mr. Harry Solomon, a former township supervisor.
13. *Yates Township Board 1970 Report*.
14. *Situational Analysis of Resort Development; Idlewild, Michigan*, unpublished report prepared by Perspectives Consulting Group, Kalamazoo, Michigan, 1989, 9.
15. Ibid., 19–20.
16. Ibid., 22–24.
17. Thomas DeVier, "Idlewild Shakes Free of Past," *Detroit News and Free Press*, 3 March 1991.
18. Ibid.
19. Betty DeRamus, "Old Resort Looks to the Future," *Detroit News*, 29 August 1998, 1C.
20. Rhonda Sanders, "Idlewild on the Mend?" *Flint Journal*, 22 January 1996, B1–B2.
21. Ron Stodghill, "Letter from Michigan: A Return to the Black Eden," *Business Week*, 30 October 1995, pp. 20–21.
22. Eric Freedman, *Detroit News*, 15 July 1994, B-1.
23. Mid-Michigan Idlewilders Club Constitution, 1.

24. *Midwest Business Association Journal* 3, no. 8 (October 1999): 10.

25. *Lake County Star*, 12 August 1999, 14.

26. Historic Idlewild pamphlet.

27. *Lake County Star*, Thursday, 12 August 1999, 3.

28. Buck VanderMeer, "Idlewild Museum Holds Open House," *Lake County Star*, 5 August 1999, 13.

29. Letter to the Editor, "Lot Owners Appreciate Help," *Lake County Star*, 14 October 1999.

30. *Lake County Star*, 5 August 1999, 7.

31. "With Time-Honored Values, Idlewild Nurturing Summer Place for African Americans," Internet, *http://www.freep.com/fun/travel/qdesx14.htm*.

32. Ibid.

33. *Lake County Star*, 12 August 1999, 14.

34. "Decades of Services: More than 30 Years of Making a Difference and Helping People Reach Their Full Potential," FiveCAP brochure, n.d.

35. *Lake County Enterprise Community* 1 (summer 1996): 3.

36. Ibid.

37. Ibid.

38. Lake County, Michigan, "The Plan," unpublished document, 141.

CHAPTER 8

1. Bobby William Austin, ed., *Repairing the Breach: Keys to Support Family Life, Reclaim Our Streets, and Rebuild Civil Society in America's Communities* (Chicago, Ill.: Noble Press, 1996), 122–23.

2. Edward J. Annen Jr., "Forever-Young Dorothy Dalton without Peer," *Kalamazoo Gazette*, December 1999, A1.

3. Austin, *Repairing the Breach*, 123–24.

4. Ibid.

5. Interview with Bill McClure, November 1999, Idlewild, Michigan.

6. Interview with Audrey K. Bullett, Idlewild, Michigan.

7. *Christianity Today*, 14 June 1999, 38. AOL keyword: CT. *www.ChristianityToday.net*.

8. Ibid., 35–36.

9. Ibid., 37.

10. Ibid.

11. *Metro Detroit Visitors Guide*, winter 2000, 6.

12. Ibid.

13. Ibid., 45.

14. Garrison Wells, "Morals Aside, Casinos Fill Pocketbooks," *Kalamazoo Gazette*, 5 September 2000, A3.

15. Edward Hoogterp, "Babcock House Museum, B&B Highlight Manistee Trip," *Kalamazoo Gazette*, 26 March 2000, H1, H3.

16. "Michigan Population Update, December 1995," Internet, *http://www.mdch.state.mi.us/mass/DPOPUP/popup954.html*.

17. Ibid.
18. Austin, *Repairing the Breach*, 132.
19. Lake County, Michigan, "The Plan," unpublished document of Lake County, Michigan, 95–137.
20. Michael H. Shuman, "Reclaiming the Inner City through Political, Economic, and Ecological Self-Reliance," unpublished paper, 37.
21. Lewis Walker and Douglas Davidson, "Outside the Dark Ghetto: Salient Economic Issues Facing African Americans in Southwest Michigan," in *The Small and Regional Community*, volume 10, ed. Thomas Van Valey, Sue R. Krull, and Lewis Walker (Stevens Point: University of Wisconsin-Stevens Point, 1993), 54–55.
22. Colin Powell, *In My American Journey: An Autobiography of Colin Powell* (New York: Ballantine Books, 1996), passim.

CHAPTER 9

1. Kim Fendley and James A. Christenson, "Rural Reflation: An Idea for Community Development," *Journal of the Community Development Society* 20, no. 1 (1989): 103.
2. *FiveCAP/Lake County, Michigan Enterprise Community pamphlet*, n.d.
3. Interview with Mary Trucks, August 2000, Scottville; October 2000, by telephone.
4. Ibid.
5. Ibid.

Index

About the Authors

LEWIS WALKER received his Ph.D. from Ohio State University and is presently Chair Emeritus and Professor of Sociology at Western Michigan University. He has authored several books and various articles within the field of race relations and he serves as a consultant to public, private and education agencies on race and ethnic relations.

BEN C. WILSON received his Ph.D. from Michigan State University. He is the chair of the Africana Studies program at Western Michigan University and is the author of several books on African American heritage in Michigan. He has produced twenty education audio-visual modules on Michigan's black experience.